Exiting Vietnam

ALSO BY MICHAEL A. EGGLESTON
AND FROM MCFARLAND

President Lincoln's Recruiter: General Lorenzo Thomas and the United States Colored Troops in the Civil War (2013)

The Tenth Minnesota Volunteers, 1862–1865: A History of Action in the Sioux Uprising and the Civil War, with a Regimental Roster (2012)

Exiting Vietnam

*The Era of Vietnamization and
American Withdrawal Revealed
in First-Person Accounts*

MICHAEL A. EGGLESTON

McFarland & Company, Inc., Publishers
Jefferson, North Carolina

LIBRARY OF CONGRESS CATALOGUING-IN-PUBLICATION DATA

Eggleston, Michael A., 1937–
    Exiting Vietnam : the era of Vietnamization and American
withdrawal revealed in first-person accounts / Michael A. Eggleston.
        p.   cm.
    Includes bibliographical references and index.

    ISBN 978-0-7864-7772-2 (softcover : acid free paper) ∞
    ISBN 978-1-4766-1458-8 (ebook)

    1. Vietnam War, 1961–1975—United States.   2. Vietnam War,
1961–1975—Peace.   3. Agreement on Ending the War and Restoring
Peace in Vietnam (1973)   I. Title.
    DS558.E35 2014
    959.704'3—dc23   2014010661

BRITISH LIBRARY CATALOGUING DATA ARE AVAILABLE

Cover photograph: *The Three Soldiers* bronze statue on the National Mall
in Washington, D.C. (Department of Defense)

Printed in the United States of America

*McFarland & Company, Inc., Publishers
    Box 611, Jefferson, North Carolina 28640
    www.mcfarlandpub.com*

Acknowledgments

I would like to thank my wife, Margaret, for her endless patience and for her comments on and edits to this book. I would also like to express my gratitude to all who contributed their memoirs for this book or helped in its preparation: Forrest "Sonny" Ashcraft, Charles F. Bernitt, Paul Michael Bryant, Sr., Michael Cason, Bill Comrey, Paul G. Dailey, Connor Eggleston, Pat Eggleston, Mac Eggleston, Raymond N. Fraley, Ken Fugate, Bill Garbett, Jack Harrigan, Loren J. Kindler, James Allan Long, Jim Lovins, Olen C. Phipps, Jr., Danté M. Puccetti, Frances Rogers, Ronald S. Simpkins, Sr., Jim Van Alstin, Professor Robert Wilensky, and Meaghan Witt.

Table of Contents

Preface

This history is focused on the end of the war in Vietnam from the perspective of the United States. To do that, I had to go back to earlier days to explain how we got involved and what forced us to withdraw, including lack of support for the war by the American people.

Someone asked me, after half a century and my years of service in Vietnam, "Was it worth it?" My answer was, "I don't know now and probably never will." I can only quote Mark Twain in defense of my answer:

> The eight years in America from 1860 to 1868 uprooted institutions that were centuries old, changed politics of a people, transformed the social life of half of the country, and wrought so profoundly upon the entire National character that the influence cannot be measured short of two or three generations.

Publishers would call this book a hybrid because it merges the official history of the war with the accounts by historians, but more important, it is the oral history of people who were there. There are hundreds of memoirs of Vietnam infantry soldiers who describe slogging through the jungle, ambushes and all of that, but this book describes what was going on from a different perspective: combat support such as advisors, supply, and communications. The important point is that while these soldiers accomplished their support duties, they were also called upon to fight as infantry. I have included the recollections of many Vietnam veterans, including my own. That is what is different about this book. Some books provide the official history while still others are memoirs. This book consists of both. Some of the memoirs are brutal, others may appear mundane, while still others are humorous. Gallows humor among soldiers is legendary. It kept us sane. In all cases, we have done our best to tell what we saw.

1

In a *60 Minutes* interview on 4 November 2012, historian David McCullough provided his insight:

> The only way to teach history, to write history, to bring people into the magic of transforming yourself into other times is through the vehicle of the story. *It isn't just the chronology, it's about people. History is human.* Jefferson said "when in the course of human events ..." "Human" is the operative word here. "Human" rhymes with "Truman." The underlying factor in the presidential election. Every candidate running for any office ought to study Harry Truman's 1948 campaign. He ran by being himself: "I am going out there and saying what I mean." Can you imagine? A politician doing that as an approach? The people loved it. It was the first time any president had ever done that.

This book tells the human story of some of the people involved in the Vietnam War during the period 1961–1975 through their letters, memoirs and histories. This book was written for people who want to learn more about the war in Vietnam. For this reason I summarize some of the background and history of the war. That way, all have a common frame of reference before launching into specific events. I am indebted to the veterans who provided the recollections incorporated in this book. I have also quoted published memoirs of others who served in Vietnam.

I served two tours of duty in Vietnam during the periods 1965–1966 and 1970–1971. The first was as an advisor to a South Vietnamese battalion at Pleiku during the U.S. buildup. My second tour was also at Pleiku as the executive officer of a U.S. battalion during the period of Vietnamization (which meant then and now how the United States would hand over the war to the South Vietnamese and depart). I later realized that this was a very rare opportunity to see the war from the same location separated by four years. I have many unpublished letters and papers written during these two periods and since. Many are included in this book. I was also able to obtain the published recollections of South Vietnamese, North Vietnamese and Vietcong soldiers who served.

I spent most of my career as a Signal Corps officer, but I am a "grunt" at heart because of my early career. "A grunt" means a foot soldier, a U.S. Army infantryperson or a marine focused on completing a military mission while taking care of his troops. I enlisted in the 47th Minnesota National Guard "Viking" Division when I was sixteen in 1954.

My first day in 1954 in the 47th was a treat. My new platoon leader told me that I had to have a pair of balls to move my jeep as fast as I could since I was the lead scout driver ahead of the division. If I could not do that, he would find someone who could. I told him that I did have a pair of balls. In spite of my arrogance, I got the job. I was looking up at the ceiling and the lieutenant asked if I was bored and I replied, "No, sir, no

47th Minnesota National Guard "Viking" Division reconnaissance company in 1957, author in the first row on the right (author's collection).

problem." Actually, I was thinking, Thank you, God; at last I have a chance to drive recklessly at government expense. I did have a few wrecks, which the government paid for, but these were not serious. I did not kill or injure anyone; these were fender benders.

A scout driver was a soldier who went ahead of the recon company that went ahead of the infantry division that was often the first division in the attack. The purpose was to locate the enemy division up ahead. It did not take me long to figure out that I was the upfront guy going up against a whole enemy division that was waiting to kill me. My best chance is that they would let me pass in order to let others kill me later while they focused on the columns that followed me. The first thing I did was to put in an increase to my life insurance.

One of my sons is an army officer and I felt compelled to relate to him what my sergeant told me sixty years ago. I know that my son is probably one of the best-equipped and trained soldiers as are all of our soldiers in the U.S. Army today, but here is what I learned over sixty years ago:

After I enlisted in the Minnesota National Guard, our sergeant who ran the company arms room realized that I was far too young to be a soldier and he decided to sit me down and explain to me the rules of engagement. He was a highly decorated World II veteran. He was an infantry soldier and told me that he had killed over a hundred Germans during the war and had been wounded several times. I thought at the time that my score was zero and would not improve any time soon. Here are his rules.

1—Never volunteer for anything, it will get you killed.

2—Your rifle is the most important thing that you have. Check and clean it as often as you can. If it jams you will be killed.

3—Make sure you never run out of ammunition. When you get your basic load, go back and get more, if you can. If you run out of ammunition, it could get you killed.

4—Don't stick your head up. Wait for the signal from your squad leader. If you don't follow his lead you could get killed.

5—Don't forget nothing as you go into battle. If you do, you could get killed (this from Roger's Rangers rules over 250 years ago).

6—**You are an Infantry soldier.** Next to your rifle, your feet are the most important thing that you have. Check your boots and feet as often as you can. Change socks frequently. Keep spare socks stuffed in condoms so that when you cross a creek, they stay dry. If you fall behind because of blisters, you will be killed.

7—Watch how you eat. Don't light a fire, but eat cold rations. The enemy is watching. If they see smoke, they will know where you are and you will be killed.

8—Treat every mission as though it was a Long Range Reconnaissance Patrol (LRRP). You need to be self-sufficient and prepared for anything.

Since I compiled what the supply sergeant told me in 1954, Vietnam veterans have added to the list. Number 9 is probably the best advice that I could give any to soldier.

9—Train yourself out of a job. Make sure your soldiers at every level can function and carry on the mission if the leaders are removed.

10—Learn to play chess. It teaches you tactics and thinking 3 or more moves ahead of your opponent [*Mike Eggleston, 2013*[1]].

    I started as a private and got my sergeant's stripes by 1957. This was an incredibly big deal. The most important thing that I learned during these years was the importance of training. My squad leader and platoon sergeant kept pounding tactics into my head to the point that I could act instinctively without thinking when there was no time to evaluate alternatives. I was trained to disassemble and reassemble my M1 rifle in record time blindfolded. Sometimes they would stick a bug in the rifle, which I would need to clear while blindfolded. The result of this training is seen in an incident that occurred during my first tour in Vietnam.

    Fast-forward to 1966. I was an advisor in Vietnam and a colonel asked me to drive him to a meeting some distance away. I knew my way and traveled what I thought was a safe route. It was not. We got ambushed and while the colonel was having something like a stroke, since he had never heard a shot fired in anger, I instinctively did a 90 degree turn off the road into a banana plantation. I was on automatic pilot. We careened through the bananas as the VC fired. The jeep took hits, but we did not. This was a long ride through the plantation and the bananas kept piling up on the windshield and my face. I put the windshield wipers on, but they did not do much good, if you can imagine a banana squished on your windscreen. These were those small Asian bananas with big pits and not much to eat. We finally sailed out of the plantation, airborne, and landed hard on the road below. The VC were long gone and I got out to check damage. The jeep was okay and the colonel was groaning, so I moved quickly to our destination. He got out and went to his meeting while I went to the motor pool. I gassed up and started hosing down the vehicle. There were a lot of banana parts on the motor pool pavement when I finished. The motor sergeant watched, smiling, and I asked him to hose me down as well, which he did.

I waited for the colonel and realized how lucky I was. I had nearly three years of training as an infantryman and scout driver. Lessons were drilled into my brain so that when confronted with a situation I reacted instinctively (like the banana thing). This may well have saved our lives. This is nothing new. The army trains on that basis. After that I had the advantage of four years at West Point. My point is that during the Vietnam conflict there was little time to adequately train our draftees. It was up to the squad leaders and platoon sergeants to do that and they did a great job, but many "newbies" died before they could learn. For the South Vietnamese, the situation was much worse. I recall chatting with some RVNAF soldiers. As I walked away, I thought, Shit, these kids won't make it. Everyone needed more training time. We could have used a little bit more leadership and training. I am not complaining. That is just the way it was. Also, I hate bananas.

While I was in the Minnesota National Guard, I got an appointment to West Point and graduated in 1961. I had more education and many good assignments that spanned nearly thirty years in the U.S. Army. I was always grateful to the U.S. Army for my assignments. I never had a bad job. At the same time, I am critical of the job that I did and that of the U.S. Army in Vietnam, as seen in this history. The reader will find that I attempt to present a balanced view.

I met some amazing people along the way. Frank Reasoner was a cadet at West Point when I was there. He was an outstanding boxer and about the toughest person I ever met. We fought in different weight classes, thank God. If I ever went against Frank Reasoner, I am convinced that I would have ended up in the hospital. Over several years, I won the boxing championship in my weight class and he in his. Frank chose to be commissioned in the U.S. Marine Corps and I in the U.S. Army. We were both in Vietnam at the same time (1965), but he was in I Corps and I was in II Corps. What happened to Frank is well documented. During a marine operation in I Corps, one of Frank's marines was hit and went down. Frank, as those who knew him might expect, went out under heavy fire to save his comrade. Hit and killed, Frank was awarded the Medal of Honor for his valor. Author Philip Caputo gives a brief account of Frank's valor in his book titled *A Rumor of War*.[2] Frank is remembered by all of us who knew him.

There were atrocities committed by both sides, such as My Lai,[3] but the overwhelming number of murders were committed by the Vietcong, whom I sometimes refer to as murderous thugs, a reputation well deserved. I included within this book the atrocities by the Vietcong that I observed. The following is an example.

I was acting battalion commander because the battalion commander had been fragged and I had temporarily taken over his duties (he later returned to duty). I needed to move from our headquarters at Pleiku to An Khe, where we had two companies. This was in early 1971. My driver and I left early, behind the military police who would check the road, so we were the first in the convoy behind the MPs. The MPs suddenly stopped and we instantly deployed to the side of the road, ready to fire. Rule one: Never stop on Highway 19, because you will be an easy target for the Vietcong. The French Mobile Group 100 was slaughtered during the French war close to this place (Mang Yang Pass). After a short delay, the MP sergeant came to me and said, "Major, you need to see this." What I saw was burned into our memories. I walked upon what I can only describe as a field of blood. A Vietnamese bus was at the side of the road. The doors were open and the driver was shot dead. Beyond the doors were dozens of South Vietnamese executed by the Vietcong. They were men, women, and children. It was difficult to see young children with their heads blown off by the Vietcong. We later found out that the Vietcong had issued an edict that no one was to travel on the road during Tet, a religious holiday. All families wanted to reunite during this period, so when this busload of people was stopped the Vietcong decided to prove their authority by killing everyone on board.

A year or so ago, one of the Vietnam vets asked me if I would care to return to Vietnam, since he was setting up a tour. My answer was very clear: "I do not have Vietnam on my bucket list of places to visit. I will never return." But many Vietnam veterans do return and provide amazing accounts of Vietnam today, where 65 percent of the population was born after the war. Photos of battle sites from the 1960s and 1970s are also brought back from these visits. I have included some of these in this history.

I have chosen to include the anti-war sentiment of the U.S. troops in this war because it was a major factor that influenced us during the war. Many soldiers volunteered and more were drafted, but when we arrived and saw the corruption of the South Vietnamese and the incompetence of the U.S. Army senior commanders and the U.S. government many of us turned against the war, but we did our job as seen in the oral history contained in this book.

You will find many abbreviations in this book. These are defined in Appendix A. You will also see a thread of what can only be described as "survivor's guilt" in much of the oral history. When someone got killed we always pondered, What could I have done better to avoid that? or, Why was he killed and not me? It is a persistent theme in oral history. Paul G. Dailey summarized:

> You are not and will never be alone in your feeling of guilt for what we may have or may not have done during our Service in Vietnam…. We each hold a dark experience that we fight through regardless of our position in duty stations, we were all treated like crap for our service because of what a few did that society could not handle or understand [*Paul G. Dailey, 1968–1969*[4]].

As the fortieth anniversary of our final withdrawal from Vietnam, approaches, the below quote from *Henry V* seems to apply. We were all members of the Band of Brothers.

> "To-morrow is Saint Crispin's": Then will he strip his sleeve and show his scars, And say, "These wounds I had on Saint Crispin's day." Old men forget; yet all shall be forgot, But he'll remember with advantages, What feats he did that day; then shall our names, Familiar in his mouth as household words, Harry the King, Bedford and Exeter, Warwick and Talbot, Salisbury and Gloucester, Be in their flowing cuts freshly remember'd. This story shall the good man teach his son, And Crispin shall ne'er go by, From this day to the ending of the world, But we in it shall be remembered: We few we, happy few, we band of brothers; For he to-day that sheds his blood with me Shall be my brother: be he ne'er so vile, This day shall gentle his condition; And Gentlemen in England now abed Shall think themselves accursed they were not here, And hold their manhood's cheap whiles any speaks That fought with us upon Saint Crispin's day [*Henry V*, Shakespeare].

Introduction

Many soldiers have contributed their memoirs to this book. The format of this book is to provide the historical account of the events such as Tet 68, followed by the memoirs of the soldiers who served there. The focus of the book is the U.S. exit from Vietnam, why we left in haste in fourteen increments over three years. It also explains how it was executed and the impact of our withdrawal on the war. To do this, it was necessary to explain what was happening on several fronts: the earlier war, the U.S. government's policy, the home front, and the soldier in the field.

To make sense of all of this, it was necessary to provide background, returning to the account of our early involvement and how this changed from an advisors' war to a massive influx of U.S. troops to take over the fighting of the war and finally Vietnamization and our withdrawal: the focus of this book. Our objectives in fighting in Vietnam are important and should be documented before considering our exit from Vietnam. The best list of our objectives that can be captured from multiple sources is seen here. Compare these and measure whether or not we achieved our objectives as seen in Chapter 8:

—To meet our treaty agreements to support the government of South Vietnam.

—To prove that communist wars of liberation can be stopped by the free world.

—To demonstrate to the Soviet Union that the United States would oppose by force any attempt by the Soviet Union to expand its sphere of influence.

—To assist the South Vietnamese government in improving the social and economic situation of its people in order to win their support.

—To persuade the government of North Vietnam to end their aggression against the South.

—To assist the South Vietnamese government in destroying or winning over the Vietcong forces that operated in South Vietnam and the NVA (North Vietnamese Army) invading from the north.

Stating objectives and achieving them relies upon a strategy to do that. The U.S. strategy over time appeared to be driven by political considerations of the impact on the U.S. public rather than being a consistent strategy designed to meet the objectives. This is neither new nor a revelation. This is best seen in General Westmoreland's emphasis on body count, which made no sense given the fact that Hanoi had no concern about the human cost of their invasion of the South. They simply sent more people south along the Ho Chi Minh Trail. Literature tends to make people believe that the Ho Chi Minh Trail was a single thread that was used by Hanoi. It was more than that. It was a network of trails and later roads leading north to south. This meant that when the U.S. Air Force identified a trail and often hit it with devastating result the NVA merely moved supplies and people to a different part of the network. This is seen in this history especially when the United States invaded Cambodia and the RVNAF (Republic of Vietnam Armed Forces) invaded Laos late in the war.

In Vietnam I worked with some famous people, like John Paul Vann. Much has been written about Vann. He was an amazing person and I have tried to capture my discussions with him and his impact on the war.

My problem has always been deciding whose account I should trust. I exercised a great deal of caution in quoting senior officials. Many are of questionable reliability, since they were often more concerned about protecting their reputations than with telling the truth and they would and did tell the most outrageous lies. A good example is General Paul Harkins, the U.S. Commander in Vietnam in 1963 after the disastrous defeat at the hands of the Vietcong at Ap Bac. He sent glowing reports of victory to Washington. The press exposed his outrageous lies and they proved to be a major embarrassment to President John F. Kennedy.

Throughout the entire Vietnam conflict, the best judgment that I would trust was that of the veterans. U.S. government and South Vietnamese accounts are often self-serving, as will be seen in the chapters that follow. The members of the Army of the Republic of Vietnam (ARVN) tended to blame the U.S. for their defeats and seldom acknowledged the corruption in Saigon and incompetence of many RVNAF commanders in the field. RVNAF accounts are very often riddled with errors and generally avoid responsibility for their failures. This is tragic and very unnecessary since there were many outstanding RVNAF accomplishments and victories that are well documented and are addressed within this book, but when readers are presented with flawed accounts they mistrust anything that the RVNAF have to say. This is unfortunate, since there are many RVNAF accounts that are scrupulously accurate. Among the best is Major General Nguyen Duy Hinh's *Lam Son 719*.[1]

The U.S. press reports are at times exaggerated. Many members of the Saigon press corps later wrote books about the Vietnam War. Stanley Karnow's is one of the best.[2] He won the Pulitzer Prize for his history.

Recollections written by soldiers after the war are the best source. Obviously, these recollections are limited in scope and lack context, but when compared and integrated into the history of the war they reveal details of what happened. But prejudices often appear. One Vietnam veteran wanted me to include his recollections that turned out to be a tirade against his commanding officer in Vietnam. Reminiscences such as these are not included.

Letters home are always a great source of information but are often less than candid. As an example, my aircraft was shot down on a mission in 1966. By a miracle and the skill of the pilot (not me), we all walked away from the crash with very minor injuries. A week later I wrote to my mom and talked about the weather and the stuff that she had mailed to me and mentioned that the aircraft that I was on last week had some mechanical difficulties [riddled by VC bullets] and had to land early before we reached our destination [we crashed]. We continued [we walked out through the jungle] and everyone was okay [but not really, as I ended up with a back problem that haunted me for years]. No problem. Moms are much smarter than we would like to think they are. A week later I got her letter, which simply asked: "How bad were you wounded and will you get medevaced back to the states?" The answer I mailed was the usual: "No problem, everything is fine here."[3]

This is a memoir of all of the Vietnam veterans who are quoted within this book. I also captured quotes and testimony of many people such as Henry Kissinger, Alexander Haig, Richard Nixon, William Westmoreland, Bruce Palmer and others who participated in the war. This is not a fault-finding excursion or a negative book about what went wrong in Vietnam. It is instead a record of what happened in the words of many of the participants and many historians who have written about the war.

Sometimes the comments are brutally frank, such as mine and that of Tom Marshall, who was a helicopter pilot in 1971 moving RVNAF out of Laos during Lam Son 719 (see Chapter 7) and wrote a book about it:

> I'm not saying it's the ARVNs' fault as much as it is the command's fault. The command doesn't even know what the hell it's doing. I mean, it throws them out there on the damn mountaintop and expects them to do damn wonders. It's just like throwing a bunch of dinks—eight hundred dinks—can you imagine, eight hundred RVNAFs being attacked by six thousand NVA. I mean, you can see why they're getting their asses kicked. It's just that plain and simple. It's the United States' advisers and the Vietnamese higher-ups who don't know what in the hell they're doing. They're just dicking around with people's lives.[4]

ONE

The Early Days

At the close of World War II in 1945, the Japanese who had occupied Indochina during the war were on their way home, while the French sought to reclaim their colonial empire. This was not what the Vietnamese had in mind. After having fought the Japanese through a long war, the Vietnamese wanted independence. Ho Chi Minh, the Vietnamese leader, summarized:

> If they [the French] force us into war, we will fight. The struggle will be atrocious, but the Vietnamese people will suffer anything rather than renounce their freedom.[1]

Ho's words were prophetic, as would be proved thirty years later when North Vietnamese tanks rumbled through the gates of the South Vietnamese palace in Saigon, ending the war. In August 1883 a French fleet arrived at the mouth of the Perfume River near the imperial capital of Vietnam, Hue, and demanded the surrender of the government. Before the Vietnamese could respond, the fleet opened fire, murdering thousands of unarmed Vietnamese.[2] The French seized Vietnam and turned it into a colony of France. There were many riches that France wanted to exploit, as most colonial powers do. Rubber, tea and rice were not the least of these. Vietnam had been invaded and occupied over the past few thousand years, but the French occupation was the most recent. As a result of the slaughter of Vietnamese in Hue in 1883, the Vietnamese capitulated and the French took over and declared that Vietnam was now their protectorate, sending in troops. What followed was over fifty years of French exploitation of Vietnam that ended when the Japanese took over.

Along the way there were some strange occurrences. At the World

War I peace conference at Versailles in 1919, a very young man attempted to see President Woodrow Wilson. The young man, whose name was Ho Chi Minh,[3] wanted to argue for the sovereignty of Vietnam, but Wilson refused to see him.[4] Had Wilson done so, the history of Vietnam may have been different, but that was very unlikely. Most say that Ho was a communist, while others argue that he was a nationalist. Today it does not really matter, given the outcome of the war, but his political leanings did change over time.

A very strange situation emerged in Indochina during World War II. The Japanese left the French bureaucratic colonial administration intact to rule Indochina while they directed its activities.[5] This was a decisive period of time. The Vietnamese realized that the French were defeated and incompetent and could not fight (as seen in the fall of France in 1940). The French bureaucracy and planters wanted to protect their interests. While the Japanese exported their plunder from Vietnam nearly 20 percent of the population in the North died from starvation.[6] The reason for the starvation was crop failures in the South. The North was not self-sustaining and suffered the most since it was relying on crops from the South. Years later, the mayor of Hanoi described the scene:

> Peasants came in from the nearby provinces on foot, leaning on each other, carrying their children in baskets. They dug in garbage piles, looking for anything at all, banana skins, orange peels, discarded greens. They even ate rats. But they couldn't get enough to keep alive. They tried to beg, but everyone else was hungry, and they would drop dead in the streets. Every morning, when I opened my door, I found five or six corpses on the step. We organized teams of youths to load the bodies on oxcarts and take them to mass graves outside the city. It was terrifying—and yet it helped our cause because we were able to rally the nation.[7]

In August of 1945, after the U.S. Army Air Corps had incinerated the Japanese towns of Hiroshima and Nagasaki with nuclear weapons, the Japanese decided to surrender, unconditionally.[8] Bao Dai was the titular leader of Vietnam throughout the war. He resided in Hue, the traditional capital of Vietnam, and also spent time at his hunting lodge at Ban Me Thuot. When World War II ended he moved to Hanoi and became the pawn of the Vietnamese nationalist movement under Ho Chi Minh. He was a playboy who did very little, but the Vietminh, the nationalist group led by Ho Chi Minh, used him to their advantage. They appointed him as "Supreme Advisor" and manipulated him for their own purpose.[9] When asked, he sent the following letter to Charles de Galle in France:

> You would understand better if you could see what is happening here, if you could feel this yearning for independence that is in everyone's heart, and which

no human force can any longer restrain. Should you re-establish a French administration here, it will not be obeyed. Every village will be a nest of resistance, each former collaborator an enemy, and your officials and colonists will themselves seek to leave this atmosphere, which will choke them.[10]

Nothing came of this. France was committed to retain their colony of Indochina. By the fall of 1945, it was clear that a war between the French occupiers and the Vietminh was imminent. As the French general Etienne Valluy summarized: "If those gooks want a fight, they'll get it."[11]

The French got their fight. At the same time, Ho appealed to the United States to recognize his cause. At this time, U.S. President Harry Truman was not inclined to support an avowed communist such as Ho against a very weak ally: France.

In the postwar period, the French strengthened their control of Vietnam without regard to the Vietnamese people. Atrocities were committed by both sides, including the massacre of about 150 French civilians in Saigon.[12]

Many French plantation owners applauded the return of the French, but their joy was short-lived when the French were later defeated. Nevertheless, twenty years after the defeat of the French the French plantation owners were still in Vietnam exploiting its resources. It was not until 1975 when the Saigon regime collapsed that the Vietnamese were able to get rid of most of the French. Even so, a residue of French planters remain to this day in Vietnam.

The French sought a "Set Piece Battle" with the Vietminh. This meant a conventional fight in which both sides faced off and fought it out in a battle, one side losing or the other. The Vietminh did not fight that way. It came down to guerrilla warfare with ambushes on the French, and the Vietminh then fading away. The best example of this is the destruction of the French Mobile Group 100 that Dr. Bernard B. Fall described in his book *Street Without Joy*.[13] Dr. Fall was killed when he later stepped on a land mine. Hollywood re-created a part of this massacre in the Mel Gibson movie *We Were Soldiers*. The film was based upon General Harold G. Moore and Joseph L. Galloway's book, *We Were Soldiers Once ... and Young*.[14]

The war with the French would drag on for nine years. Ho made it clear to the French: "You can kill ten of my men for everyone I kill of yours, but even at those odds, I will win."[15] Bao Dai was a playboy, but he was no fool, and he fled to Hong Kong when it was clear that Ho would defeat the French. S. J. Perelman, the U.S. humorist, author and screenwriter, met Bao Dai in Hong Kong at that time and recorded what he saw:

The pleasure dome where His Majesty frolicked nightly turned out to be a somewhat sedater version of Broadway's Roseland.... Bao Dai was seated in a snug alcove surrounded by several hostesses whose skinny necks and high-pitched avian cackle lent them more than a passing resemblance to a flock of spring fryers. The royal exile, a short, slippery-looking customer rather on the pudgy side and freshly dipped in Crisco, wore a fixed, oily grin that was vaguely reptilian. Since he spoke almost no English, the interview was necessarily limited to pidgin and whatever pathetic scraps of French we could remember from Frazier and Square. To put him at his ease, I inquired sociably whether the pen of his uncle was in the garden. Apparently the query was fraught with delicate implications involving the conflict in Indochina, for he shrugged evasively and buried his nose in his whiskey-and-soda.[16]

As a humorist, S. J. Perelman was unsurpassed, but for those of us who suffered terribly through basic French class and hated it, this famous statement translated from French was "The pen of my aunt is on the table [or bureau] of my uncle." Perelman was so clever that he altered the French quote and Bao Dai never picked up on that and probably did not care. Bao Dai was lured back by the French and served as chief of state (doing nothing) until the final French defeat and withdrawal in 1956. Bao Dai was the last emperor of Vietnam. Among the people in Bao Dai's cabinet was a bureaucrat named Ngo Dinh Diem. Diem would play a key role in the history of Vietnam.

There was much bad news for the West in the 1949–1950 time frame, all of which influenced Vietnam. Chairman Mao defeated the Nationalist government in China and stationed his troops along the border of Vietnam. They were ready to provide support to the Vietminh in spite of the fact that the Chinese had been traditional enemies of the Vietnamese. Soul-searching in the United States revolved around who lost China. With Senator Joseph McCarthy initiating a red witch hunt in the United States, there was no sympathy for anyone such as Ho, who could be viewed as a communist. President Truman had no interest in initiating any contact with or negotiating with Ho. This was also a Cold War issue. The United States would support the French in Indochina, and in return the French would support the U.S. doctrine in Europe for containment.

The Soviet Union had constructed and detonated its first nuclear weapon thanks to input from traitors in the United States and United Kingdom. The United States had lost its sole possession of nuclear technology, and with that went an enormous bargaining chip that could have been used to negotiate a settlement in Vietnam if Truman had wished to do so.

The French continued to drain their military resources fighting a losing war in Vietnam. By 1950, French losses exceeded 50,000 and the Vietminh were killing French officers at a rate faster than they could be graduated from officer schools in France.[17] This reduced the ability of France to meet their NATO requirements in Europe. By late 1952, French casualties (dead, wounded, and missing) were up to more than 90,000.[18] By this time, the United States was funding most of the cost of the French war but had not committed any ground forces.

The war in Korea had an effect on Vietnam. When the North Koreans invaded South Korea in June 1950 the United States responded by moving thousands of troops to defend their ally South Korea, and this was one of the most curious wars in recent history. It was called by the United States a "Police Action." Some background is relevant. In 1950, Dean Acheson, the U.S. Secretary of State, announced that Korea was outside of the U.S. "Defense Perimeter." This occurred during his Press Club speech on 12 January 1950. The North Koreans believed what Acheson said and viewed his statement as a green light for them to invade the South. They should not have believed Acheson's statement. The United States, as it turned out, would fight to defend its ally. Acheson would later deny his statement and indicated that his Press Club speech was "grossly distorted."[19] This was symptomatic of the U.S. view of Asia during the 1950s. Korea and Vietnam were sideshows that did not deserve much thought or time until major conflicts erupted. The focus was on the Soviet Union and Senator Joseph McCarthy (called "Tail-Gunner Joe" because he claimed that he was a tail-gunner in a U.S. aircraft in the Pacific during World War II: He flew one mission). These two were the major threats to our democracy. U.S. troops were tied up in Korea and the United States had a reduced capability to assist France in Vietnam, except for funding and some air support missions.

Dien Bien Phu

The French demonstrated that they never understood their enemy during the conflict in Indochina, as seen in their last battle. The French decided that they would establish a base camp west of Hanoi in a valley called Dien Bien Phu.

This was intended to block the return of Vietminh General Vo Nguyen Giap into Laos, which he had easily accomplished in 1953 but had withdrawn from because of the rains.[20] This was similar to the situation experienced by the RVNAF and NVA, as seen in the battle of Lam Son 719 in 1971 (see Chapter 7). In this way, the French hoped to entice the Vietminh to attack them and for the French it would become a "Set Piece Battle." The French got their wish. Giap marshaled his forces around the French garrison. By 13 March 1954, Giap was prepared to attack. He had assembled 50,000 troops at Dien Bien Phu. The French had 13,000, about half of whom were fighters.[21] One of Giap's soldiers recalled:

> We had to cross mountains and jungles, marching at night and sleeping by day to avoid enemy bombing. We sometimes slept in foxholes, or just by the trail. We each carried a rifle, ammunition, and hand grenades, and our packs contained a blanket, a mosquito net, and a change of clothes. We each had a week's supply of rice, which we refilled at depots along the way. We ate greens and bamboo shoots that we picked in the jungle, and occasionally villagers would give us a bit of meat. I'd been in the Vietminh for nine years by then, and I was accustomed to it.[22]

The French battle plan was a soldier's nightmare. The French established their camp in a valley, which meant that any force on the surrounding hills could destroy the French. If the Vietminh closed in, the French would have to rely on air resupply and had limited assets, although the United States agreed to provide some airlift capability. The French thought that this would be a perfect "Set Piece Battle." It was.

The French commander, Colonel Christian de Castries, had established strong points on the hills surrounding Dien Bien Phu. As one might expect, he named these for his French mistresses. Perhaps like his mistresses, it was a French fantasy: The outposts could be easily overcome by the Vietminh, and they were. The greatest miscalculation was artillery. The French concluded that since the Vietminh had no artillery at Dien Bien Phu and the French had air support, Dien Bien Phu could survive an attack by the Vietminh.[23] Giap solved the problem for the Vietminh. The troops dismantled their artillery pieces and humped them up the mountains to overlook Dien Bien Phu. Vietminh artillery overlooking Dien Bien Phu fired at will. It was a "turkey shoot."

Giap's battle plan was simple:

> By launching a big offensive with fresh troops, we could have fore-shortened the duration of the campaign, and avoided the wear and tear of a long operation.... [But] we saw that these tactics had a very great, basic disadvantage. Our troops lacked experience in attacking fortified entrenched camps. If we wanted to win swiftly, success could not be assured.... Consequently, *we resolutely chose to strike and* advance surely ... strike to win, strike only when success is certain. If it is not, then do not strike.[24]

Initially, Giap lost heavily and changed his battle plan. A veteran of the battle recalled:

> General Giap changed the entire plan. He stopped the attack and pulled back our artillery. Now the shovel became our most important weapon. Everyone dug tunnels and trenches under fire, sometimes hitting hard soil and only advancing

five or six yards a day. But we gradually surrounded Dien Bien Phu with an underground network several hundred miles long, and we could tighten the noose around the French.[25]

It was a hard fight. Giap's infantry moved through the tunnels and trenches to the French line while his artillery pounded the French position. Bad weather limited air support for the French. Two U.S. Air Force officers were killed at Dien Bien Phu while attempting to resupply: Captain James McGovern and his copilot, Wallace Buford, died when their supply aircraft was shot down by the Vietminh. These were among the earliest U.S. casualties in the Vietnam War. Over 58,000 U.S. dead would follow after the French war.[26]

The French artillery commander faced with defeat committed suicide. The French defenses were easily overcome. On 7 May 1954, the French surrendered at Dien Bien Phu and thousands of the surviving French soldiers became what were known as "pearls." This meant that they were hostages until France paid a ransom for their release. Ten years later, as I drove around Saigon I saw at intersections small tombstones to French soldiers killed in Vietnam. I often wondered if anyone in France cared about these people. They were for the most part legionnaires, people whom the French hired to fight their wars. They were quickly forgotten by the French, but not by their relatives in Germany and elsewhere.

While Giap and the French were fighting at Dien Bien Phu, a peace conference was scheduled in Geneva, Switzerland. The peace conference started on 7 May 1954, the same day that the French surrendered at Dien Bien Phu. The French would soon be out of Vietnam and the forces left behind would be those of Ho in Hanoi and Bao Dai enjoying the life of a playboy in Paris. Bao Dai appointed Ngo Dinh Diem, the Nationalist, as his prime minister for South Vietnam. Diem would reside in Saigon. Diem had an inflexible personality and was a Catholic in a predominantly Buddhist country: two items that would haunt the United States years later.

The peace conference was short as most conferences go and was concluded in July 1954. One observer at the peace conference had stated: "You cannot expect to negotiate at the conference table what you have lost on the battlefield." This was proved wrong. Vietnam would be partitioned at the seventeenth parallel (north of Hue) with the Vietminh controlling the North and Boa Dai in the South. The plan was for free elections to be conducted two years later to reunify Vietnam. The Soviet Union and China had dominated the discussions. The Vietminh would leave the South and the French would leave the North. Few participants were happy with the outcome. The Vietminh were outraged. After winning Vietnam on the battlefield, the Vietminh now had to settle for a divided country. Pham

Van Dong, the Vietminh representative, speaking about China's Zhou Enlai simply said, "He has double-crossed us."[27] Zhou supported the partition of Vietnam. The migration of people between the North and the South had started. Added into the mix were Vietnamese nationalists and Catholics who fled south rather than live under Ho's Communist regime.[28] Diem consolidated his power in the South while Ho did the same in the North. The planned elections to reunify the country in 1956 never occurred. In April 1956, the last French soldiers left South Vietnam. The United States inherited Diem's anti-communist regime in the South.[29]

In the years that followed the Geneva Accords, the United States increased aid to Diem while Ho infiltrated more troops into South Vietnam. In December 1960, Hanoi established a new organization in the South: the National Liberation Front. Its purpose was to unify the various groups opposing Diem.[30] At that time, the United States was involved in a major effort to train the South Vietnamese Army.

Counting Dominoes

Until the French defeat, the United States had provided funds and hardware, including aircraft, to help the French fight their war against the Vietminh. The South would be governed by Ngo Dinh Diem. Diem was an unpopular leader hated by both the North Vietnamese and the Buddhists in the South. As Secretary of State John Foster Dulles put it: "Americans had underwritten Diem because we knew of no one better."[31] The Joint Chiefs opposed any support of Diem until he proved that he had a stable government, something that never occurred. Eisenhower embraced the regional domino theory and explained it with his metaphor: "You have a row of dominoes set up, you knock over the first one, and what will happen to the very last one is that it will go over very quickly." In other words, if South Vietnam fell to the Communists, so would Southeast Asia. This would lead to a global bandwagon effect with countries appeasing and joining the Soviet Union since the United States could not be trusted.

Each president following Eisenhower embraced the domino theory, which was flawed. It assumed that all nations had the same culture, background and aspirations, which they did not. Vietnam, Laos and Cambodia fell, but the rest, such as Thailand, did not. With the defeat of the French, the conclusion was that the United States would need to shore up the Diem regime to prevent the South Vietnam domino from falling to the North.

TWO

The Advisors

After Ngo Dinh Diem took over as president of South Vietnam in 1954, there were a few years of peace while Ho rearmed in the north and Diem cleaned out stay-behind enemies of his regime now known as the Vietcong. Diem ran a corrupt, autocratic regime and operated similar to a Chinese mandarin. His regime had many problems, such as lack of popular support and his repression of the Buddhist majority, who did not trust him since he was a Catholic. While the United States was sending more advisors, the RVNAF appeared to be losing while the Vietcong were gaining confidence and increasing their numbers. By the end of 1962, the United States had 11,300 people in South Vietnam.[1]

Military Assistance Command, Vietnam Patch (author's collection).

Ap Bac

David Halberstam was a journalist in Saigon during the early years of the Vietnam War. His book *The Making of a Quagmire* was published in 1964, before many of the significant events of the war had occurred. Halberstam covered the Battle of Ap Bac, January 2, 1963. Lieutenant Colonel John Paul Vann was advisor to the South Vietnamese 7th Division.

A force of 2,500 members of ARVN, supported by U.S. helicopters, ARVN armored personnel carriers, and advisors, was defeated by three hundred Vietcong. As the ARVN force moved in on the Vietcong, the Vietcong opened fire. One VC leaped up and tossed a grenade at the advancing armored personnel carriers (APCs), which did no harm but encouraged other VC to do the same.[2] This stopped the ARVN advance. Nothing could persuade the ARVN officers to move forward. The ARVN under Ngo Dinh Diem, the South Vietnamese president, was accustomed to avoiding combat and faking operations.[3] The battle was a disastrous defeat and it demonstrated that the war was rapidly being lost, something that few in the Kennedy administration wanted to hear. After briefings and efforts to get official recognition of the problem without success, John Paul Vann went public about the situation in discussions with David Halberstam and Neil Sheehan. It made news in the States and Halberstram got the Pulitzer Prize for reporting after he returned to the States in December 1963.

Ap Bac was a turning point in the war. Until then, it had been a war on the cheap for the Kennedy administration. U.S. aid and advisors were sent, but the war was well down on Kennedy's list of priorities and received little press coverage. Earlier, Kennedy had decided to let Robert McNamara, the Secretary of Defense, "handle the war." This was not working. McNamara knew nothing about Ap Bac until he read about it in the *New York Times* (Halberstam's article). Now people, Vann and others, were publicly stating the war was being lost: "*New York Times ...* headline noted that five helicopters had been downed and another nine hit. The subhead was uncompromising: 'Defeat Worst Since Buildup Began—Three Americans are Killed in Vietnam.'"[4]

At first the U.S. military shrugged off the results of Ap Bac. General Paul D. Harkins, commander of MACV, called the Vietcong "those raggedy-ass little bastards."[5] In a comment worthy of Diem, Admiral Felt, CINCPAC, stated: "The Viet Cong left the battlefield, didn't they?" It was apparent to Kennedy that the military (and perhaps McNamara as well) had become detached from reality. General Harkins, was still claiming victory: "Yes, I consider it a victory. We took the objective." What Harkins did not say was that the ARVN occupied Ap Bac two days after the victorious Vietcong had conducted an orderly withdrawal.[6]

Kennedy had always liked and trusted journalists. He told his friend in the press corps Charles Bartlett: "We don't have a prayer of staying in Vietnam. Those people hate us. They are going to throw our asses out of there at almost any point. But I can't give up a piece of territory like that to the Communists and then get the people to reelect me [in 1964]." To his aide Kenny O'Donnell: "If I tried to pull out completely now from

Vietnam we would have another Joe McCarthy red scare on our hands, but I can do it after I'm reelected. So we better make damn sure that I *am* reelected."[7] Kennedy was getting input from many sources after Ap Bac. While the military argued for more advisors, helicopters, and weapons, the Harriman group argued against a purely military solution. Nation building and civic action programs were the answer: "What was needed was a consuming motive to lead South Vietnamese to fight for Saigon. Why, for example, should peasants die for a government which, when it recovered territory from the Viet Cong, helped the landowners collect back rent?" In the end, Kennedy settled for a modest increase in the number of advisors while he waited for his second term, which would never arrive.[8]

The era of charm and easy deceit by the U.S. government was coming to an end. In the long term this may have been one of the most significant outcomes of Ap Bac. It started a trend in the press and later in the entire nation to believe that the government could not be trusted to tell the truth, a fact that subsequent events would prove was correct. Newspapers were now pressing for answers and Military Assistance Command, Vietnam (MACV) continued to blame correspondents for bad press. If there was a time for the United States to abandon Diem and leave Vietnam it was now. Diem's actions after Ap Bac further condemned him and his regime. Journalist Deborah Shapley explained what had happened:

> The officers of the Seventh Infantry Division who performed so ignominiously at Ap Bac—were later decorated by Diem, for they seized the Viet Cong radio transmitter that afternoon—had been chosen by Diem for their loyalty to him, for coup insurance, not courage or proficiency in war. Neil Sheehan, the young UPI reporter in Saigon at that time [Sheehan would later write the history of the Vietnam War and John Paul Vann], would later learn that Diem had promulgated a secret order to his trusted officers the previous fall: they were not to take casualties on their own side. Casualties would make army service unpopular, and Diem needed a loyal army so that his family could stay in power.[9]

Stanley Karnow's history of the war was published in 1983 and is considered by many to be the most complete description of the war. It won the Pulitzer Price and was the basis for the public television series *Vietnam: A Television History*. Karnow served as chief correspondent for the series. He claimed that he had no cause to plead in writing this book,[10] but he had biases that become apparent in reading his history. He demonstrated that the United States made every mistake possible in fighting this war, Ho Chi Minh was a nationalist who should be admired and the Nixon administration was self-serving (this last may be due to the fact that Nixon had Karnow on his "enemies" list).[11] In 1959 Karnow wrote the dispatches on the first U.S. deaths in Vietnam.[12]

The outcome at Ap Bac aggravated the friction then growing between the American government and the news media. Neither Kennedy nor his successors would impose censorship, which would have required them to acknowledge that a real war was being waged. Instead, they wanted journalists to cooperate by accentuating the positive.[13]

That did not happen. Correspondents simply told the truth, with their own twist, which is their privilege. I met with a correspondent after Ap Bac and accused him of being a journalistic prostitute who would write anything just to sell newspapers. He swilled his scotch (I was buying), pushed back from the table, laughed and said this: "Captain, everything that I write needs to be checked out [vetted] and if I screw up and lie, I lose my job. More important, what is going on in Vietnam is so outrageous that all I have to do is tell the truth and my story gets filed along with many others." Just after the Ap Bac battle, when Peter Arnett of the Associated Press asked him a tough question, Admiral Felt shot back: "Get on the team."[14]

Sheehan's coverage of the Battle of Ap Bac is quite lengthy, possibly because of Vann's involvement. Vann was in and out of Vietnam a number of times before he was killed in a helicopter crash in 1972. His extensive and important service is seen in Chapter 8. Sheehan's thesis is that Vietnam was a wrongful war and he uses military reports to prove his point, as seen later. Sheehan quotes the story making its rounds after Ap Bac:

A Viet Cong porter spends two and one half months toting three mortar shells down the mountain and rain-forest tracks of the Ho Chi Minh Trail. He finally reaches a battle and hands them to a mortar man, who fires them off faster than the porter can count and says: "Now go back and get three more."[15] Sheehan always captured humor, and this makes his history very readable.

Francois Sully (a correspondent for *Newsweek*) clashed with U.S. ambassador Nolting over the Strategic Hamlet Program (a colossal failure). The Strategic Hamlet Program was designed to concentrate rural populations into camps where they could be isolated from the Vietcong. The problems were that it uprooted the rural populations from their traditional lands where their ancestors were buried and there was no way of knowing how many of the people in the camps were VC. Nolting asked, "Why, Monsieur Sully, do you always see the hole in the doughnut?" Sully replied, "Because, Monsieur l'Ambassadeur, there is a hole in the doughnut."[16] To the relief of Nolting, Diem expelled Sully.[17]

The result was changes by Kennedy including the removal of General Harkins and his subsequent retirement. It appears that Harkins was the only person of any rank who believed that the South Vietnamese had won a victory at Ap Bac. After Harkins returned to the United States, a common phrase in the army upon screwing up was "I just pulled a Harkins."[18]

A fascinating view of Harkins is provided by Lewis Sorley: Many of the lies Harkins was sending to Washington were in response to back channels (informal flag officer messages) from his mentor, General Maxwell Taylor, who wanted to present a rosy picture of progress in the war.[19] Taylor acknowledges in his memoir that he sent a private cable to Harkins asking for his assessment but obviously makes no reference to any pressure on Harkins for a favorable report.[20] The reports that Harkins sent were mixed. McNamara told LBJ that Harkins was sending false reports to Washington, but McNamara may have had a hand in the false information that was circulating.[21]

The Battle of Ap Bac was a decisive event. Most scholars agree that it proved that Diem was losing the war, but historian Mark Moyar refutes this view in two ways. Moyar claims that Halberstam and Sheehan were young reporters who were misled by John Paul Vann and they mounted a smear campaign against the South Vietnamese government.[22] Moyar fails to tell the reader that Halberstam received the Pulitzer Prize for his reporting. Moyar blames Vann's actions for the defeat but does not tell the entire story of Ap Bac. Author A. J. Langguth provides a complete summary of Ap Bac that includes interviews he conducted in Ho Chi Minh City in 1996. Moyar's alternate view of Ap Bac is based upon a primary source and perhaps two secondary sources. Langguth's account of the battle appears more credible. He points out that the Vietcong were well trained and states: "The RVNAF displayed the result of their own brand of training—months of avoiding casualties ... making a priority of pleasing the palace, not fighting the war."[23] Langguth points out that Halberstam and Arnett got a major input from angry helicopter pilots as they flew back from Ap Bac and also queried other military contacts. Sheehan had traveled to Tan Hiep to piece together the details of the Vietcong victory.[24] The defeat was so bad that the ARVN left their dead and wounded behind and fled in panic. U.S. brigadier General Robert York later visited Ap Bac and found that the ARVN dead still littered the battlefield. U.S. advisors loaded about twenty ARVN dead on a vehicle and departed.[25] It got worse. When Harkins and Diem trumpeted victory, the Vietcong commander challenged the ARVN to a rematch and returned to Ap Bac with his battalion. The RVNAF took no action on the VC challenge.[26] The negative view of the RVNAF was not a case of two young reporters misled by John Paul Vann. Twelve years later, those ragged-ass little bastards would kick our ass.

The Fall of Diem

Following Ap Bac, the situation did not improve for the RVNAF. Faking operations and promotions of RVNAF generals based upon loyalty to Diem and not military competence took their toll. For Diem, it was a family experience. His brother Nhu was a good organizer and expert at intrigue, which helped the regime remain in power.[27] Worse, Diem's repression of the Buddhists had caused a violent reaction. The world press saw the self-immolation of Buddhists in the streets as a way of protest. Madam Nhu, the wife of Diem's brother, in her best style offered that if the Buddhists needed more gasoline to kill themselves she would be happy to provide it.[28] Some RVNAF generals, perhaps motivated by hope of promotion or a realization that the war could not be won by Diem, planned a coup. The United States cooperated. Henry Cabot Lodge, the U.S. ambassador in Saigon, summarized. "We are launched on a course which there is no respectable turning back: the overthrow of the Diem government.... There is no possibility, in my view, that the war can be won under a Diem administration."[29]

Kennedy had hoped for a sort of "Bloodless Coup" in which Diem would be deposed and given an airplane ticket to live elsewhere and a military junta would replace him. The RVNAF military was not that stupid: If you depose someone, you want to make sure that they do not return later and depose you. The coup was executed on 2 November 1963. Diem and Nhu fled to a Catholic church in Saigon and hoped to escape from there, but they were trapped and surrendered to the insurgents who offered them some sort of safe conduct. Diem and Nhu were loaded into the back of an APC and were murdered there. Photos of their riddled corpses circulated around the world.

Kennedy was horrified.[30] He had not expected this. Less than three weeks later, Kennedy was killed in Dallas and Vice President Lyndon B. Johnson assumed the presidency. In less than a month, two heads of state had been murdered. The war in Vietnam was now under new management.

What followed was a succession of RVNAF generals who took over the government and were in turn replaced by other RVNAF generals. The first to lead the military junta was General Duong Van Minh, called "Big Minh." He lasted only a few months before he was replaced. This was not helpful to the war effort.

Following the death of JFK, Vietnam appeared to be the last priority of the new president. LBJ was more concerned about civil rights and economic issues. He continued Kennedy's policies in Vietnam. It soon became apparent that the situation in South Vietnam had been degenerating since the death of Diem. The Strategic Hamlet Program[31] started by Diem and hated by the peasants who were forced to live there was in shambles. Many of the RVNAF in the field were pulled back to Saigon to participate in coups attempts and other activities that made it more difficult to defend the hamlets. By December, in one area three-quarters of the hamlets had been destroyed by the VC or the inhabitants themselves.[32] Word finally reached Washington that all was not well in South Vietnam. LBJ sent Secretary of Defense McNamara to South Vietnam for an assessment. He blamed poor U.S. leadership (no surprise: Harkins) and also indicated that the situation should be monitored. If there was no improvement, stronger measures should be taken. The JCS argued for stronger measures. General Curtis "Bombs Away" Lemay, the Air Force chief, argued for bombing North Vietnam, as one might expect: "We are swatting flies when we should be going after the manure pile."[33] By early 1964, the JCS proposed a plan to LBJ. The most extreme measure was the introduction of U.S. troops to take over the war. The United States would accomplish the direction of the war. The war would become "Americanized." LBJ did not approve the plan at that time. It was before the election. LBJ's thought was that *wars are too serious to be entrusted to generals.* He also knew that the armed forces "need battles and bombs and bullets in order to be heroic."[34] This is not far from President Eisenhower's warning when he left office about the threat of the military-industrial complex.

Several things happened that forced LBJ's hand. The effectiveness of the South Vietnamese regime continued to plummet and it was clear that South Vietnam would soon lose the war. In August 1964, Hanoi handed the United States a gift that provided the United States with an excuse to intervene in a major way in the war in Vietnam. Many of the details have been contested ever since. North Vietnam torpedo boats attacked a U.S. destroyer in international waters in the Gulf of Tonkin. U.S. warships returned fire. There were claims that a second attack followed, but these were false. Both sides contested the events, but this was an election year for LBJ, so he needed to appear as a firm leader. The United States retaliated with air strikes that blew up boats and did other damage, but further actions by the United States were more serious. LBJ presented to Congress what has been called the "Gulf of Tonkin Resolution." It was approved by Congress on 7 August 1964 and gave LBJ the authority to deploy troops without declaring war. LBJ ordered the deployment of U.S. troops to rescue a corrupt regime in Saigon. Over ten years later, in 1975, the fantasy ended when NVA tanks rolled into the palace in Saigon and ended the war. Between the two dates, over 58,000 U.S. citizens and over a million Vietnamese people died.

By 1965 when I arrived in Vietnam it was difficult to determine who was in charge of the government of South Vietnam. I was assigned as an advisor to a Vietnamese battalion at Pleiku. I met my ARVN battalion commander and realized that he was a man of many interests who had served years as an ARVN officer.

Until Ap Bac, U.S. forces were composed of advisors and Special Forces units. Among the first U.S. units deployed was the 1st Air Cavalry Division, which set up a base camp in the Central Highlands near the town of An Khe. In November of 1965, U.S. forces received intelligence that the North Vietnamese were assembling troops in the Ia Drang Valley southwest of Pleiku and a strike was planned using the advantage of the helicopters to move troops in to surprise and defeat the enemy. Lieutenant Colonel Hal Moore's 1st Battalion of the 7th Cavalry (which had a heritage back to Custer's old outfit) was airlifted in to trap the North Vietnamese. The result was a major battle called the Ia Drang.

All advisors had strange experiences during those early days in 1965–1966 and I had several that stuck in my mind.

I was assigned to Vietnam as a battalion advisor in the Central Highlands. I arrived in November 1965. I recall leaving the United States where it was a bit chilly and arriving in Saigon by air. When they opened the cabin door I walked out into what I can only describe as a blast furnace. I instantly decided that I did not like this place. One of my West Point classmates met me and drove me to the MACV compound, where I was issued an M2 carbine, 90 rounds of ammunition and two sets of jungle fatigues. They then gave me a survival kit and I got a bit unglued: Why would I need a survival kit? I am just an advisor who is supposed to dispense wisdom to my Vietnamese counterpart. He will take care of me, right? As I was receiving my equipment at the MACV compound, I was told that there was a big fight going on near Pleiku in the Ia Drang Valley and all hands were to fly out early in the morning to help out with the battle. That night I had a small cell in a hotel with all my gear packed and ready. I had a bit of trouble getting to sleep as I watched these strange Asian salamanders running across the ceiling. I don't know how they did that. Maybe suction cups at the ends of their paws. As I went to sleep, I figured that if one of these creatures dropped on my back he would own the bed and I would be on the ceiling.

As planned, a group of us flew out of Saigon with a stop at An Khe on our way to Pleiku. As we refueled at An Khe, the 1st Air Cavalry Division was still setting up their base camp. I remember that they had a huge 1st Air Cavalry patch made of plastic or something that they were trying to install on the side of Hong Kong Mountain that rose above their camp.

It kept getting blown down. It was entertaining us as we were waiting for the aircraft to be refueled. I don't know if they ever got it right. It seemed to me at the time and since that this was a total waste of time, like painting rocks. All it did was give the Vietcong a good aiming point for their rockets.

We landed at Pleiku and each of us went to our assigned duties. I met my Vietnamese counterpart whom I was supposed to advise. I'll never figure out how a young brand-new captain like me who had never heard a shot fired in anger and didn't speak the language was supposed to advise a Vietnamese major who had been fighting the Vietcong for ten years.

My new counterpart suggested that I might want to get rid of the M2 carbine in favor of something that might be more lethal.[35] With that, he had his soldiers open his armory and let me go through and pick out anything that I wanted. I was like a kid in a candy store with unlimited cash. I picked out a Thompson submachine gun (gangster gun) and several thousand rounds of ammunition and then moved to grenades and explosives. By this time I was doing mental math. I weighed 145 pounds and might have a problem if I was humping more than my body weight in the jungle. I loaded up with grenades but skipped the explosives because I was afraid of them. By this time I believe that my weight, including all of my baggage, was well over 300 pounds. This was nothing new. I had humped more than

Duc Co Special Forces Camp (courtesy of Olen C. Phipps, Jr.).

that in training, as most soldiers do. Finally, I profusely thanked my counterpart and went to the MACV compound to find out what I was supposed to do. It was less than 24 hours since I had arrived in Saigon and I was sweating profusely. I was a bit nervous. The senior advisor, Colonel Ted Mataxis, told me that my job was to go to the Duc Co Special Forces Camp and help with its defense and he wanted me there now. He must have wondered if I would come back alive. He let that thought pass, but I did not.

Duc Co Special Forces Camp was on the Cambodian border and was close to the Ho Chi Minh Trail, which our people monitored and could call in air support to disrupt. This annoyed the enemy since they were staging a major camp in the Ia Drang Valley to attack the South Vietnamese. Duc Co was a sideshow, since all of the action was with Hal Moore's 7th Cavalry in the Ia Drang (there were other battalions involved not shown in the film), a few kilometers to our south. All of us at Duc Co did not view this as a sideshow. By this time, because of incoming artillery and rockets Duc Co was a sea of mud. It must have rivaled a scene from World War I.

I choppered in with a few others to Duc Co. I was fully loaded with more than my body weight of weapons and ammunition. There was so much incoming artillery that the helicopters did not land to discharge cargo but shoved the cargo (including me) out at about ten to thirty feet above the ground.

In combat, helicopters do not land with the captain saying, "Passengers, you may now exit the aircraft." Instead, the aircraft hovers ten to 20 feet in the air. Cargo is shoved out and passengers jump. The nasty part is that if you hesitate and don't jump when told to do so your next opportunity may be 20 to 30 feet ... then 30 to 40 feet, and so on, because the helicopter is ascending fast. The idea is to get the chopper out of there real fast so it does not get hit. Pilots like that approach.

I landed in the mud, and because of the weight of ammunition and equipment I sank down to my hips in mud. The chopper crew smiled and waved as they left in a hurry. Artillery rounds were coming in and I was stuck in the mud. This was a very serious situation and I did not appreciate the smiles and laughter of the helicopter crew as they sped off. The Special Forces commander observed what was going on and realized that he could use the weapons and ammunition I was carrying and sent several Vietnamese out to retrieve them. If they could drag me in as well, that was good; if not, no problem. The four Vietnamese arrived and tried to pull me out because much of the ammunition and equipment was stuck to me. It was similar to Gulliver's Travels only instead of tying Gulliver down, they were trying to drag Gulliver (me) out. They succeeded and we rushed to the operations center inside the bunker.

As I entered, I must have looked like a giant Fudgsicle with legs. As soon as I was indoors I noticed a very overpowering smell. It was me. When I arrived, I noticed that work seemed to stop and everyone was looking around and finally focused on me. Everyone was eager to tell me that I had landed in the area where the water buffalo and God knows what else liked to defecate. I was treated to comments like: "Captain, you need to work on your personal hygiene," and, "Wash much?" I was ordered out of the operations center and back into incoming artillery. The only way to get to the showers (rain) was to go back into artillery barrage, but I had no choice. so I decided that I didn't smell that bad after all. Anyway, you can get used to anything if the alternative is death.

As I sat outside the bunker in the rain at the end of my first day in Vietnam watching the flash of the artillery impact, I wondered if I would get a posthumous valor award for being killed in action by buffalo shit. This is actually what happened ... no shit, please excuse the pun.

I had been in Pleiku for a month or so when the Vietnamese major stopped by my hooch. He said that he had a very urgent problem. The Montagnards nearby were very upset because a tiger was eating their livestock at night. Since he was the nearest South Vietnamese official, they were bothering him daily and were becoming very annoying and almost threatening. If I could hunt down and kill the tiger, this would be a great chance to win the hearts and minds of the people (at least the Montagnards) and I would be a hero. I said, "Sure." Up to that point the biggest game that I had ever hunted were squirrels, but I didn't tell him that. We've all seen movies where the great white hunter and his faithful native gun bearer stake out a goat at the bottom of a tree and then sit in the tree until the tiger comes for lunch. *Bang!* Instant hero. I had my plan.

I enlisted the help of another advisor with the promise that we could co-share the glory. It had to be somebody really fat. In case gunfire failed, Plan B was to run like hell, and the slower runner would become tiger chow. We told the boss where we were going. He was very supportive: "You've got to be joking. A tiger?... You're insane blah, blah ... but go ahead since you've already committed yourself to the Vietnamese." Next we visited the Montagnards for the goat. They looked very skeptical but offered up the goat, which had to be the foulest-smelling animal on the planet. Besides, the goat would probably end up on the tiger's menu in a few nights, anyway, so they had no problem handing her over. Next, we had to find a good place to stake out the goat. Close to the Montagnard village where the tiger dined every night seemed logical, but we didn't like being close to the village at night because the Montagnards would hear us and start firing thinking that we were VC or Vietnamese or the tiger or something else that they didn't like. We staked out a place not far from the village along a logical path for a tiger to use. Since we weren't tigers, it was a blind guess.

We tethered the goat at the base of a big tree and started climbing. I felt sorry for the goat. "Stop here; if we go any further, we won't be able to see the tiger when he [or she] is munching." So we stopped and set up. I had my automatic rifle, a pistol, and several grenades, just in case. The other advisor thought that grenades were a bad idea. You know, you throw the grenades down and the shrapnel comes back up. Ouch. Got rid of the grenades. Darkness set in, totally dark.

Pretty soon the other guy said, "I hear something that must be it."

No sound from the goat.

"Sssh," said I.

"He's probably right below us and you're going to give us away."

"Not below us, above us!"

"Huh?" I looked up into the biggest pair of luminescent yellow eyes that I have ever seen. They blinked. He was above us. We opened up with everything we had, firing up, down and all around. The goat dove behind the tree, covering her head with her hooves. We were out of the tree in a heartbeat on our way to the jeep.

"What about the goat?"

"Forget the goat; we're the main course this evening."

As I sprinted past the other guy I thought, Plan B is working, perfectly. As we drove off at maximum speed I kept trying to remember how fast a tiger could run and wondering if he could overtake us. I concluded he could, so I fired my remaining ammunition at the shadows behind us.

We had about half an hour to get back to the camp: plenty of time to coordinate our lies. We drove directly to the club where everyone waited. They had heard all of the firing. The colonel opened with, "Good evening, gentlemen. Should I call in an air strike or did you take care of the problem?" We assured the colonel that with all of the ammunition we had fired we must have gotten him. The colonel left and then the serious lies started. Well, it really wasn't just one tiger; it must have been at least two or three, maybe even four. We took them out as fast as they came at us. It was a slaughter. Yellow and black fur and tiger parts were flying all around us. If it hadn't been for the fact that we ran out of ammunition, we'd still be back there looking for more tigers and, in fact, the only reason we came back was to get more ammunition. *But* since the bar is open, we could be persuaded to stay awhile before returning to the kill. We didn't have to buy a drink the rest of the night, and as dawn broke and a new day started we promised to return to the scene to collect a few tiger heads and whatever was left of the goat. We returned that afternoon to find absolutely nothing except the tether and a large pile of cartridge casings piled up at the bottom of the tree. It looked like the goat had gnawed through the tether and made her escape. Good for the goat. Free to roam and do whatever goats do in the jungle. No sign of the tiger, except we did find some tracks.

I'm not sure exactly what happened, but the tiger never reappeared and we became co-heroes. My best guess is that he was probably so terrified by all the firing that he told his wife that it was time to relocate to a quieter area. He probably told her that the humans had staked out a horrible-smelling goat that no self-respecting predator would go near. He also told her that he even winked at one of the humans to let the guy know that he intended no harm. Then all hell broke loose.

The goat also never reappeared, but my guess is that she is still out there, somewhere, enjoying her freedom and chuckling about the fact that she escaped from the Montagnard cooking pot, a couple of crazy humans, and a very frightened tiger. Sometimes, when it rained heavily, I swear that I could still smell that goat with all of her wet, smelly fur.

The 8–5 Army

While the RVNAF operated on a 8–5 basis, five days a week, the VC and NVA worked 24–7 in the jungle. Of course there were combat operations by some of the RVNAF rangers and airborne units, but for the majority the RVNAF was asleep. That basis, alone, explains why the South Vietnamese lost the war. The RVNAF officers and enlisted were entrenched where they were stationed. Homes, wives, families, and careers were static. This may explain the disastrous defeat of the RVNAF. I only had a microscopic view based upon the RVNAF battalion that I advised, but from what I have heard and read from others this was the norm rather than the exception.

My ARVN battalion commander had served for a very long time at Pleiku. He was entrenched and had learned how to make money. His battalion-authorized strength was 1100 and Saigon sent him money to pay 1100 soldiers, but the number assigned was about 900. The battalion commander kept the difference. He may have split up the booty with some of his officers. This corrupt system did not encourage commandeers to recruit. He lived well in Pleiku and prospered. This was a signal battalion, so they did not have to go on combat operations: Man the fixed communications sites throughout II Corps and be happy. I believe that there was some training going on, but I did not see much. I did see many of the very young RVNAF soldiers in the battalion, and they were motivated. They were the same as all soldiers since time began. All they needed was leadership, equipment and training and they could conquer the world. The leadership element in the RVNAF was lacking from the top down. The lieutenants were great, but above that level it was very grim. I recall a long jeep ride to a remote mountaintop battalion site. Everything was wrong and no officer was checking. They had the greatest private soldiers in the world, as all armies do, but could not be bothered to train them or follow up with inspections. The site had antennas to relay signals throughout II CTZ. The interconnecting cables looked like half-eaten spaghetti. To this day, I am unable to understand how they could relay anything. These soldiers were on an isolated mountaintop site and had defensive bunkers around the perimeter. In a way it was like swatting flies. If the VC became annoyed for some reason, they could put in a serious number of troops to overrun the site and kill everyone. I went around the perimeter and checked the bunkers. They were well constructed, with good fields of fire, but the problem was that weeds had grown up in front of the firing positions. My estimate was that a soldier could see about five feet in front of his firing position and then everything was obscured by the foliage.

I had learned one thing by then: Be very tactful. After we finished the tour, I turned to the ARVN captain and said, "Perhaps it might be a good idea to cut back or burn off the foliage in front of the fighting positions." His eyes glazed over and he went stoic and said nothing. I knew that he would do nothing. I may have caused him to lose face, but I was outside the hearing of anyone else when I spoke with him. We drove back to Pleiku and he dropped me at the MACV compound while he drove to his home, wife and family so that he could continue to enjoy his peacetime way of life. Less than a week later, the site was overrun by the VC and everyone was killed. It may have been that the VC watched an American advisor and an ARVN captain drive up to the site and decided it was time to swat the fly.

As I said, the ARVN battalion commander was an amazing entrepreneur. This was during the period of the U.S. buildup in Vietnam in 1966. There were a number of U.S. bases being established around Pleiku City, but Pleiku City was not a secure area. The town was VC territory at night. An example was a brothel in the town frequented by U.S. soldiers. One night between ten and 20 U.S. soldiers were sleeping there after enjoying what they had paid for. Very early in the morning a VC squad slipped in and slit the throat of every U.S. soldier in the brothel. It was a terrible mess and many body bags were used to move the dead to be processed by U.S. people. None of my troops were involved.[36]

The ARVN battalion commander had a great deal of free time and decided to establish what he called his "ARVN Officer's Club." This was in Pleiku City. He promoted this to all U.S. advisors and the incoming U.S. units. It was a gold mine. Here is how it worked: Since the VC owned the town at night, he paid a tax to the VC. In return they would not interfere with the operation of the club. U.S. people could go and come without interference. The club consisted of a large bar and dance floor. It was populated by prostitutes who would sit at the bar and invite customers to sit down with them. While you drank whiskey, they drank something that looked like whiskey, but it was what we called "Saigon Tea," so that while the customer got drunk the prostitute took control and would take him to the dance floor, where he could press flesh, and then they would go to a bed elsewhere. I saw what was going on in my first visit and got the hell out of there in fifteen minutes, never to return. By this time I had malaria and dysentery and I did not want to take any other gifts like social diseases back to the U.S.A.

Four years later, in 1970, when I returned to Vietnam on my second tour, as we drove through Pleiku City I saw the ARVN Officer's Club and asked the driver to stop so that I could check it out. We got out and saw a burned-out wreck. Nothing was left standing. My first thought was that the ARVN battalion commander had lapsed in paying his VC tax. Then I thought again. Tet 1968 occurred after I left in 1966 and at that time all VC tax agreements were probably off the table. I never saw the battalion commander again, but he was a survivor. My guess is that he is alive and well in Paris or the United States enjoying his wealth.

I had a good friend in the RVNAF. He was a communications officer and a friend of the II Corps commander, General Vinh Loc. Occasionally my friend would stop by and say that he had to go with General Vinh Loc to Saigon. This meant that another coup attempt was about to occur: The coup leader needed a communications officer to seize radios and report to the nation that a new regime was now in place. This was my friend's job. The instability of the Saigon regimes was a major advantage for Hanoi.

FULRO

FULRO is a strange name not commonly understood today. It stands for Front Unifié de Lutte de la Races Opprimée and was organized on August 1, 1964. This united Montagnard front was to combine forces in order to defeat common enemies.

One morning when I was an advisor, my interpreter, Sergeant Trung, arrived late and looked worried. I volunteered the usual, "What's up,

Montagnards (courtesy of Olen C. Phipps, Jr.).

Trung?" Trung was about my age and was very shy and quiet. He was a good guy who would watch my back in nasty situations and we exchanged information daily … what the advisors were doing and what the South Vietnamese were doing. He rarely got worked up, but he was that morning. His comment: "Looks like the FULRO will have an uprising, tonight."

"What is FULRO?" I asked, and he explained that it was a revolutionary movement among the Montagnard people designed to win autonomy and freedom for the tribe. The Montagnards are a tribal people, a different race from the Vietnamese. They are very much like our Native Americans. The Montagnards were exploited and oppressed by the South Vietnamese and the VC. This generated the FULRO and a sort of war within a war in South Vietnam.

The Montagnard tribes were all around us in Pleiku. The only people they seemed to trust were the Special Forces advisors. Trung explained that they would rebel all over the Central Highlands and chop off as many South Vietnamese heads as they could find. I started to smile until Trung told me that since I was an advisor to the South Vietnamese my head would be included among those removed. I lost the smile, fast. This was underscored when I was patrolling in my jeep one night and got stopped by an armed Montagnard soldier who knew that I was an advisor to the Vietnamese. He walked over and put his gun to my head. My carbine was about six inches from my hand, but his pistol was one inch from my head. We exchanged glances and each of us tried to figure out what we would

Montagnard Home (courtesy of Olen C. Phipps, Jr.).

Montagnards preparing for the feast (courtesy of Olen C. Phipps, Jr.).

do as I inched my hand toward my carbine. For me this was a losing deal. I did not have a round chambered in my carbine. Neither one of us wanted to kill the other, but something would have to happen or I would be headless. At this point, a Special Forces captain, a friend called "Scotty," arrived and put his hand gently (thank God) on the shoulder of the soldier and told him to "stand down." Scotty knew me and knew that I would not stop going for the carbine. The Montagnard soldier knew the same. Scotty and the Montagnard waved as I continued on the patrol. As I drove on I thought, What a crazy war. You have North Vietnamese killing South Vietnamese and both are exploiting the Montagnards who would fight back against both. Added to the mix are the Soviet bloc and China providing weapons to the North Vietnamese and the United States doing the same for South Vietnam. This was 1966 and I kept thinking, When will this ever end?[37]

The problem then became what we could do to stop the FULRO rebellion. It turned out that the FULRO leadership would broadcast instructions at a certain time on a certain radio frequency, the next day. It would inform all of the Montagnards when and where to attack. Trung thought that if I could somehow get the U.S. brass in Saigon to jam the frequency with some of their sophisticated equipment, it would stop the

FULRO. What Trung said was backed up by a South Vietnamese colonel I trusted who talked to me later. By late morning we had the time and the radio frequency of the FULRO broadcast.

I started a long series of phone calls to Saigon and got the runaround: "Don't know what you are talking about." "We might have some of that, but it's in a warehouse and not unpacked, yet," etc. As usual, no help from Saigon. Trung then asked what *our* Plan B was. (I've noticed that when people run out of options they ask me: "What's *our* Plan B?") I told Trung that *our* Plan B was to contact the South Vietnamese, who owned a lot of radio transmitters. Trung was great with these people. Within a few hours, word had been disseminated to all. Instructions: time, frequency, and play music, talk, do anything that you can think of to jam the frequency. That night we waited and waited. We could not hear a shot fired anywhere. All was quiet.

The next morning, Trung was late, again. "What's up, Trung?" He explained that the FULRO had failed and some of their leaders had been rounded up. In his words: "They put them in front of sandbags in Pleiku and shot them all." That seemed a little harsh, but a war was going on and the South Vietnamese did not want a second war. We never found out if our radio jam did any good or the uprising had failed for some other reason.

A week or so later, the II Corps senior advisor, Colonel Theodore C. Mataxis, called me in to show me a message that had come in from Saigon. It was from a U.S. general with no fewer than four stars (Westmoreland). It was one of those boring messages that starts out: "It has been brought to my attention…" blah, blah. Then I got very interested: "A captain, who shall remain nameless, called all over Saigon asking questions about one of our most sensitive capabilities. You should all know that that sort of thing should never be discussed on the telephone or radio …" blah, blah. "If it happens again, heads will roll."

I turned to the colonel: "The time mentioned in the message is exactly the time that I was calling all over Saigon. I think he's talking about me!"

"I think so, too," said the colonel. "Bothered?"

"Nope. If my head was going to roll, it would have already rolled."

"Don't worry about it. If there is a next time, would you do the same thing?"

"Absolutely," I said. "Only next time I'll call a different set of people in Saigon and my Plan B would be—" He cut me off, saying, "Okay, sounds good, just checking."

Trung and I had a good laugh later. After that, Trung referred to me as his Captain Nameless. It caught on and everyone started calling me

The author receiving award for Operation Masher (author's collection).

that. On the last day of my first tour in Vietnam, in November 1966, Sergeant Trung drove me to the Pleiku Airbase to catch my "Freedom Bird" back to the States (with changes in aircraft in Saigon and elsewhere along the way). He had watched my back and I had watched his for over a year. There was nothing that I could do to repay him. My greatest regret from

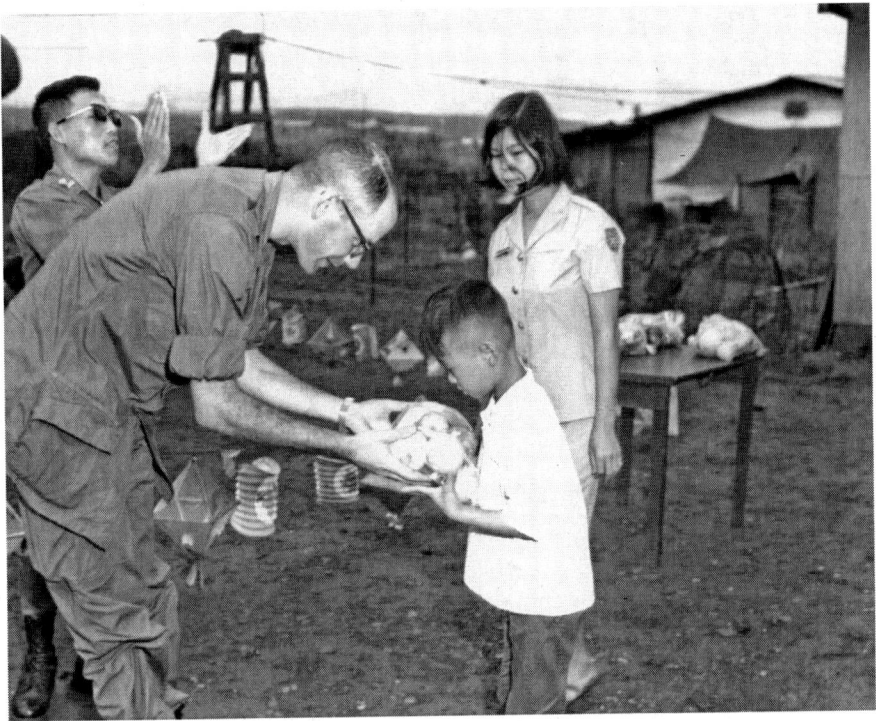

The author at ARVN Ceremony (author's collection).

my first tour is that I did nothing to contact Trung and see how he was doing. It was the last time that I ever saw or heard from Trung. When I left Vietnam, the advisors gave me a plaque that read: "To: Captain Nameless and the Head that Almost Rolled ... he always had a Plan B inside that head." I lost the plaque in a basement flood.

THREE

Taking Over the War— No End in Sight

When the United States decided to take over the war in Vietnam, two conflicting strategies developed. General Westmoreland, the commander in Vietnam, favored search-and-destroy operations to maximize enemy casualties. This was not unlike the failed strategy of the French in the earlier war. Other more thoughtful people favored a focus on pacification to make people safe and improve their lives. We called this winning the hearts and minds of the people. The United States tried to do both, but the priority went to Westmoreland's search-and-destroy concept, as seen later. Westmoreland's approach failed and cost us thousands of casualties. As Westmoreland failed in Vietnam for reasons seen later, the U.S. Army Chief of Staff, Harold K. Johnson, commissioned a study titled "A Program for the Pacification and Long-Term Development of Vietnam" (PROVN). Studies in Washington are a dime a dozen and seldom achieve anything except for letters of appreciation for those that did the studies. PROVN fared no better. It was completed in 1966 and was briefed to the JCS, the president, and others. No action was taken while Westmoreland commanded in Vietnam and he continued to pursue his bankrupt policies. When he was replaced after the Tet offense of 1968, his replacement, General Creighton Abrams, moved forward to embrace the concepts of PROVN.[1] Population security became the goal, but it was too late.

I recall in 1966 when units of the 4th Infantry Division (4ID) started to arrive in Pleiku they had a professional can-do attitude and incredible energy. I had been in Vietnam for a while as a battalion advisor and knew the terrain and the South Vietnamese. Sergeant Baxter, who was now a member of the 4ID, had been in my platoon in Germany two years earlier, reported in and with his best salute asked where the lead elements of the division could bed down. This had been preplanned, so it was easy for me to guide him to a place south of Pleiku. The 4ID was well trained and ready to fight. I would be with the 4ID at Camp Radcliff, An Khe, four years later when the division left Vietnam.

I recall meeting the 4ID advance party led by Lieutenant Colonel Ertlschwiger. They were headed for a site south of Pleiku that in those days we called Titty Mountain because it looked like that. The Vietnamese objected to the title and insisted that we call it Dragon Mountain ... no problem, whatever floats their boat. I led the 4ID advance party to a good spot below Dragon Mountain that would later become known as Camp Enari. I was helping the 4ID troops as they settled in, and as with all new troops, strange things happened. On the first night, the troops dug in and put out their barbed wire and tin cans with stones to warn of VC sneaking in while we waited. It was late night when a 4th Infantry Division soldier heard a rattle in the cans and thought that the VC were moving in. He decided that he would crawl out to see if there were any VC slipping in. He told his nearby buddies, but word spread along the perimeter. As soon as he made noise in front of the perimeter, everyone opened fire. I recall screaming, "Cease fire, friendly out there!" or something like that. A guy with an M60 machine gun said, "Okay, but can I finish my last belt, first?" I figured that this would be a very long war. I went back to the bar and got drunk, but I was amazed at the professionalism of the new units that were arriving. Ertlschwiger would play a key role in activating the 43rd Signal Battalion in Vietnam, and the history of the 43rd is described here.

The 43rd Signal Battalion was organized during World War II as the 43rd Signal Construction Battalion. It arrived in France in August 1944 and provided signal lines to connect 12th Army Group with the 3rd Army. It continued construction of signal lines until the end of the war. The 43rd was inactivated on 28 May 1946. On 16 October 1966 the 43rd was activated at Pleiku with the mission of providing adminis-

The **43rd Signal Battalion Unit Crest (author's collection).**

trative and field communications support to ARVN and U.S. units in II CTZ. It continued service in II CTZ until it was inactivated on 30 May 1971 due to the drawdown in South Vietnam. During its service in Vietnam, the 43rd was awarded two Meritorious Unit Commendations and participated in twelve campaigns.

"Camp Enari," as it was called, became the home of the 4ID, but a 43rd Signal Battalion communications site was also established there on Dragon Mountain above the camp. James Allan Long described the site and his experiences:

Long, James Allan: RA16963402 (19 Aug 66–6 Sep 67); O5347142 (7 Sep 67–31 Aug 69)

At the end of Aug 68, after a year at Ft. Bragg, NC with the 426th Sig Bn, 35th Sig Gp, I posted to South Vietnam / 43rd Sig Bn. The 43rd Sig Bn assigned me to the 278th Sig Co at Camp Enari, the 4th ID base camp south of Pleiku. The Company Commander, CPT Costello, stationed SSG Hale and I on the semi-isolated signal site on Dragon Mountain (Hill 1028). Our missions/tasks were to significantly reduce signal system and circuit outages; replace the unreliable power; and build the "gold standard" for the security and protection of our soldiers and equipment.

We, the fifteen signal soldiers, SSG Hale and I, assessed the operation and condition of the signal site. To accomplish the missions and tasks, three teams were formed: two 12-hour operations shifts; and a projects team. The teams rotated weekly, with the projects team having Sunday off.

We were nicknamed the "Dragon Mountain Boys." Using the last rank I remember, we are/were: SGT Avila (d. 31 Mar 98, Hillcrest Memorial Park, CA); SGT Blanchard (d. 31 Oct 97, Woodlawn Memorial Cemetery, FL); SGT Collins; SGT Erpenbach; SGT Fraley; SGT Gates; SGT Gray; SGT Jelks; SGT Lewis (generator operator); SGT Lundgren; SP4 McDonough; SGT Price; SGT Reeves; SGT Rhodes; SGT Robinson; SGT Schmid; SGT Starks (d. 11 Jan 99, Calverton National Cemetery, NY); SGT Smith; and SFC Winford.

The next three months, a generator pad large enough for three 45 kW diesel generators, was excavated by manual labor in the side of the mountain. It required moving over 50 cubic yards of Vietnam dirt, and the pouring of a concrete pad and building PSP walls and roof. An 80 ft. pole tower/platform was erected and over twenty antennas mounted. For the protection of the signal vans and personnel, a 3 foot wide, 12 foot tall, dirt filled PSP wall was constructed around the signal vans.

The determination and dedication of these fine soldiers, with the support of the Commanders of the 278th Sig Co, CPT Cavin, and 43rd Sig Bn, LTC Motsko, turned the neglected and marginally supported Dragon Mountain Signal Site into the best in the 43rd Sig Bn. This happened at a critical time, as the location, elevation and capabilities of Dragon Mountain provided the 43rd Sig Bn with the flexibility to adapt to and fulfill changing missions and requirements.

James Allan Long with ARVN Officer (courtesy of James Allan Long).

We didn't experience any racial conflict. Maybe it was not harmony, but we were a close knit group—had to be. We worked together; ate together; relaxed together; and slept in the same Quonset. A diverse group of four (4) African American; one (1) Hispanic; one (1) German national; one (1) non-naturalized, son of KIA World War II CBI (China-Burma-India) theater pilot; the remainder from the four corners of the U.S.

All were "RA" (Regular Army) enlistees. The Hispanic, the non-naturalized offspring and the German national, who were not U.S. citizens, but still subject to the draft [a little-known fact], elected to enlist. In May 1969, The 1st Signal Brigade assembled all non–U.S. citizens; flew them to Guam; administered the oath of citizenship; and returned them to duty. We all were proud that, unlike the draft dodgers and lack of support on the home front—the U.S. Army was taking care of its own. What a dichotomy. These new citizens embraced, supported and risked their life for their new country—while other so-called citizens fled to Canada.

Drugs, especially marijuana, were a huge problem. The REMF [rear] areas, Camp Enari and Pleiku, where troops had down time and boredom—were a problem waiting to happen. We were vigilant to keep the drugs off Dragon Mountain. A very difficult task as nightly, to man the bunkers, Camp Enari dispatched the guards and all the baggage they brought with them. As the perimeter and bunkers were "danger close" to our signal vans and billets, SSG Hale and I checked the guards almost every night. Didn't want our troops to wake up dead!

There are many recollections and memories of my tour in Vietnam. Over the years, my memories of this time gravitate to the significant. May 18, 1969 (Sunday). I left Dragon Mountain to participate in a volleyball game with the 4th ID, 124th Sig Bn at Camp Enari. These were welcome distractions after nine months on the mountain. However, that night the shit hit the fan! Watching helplessly, as "my mountain" was attacked. Camp Enari employed suppressing fire—until a AH-1 Cobra crashed into Dragon. The next day, I assisted in the recovery of the remains of the Warrant Officer crew, CWO Gregory George Beck and WO James Patrick Casey (Vietnam Memorial Panel 24 W, Rows 36 and 37). I will never forget.

May 24, 1969 (Saturday). Again, I left Dragon Mountain for Pleiku Air Base, for a flight to Cam Ranh Bay and then a flight to Honolulu, Hawaii, where my bride awaits for a delayed R&R. That evening, sitting in the club, I looked out to see a tongue of tracers from a mini-gun licking "my mountain." Immediately calling the signal site, I was informed that it had just been attacked. Satchel charges, many unexploded, and B-40 rockets / RPGs had damaged the 362nd Tropospheric Scatter Co site at the other end. No damage to the 278th site, because of the improvements we had made to the security and protection.

To this day, I believe these attacks were because I was not on the mountain. Someone knew! I moved to the 43rd Sig Bn Technical Control facility on Tropo Hill in Pleiku when I returned from R&R.

Late August 1969, I was a "short-timer"—soon to return to "the land of the big PX." One morning in the Tech Control Facility, all the circuits to the Communications Center went out. Getting with the "gray hair" Chief Warrant Officer in charge of the Com Center, we decided to move the equipment (teletypewriters and KW-7 encryption machines) to the Tech Control Facility to place the critical circuits back on-line. Good idea—until I assessed the risk of a security violation/investigation keeping me in South Vietnam longer. I posted guards with orders to shoot anyone except the Battalion Commander, LTC Martin. I was "going home!"

Out processing at Ft. Lewis, my bride and I returned to the University of Wisconsin. I had left South Vietnam and the war, but it did not leave me. Vietnam would affect me in more profound ways than having served there.

A veteran reading the political and military history of the Vietnam War would conclude the following:

The United States military did not lose the Vietnam War, the South Vietnamese military did, after the U.S. Congress cut off funding. The South

Vietnamese ran out of fuel, ammunition and other supplies because of a lack of support from Congress while the North Vietnamese were very well supplied by China and the Soviet Union.

The 1973 Agreement on Ending the War and Restoring Peace in Vietnam was a political and military farce. Leaving the North Vietnamese and National Liberation Front (NLF) "Viet Cong" forces in place; not sealing off the Cambodian and Laos borders; and requiring the legitimate government of South Vietnam to "negotiate" with the North Vietnamese and Viet Cong (NLF), both of which refused to acknowledge the government of South Vietnam—doomed South Vietnam. North Vietnamese forces were permitted to resupply military materials to the extent necessary to replace items consumed in the course of the truce. President Nixon and Secretary of State Kissinger made promises they could not keep, and as a result of the Watergate scandal, effectively abandoned South Vietnam.

In 1973/4/5, Congress, although U.S. ground combat forces had been withdrawn, in blatant retaliation of current/former administrations, betrayed the government of South Vietnam and fatally reduced the funding for their previously supported "Vietnamization." Military aid to South Vietnam in fiscal year 1973 was $2.8 billion; in 1975 it would be cut to $300 million. Once aid was

Dragon Mountain Communications Site (courtesy of James Allan Long).

cut, it took the North Vietnamese only 55 days to defeat the South Vietnamese forces when they launched their final offensive in 1975. Anti-war Senators Case, Church, and McGovern voted to cut the funding to the people of South Vietnam. They understood the consequences. They did not care.

January 27, 1977, another betrayal. President Carter, a non–hot war, non-combat Navy veteran, betrays the armed forces men and women who served in Vietnam and dishonors their finest, the 58,282 KIA (Killed-in-Action) and non-combat casualties—as of 22 Jan 13. U.S. President Jimmy Carter grants an unconditional pardon to hundreds of thousands of men who evaded the draft during the Vietnam War. He was not re-elected.

April 15, 1969, a good day in South Vietnam. SSG Hale, SGT Schmid and I are awarded the South Vietnam Signal Corps Badge, for our support to the South Vietnamese signal site on Dragon Mountain. The award was presented by Major Nguyen Khoa, Commander of the Army of the Republic of Vietnam (RVNAF) 620th Signal Battalion.

I think of Major Khoa often. He had served in the Vietnamese Army in the north before "voting with his feet" (Operation Passage to Freedom) and coming to the south in 1954 after Dien Bien Phu and the Geneva Agreement in 1954. The Viet Minh were not sympathetic to former Vietnamese Army members, especially Catholics. For reasons not known to me, his wife and children were left with family in North Vietnam. I surmise Major Khoa hoped for the elections and reconciliation that never came. He had not seen his family in over fifteen years. Unrealistically, I hope he survived the end of the Vietnam War and "Uncle Ho's" re-education camps, and was reunited with his family.

A political scientist coined the term "democide" to denote the murder of one (1) million people or more, but less than ten (10) million. Although Ho Chi Minh did not rise up to the level of Hitler, Stalin or Mao Zedong, let no one think he was not a mega-murderer. Ho Chi Minh, a nationalist, and a Communist, is guilty of the democide of well over three (3) million of his countrymen in the Vietnam War, purportedly in the name of reunification. I am confident that the majority of the 3 million would not vote for reunification at that cost.

An Army Vietnam Veteran friend when discussing the war said to me, "Let's just forget the Vietnam war." I replied that I would never forget the war—I could have died there. In retrospect, I am very fortunate that I did not die there. I experienced evil, destruction, carnage and camaraderie that unfortunately too few of my countrymen have. My countrymen ignored that if it were not for the assistance of other countries, the United States of America would have not won its freedom and independence, and through the years remained free from oppression [*James Allan Long, 1968–1969*[2]].

Mike Cason was also assigned to Camp Enari:

When I first arrived at the 43rd, I was assigned to a platoon in Camp Enari supporting the 4ID. A warrant by the name of Hartwell H. Hubbell took on the

Camp Enari (courtesy of James Allan Long).

mission of introducing me to Vietnam (the fine art of harassing a new LT). I was not there very long before being reassigned as the S-4.

At the 91st Replacement Group one night, while sleeping in a barracks in mosquito netting, someone tossed a few fire crackers in the barracks. You can imagine a pile of us frightened young men tangled in netting crawling around the floor. Can still remember the laughing outside. Then it was on to Na Trang and then Pleiku.

My most frightening experience happened early. I had come in from Camp Enari for a farewell party. Had a bit too much to drink and went to sleep in a bunk somewhere. During the night, the siren sounded. I awoke, not knowing where in the hell I was or what to do. Remember running towards a bunker in only my underwear, helmet and flak jacket (yes, I did remember my weapon). Found out shortly thereafter that I had sprinted across a field of crushed rock in my bare feet (no Purple Heart for that idiot).

Following are some events that I recall although I was either not present at all or was only involved in a very minor role:

—The Company Command HQ being destroyed by a LAW in Camp Enari.

—The attempted murder of one of our officers by tossing a grenade onto a porch of the sleeping quarters. I was the duty officer that night and hit the siren thinking it was incoming. Believe that LTC Schoebel injured himself that night.

—Sending my supply sergeant to Saigon with "off the book" supplies to trade for much needed sandbags and cement.

—Receiving a MARS message about my wife giving birth to twins. A joke that, I found out later, and I took issue with and several of my friends regretted.

—Visiting signal sites with just a driver in a very top-heavy armored jeep with an M-60 mounted. The way we drove was crazy (the almighty wisdom of the young).

—Staying up all night counseling one of my men who had received a "Dear John" letter. He was cutting his arm repeatedly but not deeply.

—Getting into the S-4 office at 06:00 to find a note from LTC Martin "chewing me out " for being such a _ _ _ _ _ (of course, I believe he then took a nap in the afternoon).

—My anger when the VC rocketed my warehouse and destroyed the latrine.

—I will never forget my admiration for the men that worked for me. Especially, my absolute conclusion that it is the Warrant Officers that actually keep the Army operational [*Michael Cason, 1970*[3]].

Early in 1966, Colonel Theodore Mataxis, the senior U.S. advisor to the RVNAF in the II Corps Tactical Zone that included most of the Central Highlands, asked me to go to Saigon and brief the MACV staff on the need for new advisor equipment. At a certain point in time, it became clear to all of us in the advisory team that the material and the supplies that we needed were not available and everything was going to the U.S. troop units that were now arriving in Vietnam. The colonel was raising hell with the brass in Saigon to no avail. We advisors had become the ugly stepchildren of the U.S. Army. He finally hit upon the idea that what we needed was a top-quality briefing for the brass in Saigon that would point out how badly we needed equipment. I was elected to do it. I thought that this was as crazy as hell. If he couldn't persuade the brass by phone, a new captain wasn't going to do it in person. Looking back at it now, I realize that it was brilliant. Imagine a skinny captain with worn boots and a patched uniform briefing a bunch of people who had never been outside of the safe haven of Saigon. I would have instant credibility and everyone would listen. By this time, just about everything I owned was falling apart. The jungle does that, even in the Central Highlands.

It was a long day sitting in the back of the air-conditioned auditorium as all of the sharp-looking briefers in their freshly pressed uniforms came in, one after another, to give their briefings to the brass and then left. I thought that I would freeze to death, and I was gradually turning blue since I was accustomed to 100–plus degrees and high humidity. Even in the Central Highlands it gets hot. I amused myself by trying to think of the reaction of the brass to a blue captain who stood up to brief. Nearly all of the briefings were about the status of incoming U.S. troop units, nothing about the advisors or South Vietnamese. When someone said that the U.S. troop units were critically short of this or that, I thought that I was going to puke. They were flooded with gear.

Finally, at the end of the day, it was my turn. Everybody was tired as I was introduced and went to the podium to show my handmade slides. I think it was a good briefing. I had two themes: The first point was that if we wanted the South Vietnamese to be able to fight better, then we needed to make sure that their advisors were properly equipped to do their job. The second point was that with U.S. troops flooding in, the role of the advisor was changing. Advisors were becoming liaison people to help coordinate combined operations with U.S. and South Vietnamese units working together and advisors needed new equipment to do that. Finally, this enormously fat colonel interrupted me with a comment that was something like: "Don't you know that the U.S. has taken over the war and we can't count on the South Vietnamese for anything?" I was shocked. I thought that if this was U.S. policy we were in for a very long war and we would fail. This was 1966, and looking back at it now, I can't imagine what people were thinking ... LBJ, the Pentagon, and the commanders in the field. You can't just prance in and fight someone else's war and then leave when everything looks swell. My thought in 1965 and since then is that the first day you arrive is the day that you finish working out your exit strategy. When I got off the airplane at Ton Son Nhut in November 1965 and the blast of hot air hit me, my thought was that we were only there to buy time for the South Vietnamese and the sooner we get out of there the better. We never did that. I would defy anyone to explain our strategy in Vietnam. What were our goals? When should we depart? All of these colonels in freshly starched uniforms did not quite get it right. The United States was not taking over the war; responsibilities had been shifted. U.S. forces would engage the enemy in the field and the RVNAF would defend the base camps and villages and support.

While the U.S. Army in Vietnam was expanded to 175,000 people in 1965, nearly an equal number of South Vietnamese soldiers deserted. While Westmoreland was pushing "body counts" as a metric of success, Hanoi was sending an increasing number of fresh troops south on the Ho Chi Minh Trail. Hanoi was not concerned about casualties. For every enemy soldier we killed, several more were sent south. For every U.S. soldier we sent to Vietnam, at least one South Vietnamese soldier deserted. It was a simple math problem and we were on the losing end. Neither Westmoreland, McNamara nor LBJ ever acknowledged this simple fact. Until 1969 no one would acknowledge the obvious solution: Declare victory and leave Vietnam as quick as you can.

As soon as I had finished the briefing and realized that I had failed, I started devising Plan B. The advisory team had sent a sergeant with me. To keep me out of trouble, I think. I knew that he would buy in.

I called the colonel back at Pleiku to report my failure. His answer was to get back to Pleiku by fastest means since I was needed. My answer was something like: "Sir, could you send down an aircraft to pick me up?"

His answer was something like: "Why the hell do you need your own personal aircraft."

"Ummm, sir, just send the aircraft, okay?"

Long pause at the other end of the line. I could tell that he had figured it out. "Okay, you've got your aircraft. Make good use of it. We have a Caribou [a twin-engine cargo aircraft that can carry lots of gear] leaving in an hour to take a bunch of Vietnamese recruits for their training. [These were young people who had never been away from their villages and were conscripted and flown to training centers. You had to see it to believe it. Rather than taking seats in the Caribou, the recruits sat on the floor, side by side, on each side of the aircraft while cargo straps were stretched across their legs and tightened down on both ends. That way, if there was turbulence in flight they were locked down and would not be injured. We called this the Vomit Comet for obvious reasons. At the end of each flight, the interior of the aircraft had to be hosed down.] Will that do?"

"Yes, sir." As I hung up I thought, this is not going to be fun. I hope the crew does a good job of cleaning up the aircraft. Next step was to visit a classmate in the U.S. division nearby. I needed a truck with U.S. markings and a uniform with a U.S. division patch on it. Anything with Vietnamese or advisor markings would not work.

Saigon Port was a place where thousands of tons of war material were off-loaded daily. I drove over with the sergeant and the truck owner from the division and started checking out the containers stacked in the port. I was trying to look very official and even had a clipboard that I occasionally used to jot down notes that meant nothing of course. I picked out two containers that had exactly the material that we needed in Pleiku. Back to the truck to write down the container numbers on an official-looking piece of paper. Just at that time, a sergeant from the port arrived with a, "Can I help you, sir?" I explained that I was here to pick up stuff for the division. "Let's see your requisition, sir." I handed over my piece of paper and started sweating. He glanced at it and said, "Sir, this is no good. Don't you have a properly authenticated requisition?"

Whatever that is, I thought. He was standing there with a clipboard on his hip giving me a very skeptical look. Time for my Plan B. "Umm, no, Sergeant." (I was known as the world's worst liar, so it was going to be very hard to be convincing.) I told the sergeant that as we came in on final approach at Tan Son Nhut Air Base we discovered that the VC had set up in the jungle at the edge of the runway and as we flew over they fired into the air with everything they had and the aircraft flew through it all, taking many hits. Metal and dust and junk were flying all around the inside of the aircraft and we were all terrified, but no one was hit. As we touched down, I suddenly realized that I urgently needed a change of underwear (this had actually happened to me a couple of weeks earlier, except for the underwear part, so I was very convincing). There was a latrine trench right near the runway and I casually walked over to clean up. Unfortunately, my properly authenticated requisition flew into the trench as I was changing and I really didn't feel up to retrieving it. "If you really need it, I can go back and get it with a twig or something to fish it out, but I really don't think you would want me to hand it over to you and you definitely would not want that paperwork in your files."

He looked at me for a very long minute and said, "Captain, you better turn your truck around and back it up so we can load your cargo." I turned and gave our driver a triumphal smirk, then froze as the sergeant said, "Wait a minute, Captain." I turned slowly as I thought, Busted. This is the end of my career and I'll get jail time for sure for this caper. He was smiling and said, "Give my best to the other advisors at Pleiku. Next time one of you come down to Saigon Port, I'd appreciate it if you could bring along one of those Montagnard crossbows or a NVA officer's belt buckle. I'd love to have that stuff. I can trade it for good whiskey from the U.S. people in Saigon that have never heard a shot fired in anger. I'm here every day, so you won't have trouble finding me. Ahh, by the way, that's the best story that I've heard, yet. Take care, Captain; try to stay out of harm's way."

We drove very fast to the airport and immediately recognized our Caribou. They had just finished hosing down the interior to get rid of the puke (thank God) and the engines were running. We loaded and took off quickly. To this day, I remember this as my triumphal return to Pleiku. Something like Caesar entering Rome after defeating the Gaels. My bar bill plummeted in the weeks after our return. Every time I tried to buy a drink, someone put money on the bar.

As the tempo of the war increased and U.S. units carried the fight to the enemy, the role of advisors frequently shifted to that of liaison between the United States and the RVNAF. U.S. casualties mounted while Hanoi poured more troops into the South.

McNamara's War

Robert S. McNamara was Secretary of Defense from 1961 to 1968. He is best known for bringing systems analysis to the Pentagon, which helped balance resources against needs. While he was in office we had a saying that if McNamara had it figured out correctly, the last rifle bullet in the inventory would be fired as the peace treaty was being signed. The fact is that war is the most wasteful enterprise on the face of the earth and the best one can do is control it a bit and McNamara did that.

If any single person can be blamed for precipitating our full involvement in the war in Vietnam it was Robert McNamara. In August 1964 the Tonkin Gulf incident occurred. NVA gunboats were alleged to have attacked U.S. ships forty miles offshore. LBJ wanted increased authority to attack the North Vietnamese without a declaration of war. He had McNamara (assisted by Dean Rusk) deal with Congress. McNamara deceived Congress by failing to mention that there was doubt that the attacks had actually occurred. Also, a separate unrelated RVNAF operation was ongoing at that time and it is possible that the North mistook our ships for a part of that operation.[4] Based upon McNamara's comments, the Tonkin Gulf Resolution gave LBJ broad powers to wage war on North Vietnam. At the start this involvement was based upon deceit.

McNamara testified in court in General Westmoreland's 1984 libel suit against CBS (see Chapter 5). He was very clever in avoiding responsibility for his decisions and actions throughout his long career. During his testimony at the Westmoreland trial, McNamara gave the CBS attorneys an opportunity to question him on broader issues. The testimony here is a remarkable example of the use of semantics to deceive. David Boies (CBS) believed he had a historic opportunity to show the world that McNamara had deceived the public. In evidence was McNamara's pessimistic memo to the president of May 19, 1967, which was declassified for the trial and of which the Pentagon Papers had quoted only excerpts. Boies's grilling aimed to show, as Judge Leval correctly interpreted the line of questioning, that "the witness is not a truth-teller."

> The listing figure in the witness box [McNamara] said he did not believe in 1967 that they had reached the "cross-over point" and were winning, as Westmoreland claimed. He said the tables attached to his May 19 memo showed this. Boies protested: But you say in the memo's text that "'we reached the cross-over point.'" 'No, McNamara shot back, "the sentence you have quoted … quotes General Westmoreland." He said he had put the statement in quotation marks in the memorandum to show it was Westmoreland's, not his own. McNamara had pulled up the blind on his semantic game, the key to the riddle.

Boies put before McNamara the transcript of the August 1967 Senate hearing on the bombing. He read out a passage in which McNamara sounded optimistic, because he told Senator Henry Jackson "from what you have heard from General Westmoreland and General [Earle] Wheeler and the other Chiefs ... each of them firmly believes we are winning." Demanded Boies: You were saying Westmoreland and the chiefs thought this? That's right, McNamara said; "that's not my judgment, that's theirs." Well, said Boies, summoning up disdain, "did you tell Senator Jackson, in words or substance, that you disagreed with the statements General Westmoreland and General Wheeler and the other chiefs were making?"

Well, said McNamara, I expressed so much skepticism during the hearing that Senator Strom Thurmond accused me of "making a statement appeasing the communists" and a "no-win" statement. Boies: When Thurmond accused you, you said, "I submit it is not a 'no-win' program." McNamara came back: When I said "not a 'no-win' program," I was referring to not only the shooting war but the "political track" as well. We had a "two-track approach," he said, finally opening up his real position on the war in 1967, the defense in *his* case.

Boies showed him an article from *Newsweek* from September 1967. In it McNamara was asked if "the war" was "stalemated"; he had said, "Heavens, no." To Boies and the jury McNamara now claimed he had been talking about the two tracks, not just the shooting war, he said. The courtroom was hushed; he was coming to life, assuming some of his old authority.

"I did say it's a no-win militarily ... I said it cannot be won by military action. We had a two-track approach, one political and the other military, and the military was designed to move us along the political track.

His subtext was: *Therefore I was being ethical. I was working for a resolution with probes to Hanoi as the carrot and military punishment as the stick. So the fighting was not in vain.* Yet it was hard to grasp, between his own digressions and the lawyer's verbal pounding. "I admit these seem like hairline distinctions," he said at one point, as Boies hung over him with body language that said, *Aren't you a damn liar, sir?*[5]

Author Deborah Shapley summarized: Most of the lessons drawn from McNamara's life had been negative: that management by numbers ruined America's manufacturing know-how; that the [World] Bank's lending left the poorest countries with crippling debt; that the deceits and subterfuges of Vietnam disillusioned a generation with government. David Halberstam has called McNamara a "dangerous figure" because it is his "special skill to fool people," to "seem better than his official acts," whereas "the real McNamara" is "someone who says one thing in public and always follows the mandate of his superiors in private."[6]

McNamara was not well liked by Vietnam veterans. His lies and duplicity had led us into a war that cost many lives. One major reason for the contempt was that years after the war he had a change of heart and decided that the buildup in Vietnam was a mistake. A suitable epitaph for McNamara occurred in 1972, as explained by columnist Greg Mitchell:

> It didn't make *The New York Times* or *Washington Post* obituaries today, but one of the most dramatic, and in some ways revealing, incidents in the long life of former Secretary of Defense Robert S. McNamara occurred in 1972—when a young man, reputedly angry about Vietnam, attempted to heave him off the Martha's Vineyard ferry, during its 7-mile voyage, and nearly succeeded. Only McNamara's tenacious hold on a railing kept him from likely death.[7]

McNamara did not press charges and his assailant drifted away.

Buildup

As U.S. forces were deployed to South Vietnam, a logistical expansion of enormous proportions was needed to support the war. Stanley Karnow described the transformation that started in the summer of 1965:

> American army engineers and private contractors labored around the clock, often accomplishing stupendous tasks in a matter of months. Their giant tractors and bulldozers and cranes carved out roads and put up bridges, and at one place in the Mekong delta they dredged the river to create a six-hundred-acre island as a secure campsite. They erected mammoth fuel depots and

Ken Fugate, riding shotgun (courtesy of Ken Fugate).

warehouses, some refrigerated. They constructed hundreds of helicopter pads and scores of airfields, including huge jet strips at Da Nang and Bien Hoa. Until their arrival, Saigon had been South Vietnam's only major port, and its antiquated facilities were able to handle only modest ships. Now, almost overnight, they built six new deep-draft harbors, among them a gigantic complex at Cam Ranh Bay, which they completed at breakneck speed by towing prefabricated floating piers across the Pacific. They connected remote parts of the country with an intricate communications grid, and they linked Saigon to Washington with submarine cables and radio networks so efficient that U.S. embassy officials could dial the White House in seconds—and President Johnson could, as he did frequently, call to check on progress. By 1967, a million tons of supplies a month were pouring into Vietnam to sustain the U.S. force—an average of a hundred pounds a day for every American there. An American infantryman could rely on the latest hardware. He was transported to the battle scene by helicopter and, if wounded, flown out aboard medical evacuation choppers known as dust-offs because of the dust kicked up by their rotors as they landed. His target had usually been "softened" beforehand by air strikes and artillery bombardments, and he could summon additional air and artillery assistance during a fight. Tanks and other armored vehicles often flanked him in action, and his unit carried the most up-to-date arms—mortars, machine guns, grenade and rocket launchers, and the M-16, a fully automatic rifle.[8]

Ken Fugate was assigned to Vietnam during the buildup and saw it:

I was deployed to RVN as commander of a Signal electronic supply and repair company, similar to one I had commanded in Germany. Almost immediately, the COSTAR restructuring of Army logistics responsibilities reorganized us as a Light Equipment Maintenance (LEM) company and we were attached to an Ordnance battalion under a Quartermaster group. You can guess how that worked out for a Signal Corps officer.

After Vietnam I served in the Army Data Command in the Pentagon, which was run by the Adjutant General. I guess the Signal Corps just gave up trying to stay in the IT business until decades later when communications became digital. Anyway, that was it for me, and the civilian world was waiting.

That said, my time in Vietnam was instructive. We arrived at Nha Trang to find the largest cache of military equipment and supplies outside the Cam Ranh Bay complex. We built our own section of the giant tent city called "Camp McDermott" and, since our equipment had not yet arrived, we went to work inventorying and establishing security over the informal depot we found. There were blocks of shipping containers stacked three high holding every kind of equipment, including weapons, and piles of soda, beer and rations under tarps sitting in the sun. There was no inventory control.

I think this must have been a manifestation of the "just ship everything you can think of" theory of logistics planning, officially known as the "Push" system. And, you can imagine the corruption attracted by this huge stockpile of stuff.

The operational philosophy of the command was not to worry about what was there or where it went, except that nothing went to the RVNAF or MACV unless it was for a friend. It was made in Heaven for scroungers.

Slowly, very slowly, equipment inventories were completed, repair parts warehoused for the maintenance teams, and what was drinkable given to the troops. A lot of stuff just went into the sea. After nine months we received an inventory control system, so by the time I rotated things were somewhat more orderly. Still, there were continuing serious shortages and the scrounge system moved as much materiel as the computer system [*Ken Fugate, 1966–1967*[9]].

As the buildup continued, all sorts of skills where needed and a variety of trained army personnel were deployed to Vietnam. Jim Van Alstin tells his story:

When I joined the Army in March of 1968. I had Basic Training and AIT at Fort Leonard Wood in Missouri and was a 63B20 Wheel Vehicle Mechanic. I was then sent to Fort Knox to Tank Repair School and became a 63C20 and a Spec 4 and was then sent to Fort Carson, Colorado. After about 6 months there, the Fort Commander put out a request for people to go to the 5th Division RECONDO School, anyone who went would receive a grade increase. I volunteered not really understanding what that would do to my MOS. I then became an 11D40 Armored Recon and sent to Vietnam. I arrived at Cam Ranh Bay and was sent to the 21st Signal in Nha Trang and then to Pleiku at the 43rd Signal BN. When I reported for duty the 1st Sgt said, "What do we need with an 11D40 Armored Recon person?" He was going to send me back to be reassigned to an Armor Unit. About a day before I was to go back, the Battalion Motor Sgt Householder came and asked me if it was OK to change my MOS from 11D40 to a 63C40 and become the 43rd's HHD Motor Sgt. Needless to say I had spent over a week through this processing and hadn't been issued a weapon yet and was feeling scared, so I said it was fine with me, still not realizing what the reassignment would have meant. I finally figured it out about 4 months later and was glad I had made that decision.

The 43rd Signal motor pool guys from mid 69 to mid 70 got along great and we always were looking out for each other. I have many fond memories of these guys but I have never been able to find any of them. The two people that I remember reporting to through my three years in the Army and really liked and respected are CSM Stallworth at Fort Carson 68 to 69 and SFC Householder 69 to 70. I always knew that they cared about their men.

I never reported this, but someone from D Company in Kontum or Dak To attempted to frag me while I was in the latrine area. I kept hearing someone outside saying "is he still in there?" to everyone leaving the latrine and felt something wasn't right so I left while there were 3 or 4 guys still in there. I shocked him as well as myself when I exited. He had a grenade in his hand and was ready to pull the pin and throw it in the latrine when I was the last guy in there. He told me with the grenade in his hand and the other hand with a finger in the pin, that this is for you. From that time forward I was never alone, I always had someone by my side. I barely slept after that and always had my M16 locked and loaded in my bed.

In December of 1969 I was sent to Saigon to become the battalion's Defensive Driving Instructor and fulfilled those duties also. My wife still doesn't believe it today. In 2008 and 2010 I went back to Pleiku. Camp Schmidt, II Corp Headquarters, 71st Eva area and Tropo Hill (without antennas) are occupied by the Vietnamese Army and off limits to include taking photos, however we did take pictures as we drove by and we weren't bothered. The Air Force Base is now the Pleiku Airport where we flew into and out of on our trip [*Jim Van Alstin, 1969–1970*[10]].

Loren J. Kindler had similar experiences:

I was with A Company of the 43rd Signal Battalion in Pleiku and the 278th Signal Company at Camp Enari from 12 January 1968 until 21 August 1969. One of my more memorable events began on 6 March 1969, when we were asked to take some worn and badly damaged electronic equipment from Company A to our U.S. Military "junkyard" in Qui Nhon. We gathered up the large load of electronic gear, loaded it in a Company A ¾ ton pickup truck and joined a convoy going from Pleiku to Qui Nhon on QL19 near Camp Holloway.

The electronic gear was to be turned over to the salvage depot in Qui Nhon. The convoy had at least 10 vehicles when it started out around 1:00 in the afternoon. I didn't have a military driver's license so I was riding along in the "shotgun" seat. We were about ⅔ of the way back from the lead truck. The 6 cylinder engine in our truck was running on 5, maybe 6 cylinders as we headed down the highway and it was not getting any better as we traveled. The truck was running so slowly that everyone else had passed us up and we were on our own.

About 5 miles North West of An Khe, the half-way point of the planned trip, a whining noise developed in the rear axle and the driver asked me, "What do we do?" I said to keep driving, what other choice did we have? A few minutes later there was a loud clank from the rear end and the truck slowed to a stop. That is when the panic set in because we had no radio to call for help and no idea if anyone would be coming down the road including "Charlie."

I thought about it for a minute, and then I told the driver to try putting the truck into 4-wheel drive. That worked and the front wheels got us to An Khe. Once there, I crawled under our truck and spotted a missing drain plug on the differential housing. The loss of gear lube had destroyed it out on the highway.

Our sister company in An Khe, the 586th Signal Company, called back to A Company for another truck which never arrived after a day long wait. We borrowed a truck from 586th Signal Company, went on to Qui Nhon and delivered our load.

Qui Nhon had a huge "junk yard" of damaged military equipment including ¾ ton pickup trucks. Seeing that, I had an idea to get a differential from them

Loren J. Kindler showing near miss (courtesy of Loren J. Kindler).

and take it back to An Khe the next day. Having grown up in the 1960s I was an old Hot Rod enthusiast from those days; so changing a differential was not a challenge, even for a 31E20 Field Radio Repairman. I replaced the damaged differential, found some new spark plugs, and that beat-up old truck engine was humming much better than when we departed Pleiku.

We planned to head back to Pleiku but got orders to go back to Qui Nhon to pick up some more items for A Company. We completed our tasks then went nonstop from Qui Nhon to Pleiku at a good speed with the engine running on all 6 cylinders. Those two days were an episode that I will never forget. .!! [*Loren J. Kindler, 1968–1969*[11]].

Ronald S. Simpkins tells his story of Vietnam and after:

Our recollections do not carry the intensity of an infantryman who deployed with us. I know a colleague (Captain, 35th Infantry at the time) who told me in recent years that he spent > 300 days of 1966 in the 'field.' Our task was to assure the readiness of their equipment. I remain best friends with the CO of the Medical Company from 1966, Captain (Doctor) Mandel Heors and his doctors were reminiscent of the MASH TV program, in that they had so little to work with other than Triage. Many memories are of the time between call-up in Hawaii, through deployment (like arriving on the hill to find the 1st Cavalry had secured it and were waiting with their choppers, for us to arrive so they could return to An Khe). Our actions in Hawaii to have some "creature comforts" when we went to VN are secure memories. The work with OC Phipps (now LTC), Lt. Denis Siok, and of course CWO Crow did in advance and in-country made our lives much more bearable (and our stories more legendary). We moved fast after the alert in Hawaii. We, in the 25th, were alerted just days after LTC Hal Moore, with his 7th Cav battalion had confirmed the existence of the NVA in the Central Highlands.

Being a forward support Maintenance Company did have many rewards. We also had a tech support group in our brigade. We sent trucks almost every day to the big supply depot at Qui Nhon. We had a Col as our brigade CO, a Colonel Stoutner (sp), to have more pull a General Walker was put in command of our bde. We also had our own shower with chrome shower heads and heated water. Generators were everywhere. When the trucks would go to Qui Nhon for supplies, they got everything that was not tied down. We got an old motorcycle engine down there and used it to pump our water up to the holding tanks. We also got several of those ole wringer washing machines. Oh we had a 1st LT. who stayed at Qui Nhon. We had it as good as anybody at base camp. As a company clerk they even got me a new typewriter. You would not believe all the stuff we would get. We even got enough lumber to build a mess hall, and when the weather was bad we would see the movies in the mess hall. Worse thing we had was those darn rats and electric wire everywhere.

We could see for miles from our hill we were on. We could see Dragon Mountain from our camp. VC and those RPG's was our biggest problem. We only got hit hard one time in April 66. The NVA and VC hit our base camp, Pleiku airport and Camp Holloway at the same time. Sadly only one casualty in our company that night. While setting up claymore's one went off in the hands of a member of our company. Army said it was static electricity?? He was immediately evac out, and I never heard any more about him. The morning report just showed him reassigned to 85th med evac at Qui Nhon. I will not disclose his name but he was a SP5 and a very good soldier. It was the worst attack we had while I was there. That was the only time I saw those C-47 Gooney Birds with all those red tracers coming down. Fighter jets also and at day break those gun ship choppers cleaned up what was left. A few VC did get inside our perimeter but were eliminated quickly. I watched all that from the Company Command bunker. I was scared YES but I had my M-16 ready. Since the attack was repelled, I don't know what I would have done if they had gotten to our bunker. There what we called the SHOTGUN volunteers from the 25th who served in late 64–65 in Vietnam. All volunteers to ride shotgun on choppers in Vietnam from the 25th. Right now I cannot remember how long their tour of duty was, 6 months? They were all volunteers from the 25th in Hawaii. But they flew in support of all units that were there. When our Div got to Vietnam they were put back in the 25th, and still rode shotgun for us.

When we got to Vietnam, Pleiku City was off limits. It took several months to get it secured, and then we could go there in the afternoons. No weapons, we parked the trucks at the MPs. When we had men in the field on operations supporting the Inf and Armor. Captain Bernitt was one who went and kept a check on them, always carrying that .45 cal machine gun. I remember when one of our tanks from 69 Armor. got hit real hard. Capt Bernitt went out to see if it could be salvaged. No it couldn't be, it was full of ammo, so they called air strikes to destroy it. When the Capt's year of duty in Vietnam was over he was supposed to be sent to Virginia for a school. The army changed his orders and he was put in charge of missile base, maintenance from Philly to New York, he was over more civilian than army personnel. He did not like that so he got out of Army after 10 years. Went to work for Kodak, spent a lot of time in China setting up plants for Kodak over there. I made contact with him after he had retired from Kodak. We exchange emails almost every day. One day in Vietnam he told me to get cleaned up the next morning to go before the board for promotion to SP5. My 1st Sgt was on the board, they had 4 openings for E-5's. There was Sgt. Major, 1st Sgts and a Major on the board, my 1st Sgt was one on the board. There were about 7 of us SP4's that went before the board. Later my 1st Sgt got back to Orderly Room and told me I made it to E-5. I was number two on the list, I was beat out of 1st place by the medical company's Co Clerk. Told me I got beat out of being number 1 was because the clerk in medical company had one year of college. I was glad to be number 2 because the medical company's clerk and me were good friends. We helped each other out when one of us wasn't sure how to do something and fill out certain forms. The head surgeon of the medical company and Capt Bernitt were best friends, so I got to know him well. After he got out of Army he opened a doctor's office in NYC. We are all retired now. Oh I also never had to pull guard duty or mess hall duty after basic training. Today I still say Capt Bernitt was the smartest man I ever met .There were a few times he got on me when I made mistakes in typing out forms that he had to sign. Good thing 'cause now I make lots of errors in spelling and typing. Oh what I was gonna tell you was I got out that 25th Inf Div yearbook this morning Oct 41 to Oct 1966 the 25 year anniversary. My name is in it. It covers the 1at and 2nd Bde's that went to Cu Chi and also the 3rd Bde at Pleiku. All of the guys who went to Vietnam in 65 and 66 are listed in the back of the book You know I am proud to have my name in that book. I hope you hear from the other Capt in our Co. a Lt Col Olen C. Phipps one of those ROTC guys. He was a good one. Retired now and I exchange emails with him. Capt Bernitt had a few months on him, and he got the CO job. He is also a real good man, hope he emails you also. He got out of the army after 10 years and taught ROTC in S. Carolina for 10 years, then went back in army. He spent nine years as a Major in Engineering. Told me people thought his first name was Major. He finally got to be a Lt Col and then retired with 20 years of service ... and 3 tours in Vietnam.

The units of the 25th that went to Pleiku were the whole 3rd Brigade with extra man power. They added about 15 more men to our company who were rotary and fixed wing repairmen. They stayed at Camp Holloway. We were a forward support maintenance company, and went to the field with the tanks, and infantry on operations all around the Pleiku area. About 15 men in our company earned Combat Infantry Badges. The General pulled that off, after operation Paul Revere which lasted about 3 months. Paul Revere was four phases. The 3rd Bde 25th participated in all 4 phases. The 4th Inf Div had two brigades that participated in it, and the 1st Air Cav participated in at least 2 phases of it. I can't remember now but Paul Revere lasted close to 4 months. I have an article about Co A 1st Bn 14th Inf, of the 25th, in hand to hand combat with the NVA at Dragon Knoll. I am now remembering things I had forgot. YES I was a draftee. I was promoted to SP5 E-5 in August 66 and in the summer of 67 I had to go to reserve camp, and was made a Sgt E-5 and sent home and was told my army reserve time was over. That was when all the politicians and big shots got their sons in the reserves to keep them out of Vietnam. I have a close friend who was in the 38th Indiana National Guard. A 1st Lt. He served with the only National Guard Unit that went to Vietnam in 1969 and pulled recon for units down there. It was Co A 151st Inf Airborne Rangers. He was wounded in Vietnam and spent over 3 years on active duty in a hospital in PA. As a member of the 3rd Bde 25th Inf Div we were sent by air to Vietnam in Dec 65 and Jan 66. At that time it was the longest and largest air lift of troops. Our tank Bn and APC's came by boat and drove by land up to Pleiku. As you remember, our base camp was located on a large hill next to Pleiku Air Base. After our Brigade became the 3rd Bde 4 Inf Div, and was moved to 4th Inf base camp. When the 3rd Bde of the 4th Inf Div came to Nam they were sent to the base camp of the 25th Div near Saigon, and became the 3 Brigade of 25th. I have been discussing this with my ex CO and another Capt from my ole company. My CO was a 1962 grad of the USMA. The other Capt in our company was an ROTC man, but he was a good one. I now exchange email with them, the ROTC Capt. was at our ole base camp during the exchange between 4th and 25th brigade changes. He was present when our colors were changed to 4th Inf Div. Said everyone was against the change. But you know the U.S. Army won, and the change was made. This Captain spent 20 years in the army and retired as an LTC (I just have to put this little funny in here. He was a Major for 9 years and told me everyone thought his first name was Major. Oh, he also taught ROTC for 10 years in S. Carolina College. Bill, I might have told you this before but I made SP5 before I had a year and a half in the Army. I was the Company Clerk for the forward support Maintenance Co. 3rd Bde 25th Inf Div. In the summer of 1967 I had to go to Camp Grayling in Michigan for two weeks, since I was a draftee we were required to be in active reserves for two years. Right before I left Nam I was promoted to Sgt E-5. After I spent those two weeks at Camp Grayling, Michigan. I was taken off the active reserves, and never had to go back again. The reserves had too many joining to keep from going to regular army and probably Vietnam. While I am on computer I want to tell you about a special friend who lives down the street from me. He is now 68 years old. He served in the only National Guard Co. that went to Vietnam for 1 year. They were Co D 151st Inf Airborne Rangers. He was a 1st Lt. They were stationed down around Saigon and did recon for several units down there including the 25th Inf Div. About a month before they were to leave Vietnam they were engaged in a large fire fight with VC. He took part of an RPG round to the right side of his body, and was evacuated out of Vietnam and ended up spending over three years in a VA hospital. He is doing okay now but has a big limp. All the time he spent in Vietnam and in the hospital was all credited to a 4 years and 3 months on active duty. He did receive a silver star [*Ronald S. Simpkins, 1966*[12]].

Charles F. Bernitt adds:

These recollections, true or stretched a bit. The runs from Qui Nhon (if I remember correctly, OC did a hell of a run through Saigon's port and got us a rough terrain forklift, and the seaborne transportation to Qui Nhon for a very modest cost) and the "mission" of then Lt. Siok are legendary only to us. What stories we could tell if we sat around a bottle of Jack Daniel's and played off each other. Don Mandel and I have shared experiences many times, over much JD. As to the picture, I have no recollection. Don Mandel arrived in country about May,

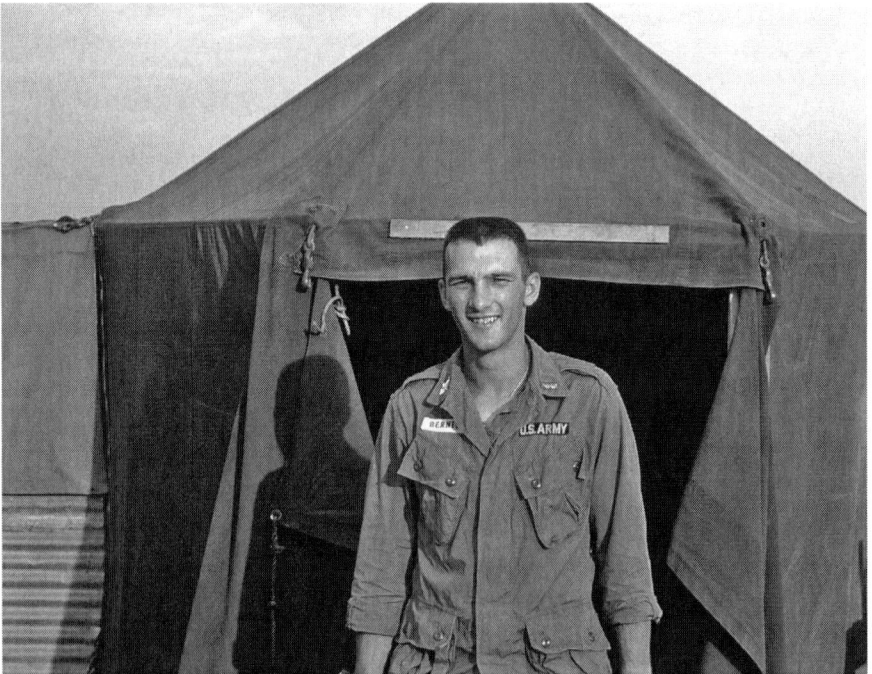

Charles F. Bernitt (courtesy of Charles F. Bernitt).

while Major Evans was still our CO. Major Housand took over in the second half of the tour. It got his 'ticket' punched as a commanding officer in a combat zone. Both were good men. I remember Herbert Evans coming to the tent OC and I shared the night before he left. He shared many personal experiences of his time with us, drank a little Jack, and wished us well. He never asked for too much detail about our mess hall, ice machines, laundry facilities, theater, showers, rough terrain forklifts, real pigs for a luau, comfortable chairs in the Medical company, licensing the doctors to drive tanks, or any other unauthorized equipment we had acquired. I'd bet 1966 was OC's best tour. The trust we all had in each other to do what was best for the troops and our circumstances was always difficult to replicate in later life with organizations I was privileged to belong. It was good to have some straight laced people to keep us in line, like you and 1Sgt Peck, and a few, like CWO Crow and SSG Ted Botelho to keep it light. Some of the finest men I ever knew were in Company D, 725th.

We were unique in that we deployed together, Nearly everyone in the Brigade knew well their counterparts in the other units and the members of our own unit. We never had contact, in any way, with our brethren in the other two brigades of the 25th that had gone to Cu Chi to fight a different enemy [*Charles F. Bernitt, 1966*[13]].

Following are notes on deployment to RVN: Delta Company, 725th Maintenance Battalion, 25th Infantry Division, by Olen C. Phipps, Jr.:

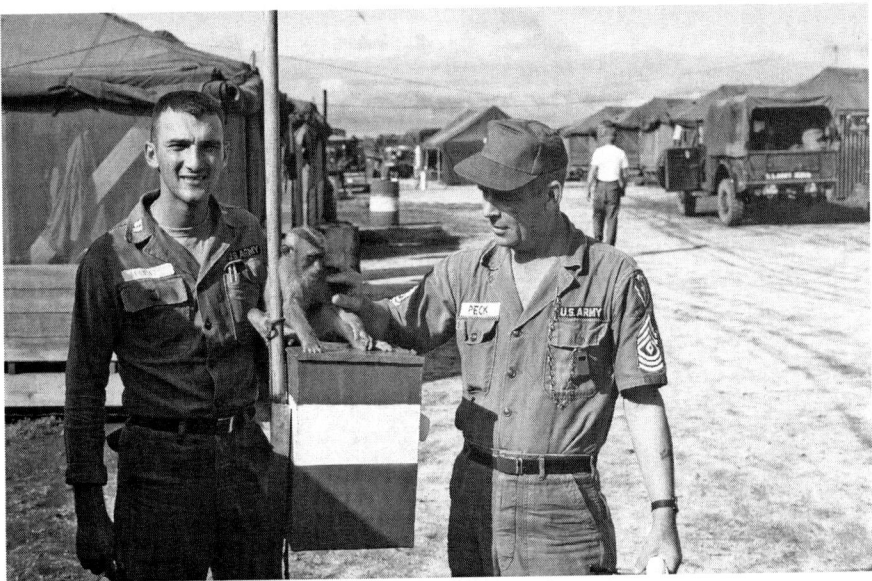

Charles F. Bernitt with First Sergeant Peck and friend (courtesy of Charles F. Bernitt).

During the Summer of 1965 we heard rumors of a possible deployment to Viet Nam and we were aware that several of our neighbors were "volunteering" as advisors, particularly from the combat units. Most of us were busy just enjoying Hawaii. As primary support units our mission was to upgrade readiness throughout the 25th Division with new arms and equipment. We tested the new (at that time) M-16's and new multifuel vehicles and began getting rid of the old stuff. This meant building a new support base which meant we were dropping support for "old family" and adding for "new." We were working two Army stock lists simultaneously.

We were finally alerted in November and began a big push to get ready. Separation of supplies and equipment took a back seat to getting stuff on the trucks and on the ships and planes. In addition to all the military provisions, local purchase options cleaned out Honolulu's hardware and supply stores.

Many families elected to stay in Hawaii but others were uprooted to return to a home base on the mainland. This was a gut wrenching period for those of us with young families. We were going off on a great adventure but wives and children only faced loneliness and separation. I argued that my family would be better served at home if something happened to me. I was fortunate but others were not. Families of two of our friends stayed at Schofield and one of them was lost. I am sure his family received much help and support but I felt home support would have been better for my family.

We loaded our loaded-down trucks and equipment on C141 transports at Wheeler AFB and Hickam AFB and saw our families off, then boarded the same C141 transports and were on our way. Arrival in Vietnam was a special treat in that the New Pleiku Air Base was a hot spot. The big planes came in as steeply as they could with their loads and slowed as they taxied down the runway. We drove the trucks and equipment off while moving and the empty planes turned at the end of the runway and took off without ever stopping. We hit the preexisting foxholes along the runway to assist in security. We were pretty surprised to find elements of the 1st Cav were there to provide security for us. As the Brigade assumed control of our new base camp, the 1st Cav guys pulled out and there we were.

We got organized pretty fast and started the process of support and making a home at the same time. We put up the tents and worked the mission out of CONEX containers and from the airlifted supplies and equipment. Lt Siok was dispatched to Qui Nhon to transship the equipment and supplies which had been sent by sea.

The company settled into a routine of backup support in the base camp and sent a contact team out with the maneuver elements. Paul Revere was our first major combat sweep and it seemed that it lasted for much of the year. Lt Nickles, the shop officer, did most of the contact team support. I can remember only two or three missions for myself and that was probably just to relieve Nick.

On one of these missions one night, we had perimeter duty for a section of the task force and a small elephant had the misfortune of walking into a trip wire. Flares went off and the guys on the M-60 machine guns opened up,

Left to right, outside of helicopter: Captain Ronald Ray Van Regenmorter, Captain Charlie Bernitt, and First Lieutenant Olen C. Phipps at Cu Chi (courtesy of Olen C. Phipps, Jr.).

followed by everyone else. I had a starlight scope and could find nothing. By the time we got everyone to cease fire the little elephant was no more. I had heard of others who had perimeters breached by tigers but that must have been a rarity. I suspect that our elephant was not wild, just unlucky.

On another, the task force moved and left some of us to guard some bladders of petrol which we had to take back to base camp. As usual the Air Force was late. They finally got there with the C-123 and the pilot promptly told me to get the men on, that he couldn't wait for us to load the bladders and stuff because he had used up his flying hours. I disagreed and he said that he would just leave us. He changed his mind when I told him he would stay with us because I'd shoot his tires out if he tried to leave us. We got out ok and I think he was just wanting to get back to happy hour.

The 69th Armor Battalion was relocated from Cu Chi to Pleiku, reversing the original thinking that tanks would perform better in rice paddies than hilly terrain and woods. Our support requirements shot up. CWO Crow handled the shop operations in base camp and my tech supply team under SGT's Burge and Jones got the Brigade Support functioning. We obtained serious equipment stockpiles. We got all the old and new family of support stocks and all the stuff Lt Siok was liberating from Qui Nhon, then we got in the second complete supply list that we had ordered prior to deployment. On top of that we got a push package which had been prepositioned in Japan or somewhere. Lots of good stuff like Arctic parkas and equipment that we had no use for whatsoever. Wait a minute! I spoke too soon. That stuff was great.

The local Special Forces A team and C teams were training and assisting the Montagnard troops and they had the old family of weapons and equipment. They just couldn't get repair parts for the stuff and they needed help and we just happened to have a whole lot of that stuff. They were very appreciative of our "support" and some of their appreciation made it all the way to Saigon in an ongoing effort to relocate needed items to the Central Highlands. Major Morris from the Battalion HQ in Cu Chi was doing expediter work for the Division(-) in the Cholon/Saigon area similar to the job Lt Siok did in Qui Nhon for 3rd Brigade. He helped me find a lot of stuff.

We had a maintenance float of weapons, tanks, trucks, jeeps and other equipment which allowed us to quickly replace combat losses. We combat-lossed a lot of equipment during Operation Paul Revere about the time the 4th Infantry Div came in-country.

That bunch was a special treat. We helped them get set up and tried to give good advice but, obviously, they figured they knew better. We warned them not to strip away all vegetation from that red clay soil because it was the slickest stuff in creation. Came the foretold monsoon and our guys had to take our two wreckers and the M-88 tank retriever over just to keep the Division street open. The Ops Officer of the Signal Battalion of the 4th Div was Major Len Riley. He was a water walker in the Signal Corps. He headed the White House Communications for a period and made BG way early. He commanded the 7th Signal Command where I was his Engineer later in life.

Between my forays to Saigon and Lt Siok's ventures in Qui Nhon, we built quite a home away from home. We had several troopers from Hawaii so naturally we had to have a luau. After the men were properly housed we undertook building a suitable Captains' quarters for Captain Bernitt and myself. Charlie had accumulated a stack of Playboys so we took the centerfolds and wallpapered the tent. Packing crates became bureaus and weapons caches. We had M1's, carbines, Thompson submachine guns and of course the authorized M16's and 45's. The bar was open.

We also took an M60 tank engine container, sealed it and made legs by welding shell casings together. We erected it with wrecker booms and used emersion heaters for hot water. Voila, water tower and community shower. I understand that the water tower was still standing when our base camp was turned into Engineer Hill after our brigade was integrated into the 4th Division in 1967.

On one trip to Saigon, I was working with Major Morris and was summoned to 1st Logistic Command HQ and offered a job as expediter for 1st Log. I suspect that Major Phil Morris was responsible for this. He had been my sponsor when we came to Hawaii so we were pretty good buds. Since I was one of four Captains in our company at this time, I accepted the reassignment and moved to

Saigon in October '66, ten months into my one year tour. Living in Saigon was different. No weapons allowed and a bustling night life are a bad combination. The cowboys (VN gangs) patrolled and the butterfly girls took full advantage of unwary GIs.

I was traveling from the Continental Hotel to my BOQ in a Cyclo and a cowboy zipped by on a Vespa. He grabbed for my watch but didn't get it. What he got was an over the head shot from a .25 automatic. The only shot it ever fired in anger. I took it home and gave it to my brother-in-law who collected guns. He died a few years back but my nephew wouldn't give the gun back to me. I gave the watch to my daughter last year. A self-winding Seiko with day and date.

At 1st Log I was placed on permanent flying orders and given a list of critical items which were "lost." That was a real treat. The most memorable "find" was a shipment of tank search lights destined for the 1st Cav. I finally found them in An Khe. The 1st Cav guys had appropriated them from themselves.

I covered a lot of territory and flew in a lot of choppers, Caribous and C 123's. I spent nights in tents on the beach at Cam Rahn Bay, Nha Trang, Vung Tau and a few other less memorable, isolated spots. Good job. When I left Tan Son Nhut in mid–December I passed on a few goodies to my trusty NCO. Among them was a jeep and a Thompson submachine gun. I didn't think they would let me bring them home with me. Love the Special Forces and combat loss [*Olen C. Phipps, Jr., 1965*[14]].

With the deployment of new units came the arrival of new weapons systems. I was on guard duty late one night when I saw a fixed-wing aircraft circling within a mile or so from our perimeter at Pleiku. Occasionally I saw what appeared to be a large searchlight switched on from the aircraft and aimed at the ground below. It was accompanied by a loud humming noise. I concluded that the aircraft was illuminating the terrain to locate VC. It was a bit confusing because I never heard of a searchlight that hummed when turned on. I contacted the command center and got a big laugh in response. The reply that I got was: "That's no searchlight; that's Puff the Magic Dragon doing its work." Later on patrol I found out what the "work" was. The terrain was devastated, with trees and foliage cut down as though by a huge scythe. I had seen the work of the new U.S. Air Force weapon system called Puff the Magic Dragon or Snoopy. It consisted of an AC-47 (military version of the very old DC-3) armed with miniguns firing through ports on the side of the aircraft so that as it circled it could lay down a tremendous rate of fire that could cut down anything in its path. The humming noise that I heard was the sound of the motors that turned the barrels of the miniguns. The tracer bullets being fired were so numerous that they appeared to be a beam of light. The VC thought that we had invented a death ray and they were terrified. Spooky saved many lives during its close air-support missions.

Tet '68 (January–February 1968)

In 1967 controversy reigned on both sides. Hanoi debated whether a return to guerrilla warfare should be pursued or a conventional military attack should be launched. The decision was to launch a conventional mil-

1. ATTACK ON TET EVE

2. ATTACK ON TET NIGHT

3. ATTACK ON 2nd TET NIGHT

4. ATTACK ON 13th NIGHT AFTER TET

DMZ

QUANG TRI

HUE PHU BAI

PHU LOC

DA NANG

HOI AN

TAM KY

CHU LAI

KONTUM

BONG SON

PLEIKU

AN KHE

QUI NHON

HAUBON
(CHEO REO)

TUY HOA

BAN ME THUOT

NHA TRANG

DA LAT

TAY NINH

PHU CUONG

DUC HOA

BIEN HOA 3

GIA DINH

LONG BINH

PHAN THIET 2

MOC HOA

SAIGON

CHAU PHU
(CHAU DOC)

PHUOC LE
(BA RIA) 3

SA DEC

MY THO

VINH LONG

TRUC GIANG (BEN TRE) 3

RACH GIA

CAN THO

PHU VINH
(TRA VINH)

SOC TRANG
(KHANH HUNG)

BAC LIEU

QUAN LONG (CA MAU)

★ PROVINCE CAPITALS AND OTHER CITIES ATTACKED

☆ MILITARY INSTALLATIONS ATTACKED

Tet Offensive of 1968 (courtesy of Hong Ngoc Lung).

itary offense in the South with the goal of causing a South Vietnamese uprising to reject their government. In the South, debates between the CIA and MACV continued over the strength of Communist forces in the South. CIA estimated a total of 430,000 in the South while MACV estimated no more than 300,000 were available. MACV realized that the higher number would indicate that Hanoi had the military strength to pursue a protracted war, something not acknowledged by Westmoreland. At this point in time U.S. public support for the war had declined. Opposition had increased from 25 percent in 1965 to 45 percent in 1967. For this reason, the CIA estimate was suppressed.[15] The number of troops available during Tet '68 were 325,000 to 595,000 Communists and nearly a million available to fight for the South. This number included 331,098 U.S. Army and 78,013 marines.

It was a strange situation. All in the South realized that there would be a major offensive during Tet, but when and where were unknown. In spite of the threat, business went on as usual. For example, Thieu insisted on sending many of his soldiers home on leave for Tet.

The South was considered unprepared for the offensive that started on 30 January 1968. There was no sense of urgency. The Communists attacked province capitals, district capitals and other targets. These were quickly retaken except for Hue, where the Communists held out for weeks while they murdered thousands of South Vietnamese who were loyal to their government.

For the North, Tet '68 was a disastrous defeat. The offense generated no popular uprising and total losses were 45,267 killed. Stanley Karnow reported a meeting in Ho Chi Minh City in 1981 with a prominent Communist figure, Dr. Duong Quynh Hoa:

> "We lost our best people," she said mournfully, recalling that Viet Cong units composed mostly of indigenous southerners had borne the brunt of the fighting and had suffered the heaviest casualties. Over the next year, she went on, the southern Communist political organization was to be badly battered by the CIA's Phoenix program, a covert campaign to uproot the Viet Cong's rural structure. So growing numbers of North Vietnamese agents were sent south to fill the vacuum. They rebuilt the Southern Communist apparatus, and they remained after the war to manage it—often antagonizing their southern comrades, who, despite an abstract commitment to national cohesion, clung to their regional identity. Many southerners viewed them as rigid, doctrinaire, alien, and even corrupt carpetbaggers, and Dr. Hoa made no secret of her loathing for them. "They behave as if they had conquered us," she told me.[16]

While the United States had won a military victory in South Vietnam, it suffered a political defeat at home. After years of promising reports by Westmoreland and others it became obvious to the American public that we were not winning the war. A "credibility gap" was widening between the government and its citizens. Photos of such images as dead VC who had broken through and were finally killed on the grounds of the embassy underscored the fact that we were not winning the war.

Walter Cronkite made a hurried tour of Vietnam in late February 1968 and shortly thereafter on national television dolorously called Tet an American defeat, saying on 27 February that "the only rational way out will be to negotiate, not as victors but as an honorable people. President Johnson watching this program lamented to his press secretary, George Christian, "If I've lost Cronkite, I've lost middle America."[17]

Forrest "Sonny" Ashcraft, a dog handler, tells his story:

My dog's name was "Inca," she was a 65 LB German Shepherd and a little on the thin side. Her number was OB76 and after I left Vietnam she was retrained with another handler, after that she was put down, if you use her OB76 number you can research her working dog history.

Us canine K-9 guys were like the LURPs, we always worked alone and we did everything opposite of normal. When the base worked during the day we slept, when the base slept we were out in the boonies or out on the perimeter all night. We ate breakfast in the chow hall alone before the chow hall was even opened for business and we were fed well before the rest of the base was even awake. As we were just coming in after 48 hours or longer out in the bad parts around the bases that we secured. We ate a good breakfast after days on C-rats, then we went and tried to sleep in the bright hot heat of the day time, and with all the normal noise of a base being active in its daily routines. No air conditioning just those huge fans one at either end of the hooch's stirring the hot humid air enough to let us catch a few hours sleep before we went out again after the sun went down that night after just coming in that morning, with our dogs. Always on patrol, always vigilant, always the first line of defense, and always the first killed if the base is attacked.

No air base, air field or any type base in Vietnam for the entire length of the war was ever overran or attacked by a major force that was guarded by the SPS Security Police Squadron Canine Units, in all of Vietnam, and of that record I am proud to have been a minuscule part.

On the one side of the base (I don't remember directions anymore) we had those huge military spotlights like you might have seen at a movie or mall grand opening shining up into the sky in the '50s and '60s in suburban America. These spotlights were huge and they shined right out into the area around the base to give us better vision to spot any enemy sneaking towards the base in a extremely dark part of Pleiku Air Base. My wonderful grandmother had sent me a care package with cans of Campbell's noodle soup, some cans of Ravioli, and cookies and newspapers from my home town. These would taste much better than the WW II C-rations we were given every night on the way to our patrol areas. I was

Forrest "Sonny" Ashcraft (courtesy of Forrest "Sonny" Ashcraft).

still a new guy at that point and someone explained to me that if you put your food in the can whether it was c-rats or in my case noodle soup on the generator that ran the spotlights muffler and left it there for a while one could have heated food, which was a treat because it got plenty chilly in the Central Highlands of Vietnam at night. After patrolling an area on the fence line of maybe a mile and a half each way back and forth and nothing going on that particular night, I decided to try heating my can of chicken noodle soup on the generator as had been suggested to me. I put the can of chicken noodle soup on a area where the can was snug up against a part of the gasoline powered spotlight engine that generated heat and started back down the fence line to continue my patrol on the perimeter when that telltale sound of incoming mortars and rockets started in another attempt by the enemy to damage the runway or anything they possibly could. The attack did not last long and the all clear was sounded and one small warehouse in my area had taken a mortar round hit but with minimal damage, and whatever else was damaged on the base was unknown to me.

The perimeter settled down and all got quiet and dark again, when there was a huge explosion on my perimeter more noise than a "shock and awe" type explosion but everyone started shooting out of bunkers and foxholes all around the base figuring an attack was imminent and a couple of choppers went up and raked the entire base perimeter and the area especially in front of my perimeter with their M-60's just to quell any attempt by the enemy to be sneaking up towards the base to make a sapper type attack.

Again the all clear sounded and the base settled down into darkness and night time normalcy. I went down to the spotlight to check on my can of soup that I had forgotten about, and the can was in two or three pieces and that was what had exploded due to being overheated, and there were noodles and chicken bits all over the muffler and the gasoline powered engine.

I figured that I just might be held responsible for the night time firefight costs and all the ammo used to fight off an invisible enemy force that night. So I spent the rest of the night picking off noodles and chicken bits off the spotlights engine with my bayonet and "Inca" was more than happy to slick the soup off the ground where I wiped my knife every time I was able to scrape some chicken noodle soup remnants off the engine and muffler area.

I never told this story until it and I were way past the statute of limitations of military responsibility for any costs that might have been passed on to me, who was just a E-3 at the time.

I/We always patrolled the barbed wire fence line perimeter patrol, alone. I always worked by myself or with my canine. Patrol, eat, sleep or try to sleep during the day in the heat and noise. Then eat some c-rations then feed and water my canine, "Inca," and get ready to patrol again that night, and every night over and over and over. That was the life of a dog soldier. It did not matter if it was a sweltering hot night, or the monsoons were at their worst, or the night was near freezing temperatures in the central highlands of Vietnam. The K-9 dog soldier and his canine were on the perimeter ... as the first line of defense, always vigilant and always alone.

I saw two Tet offensives on the fence and two Christmas's on the fence, and I turned 19 and 20 on nights like that along the fence ... always at night, and always alone, always vigilant. "Where others fear to go, the K-9 soldier walks alone...." I think once or twice a month we got one day off and that was spent getting drunk alone as everyone else I worked with was either trying to sleep during the day, or getting ready to patrol, or on patrol. For twenty months that was my life ... 66 to 68, a life like that when I was young made me a loner and a recluse and a bit of a hermit for the rest of my years and especially in my older years [*Forrest "Sonny" Ashcraft, 1966–1968*[18]].

Bill Garbett was a combat medic wounded shortly before Tet. Here is his story:

I was in A/2nd/35th. 4th ID. Was an infantry medic from time I arrived in August 1967 till I got hit on 1/10/68.

My first real experience relating to Nam occurred at Ireland Army Hospital at Ft. Knox in the intensive care ward where I was stationed in the months before going to Nam. Two patients stand out. One was Special Forces just back from Nam. He came in with a 105° temperature of unspecified origin. I was assigned to his care with the orders to get his temperature down. Actually I was surprised he was not dead. Anyway this is what I did. First stripped him naked. Packed his arm pits and crotch in ice. Turned the big fans on him. Three sponge baths an hour with ice water and alcohol. Then there was the aspirin suppository. He really knew how to cuss and threatened me with things I didn't think were possible with words, some of which I had never heard. The best part was he walked out under his own power with a normal temperature and didn't come back to rip me apart.

The second was a soldier enroute to a long term VA hospital. He had really been fucked up and had already received multiple surgeries. The time I cared for him on 3rd shift was one the proudest moments I had in the military or maybe ever. This poor guy was in serious constant pain. And had apparently received some rough handling in other hospitals. When I showed up to give him an 0300 pain shot, he started crying, asking me not to give the shot. He hurt too much when touched, especially when getting a shot. His arms had really been shot up. So I tried something a bit different. I was able to unsnap his Pajama bottoms to get access to his thigh. Then managed to get the injection in a spot that was in relatively good condition. When I was done he thanked me for not hurting him more. I felt like I should be thanking him for what he had done and letting me take care of him. The injection started to take effect and he was soon asleep. Several months later after having been hit I was able to understand how he felt. And like I said I think this was the proudest moment of my life. The Bronze Star and Purple Heart don't come close. The only thing from Nam that I treasure as much is my Combat Medical Badge.

Spent basically the whole time in the field and spent much of that as perimeter night guard . I took good care of my guys and they took good care of me. Did lose a few. Two stand out very much. I still think about them even after the dreams stopped. We had a platoon dog one of the other medics found in a Bunker. He eventually started going on patrols with us generally walking point. He was good at discovering VC caches. And on one search and destroy triggered an ambush saving a lot of lives. During the incident he was shot. A bullet through the shoulder but not very serious. I sent him back to hospital on medevac chopper. There were a lot of stories, good, bad, happy and sad.

First of all, you will not be seeing names in the following. I can only remember two names from my time in Nam, so I will not be using any names. This will be about my most intense time in Nam and possibly my return home through hospitals. Christmas 1967 I awoke to a Christmas truce and a friend opening a Christmas package from home. In the package was a restaurant size can. Inside the can was a bottle of Jack Daniel's. I got the first drink. I always said that as a medic I took good care of my guys and they took good care of me. Later in the day a very Irish chaplain appeared. He was sharing his canteen with the troops. The canteen contained Jack Daniel's on the rocks. Not sure which was appreciated more, the bourbon or the ice floating in it. He then said mass with ammo crate

as an altar. Various denominations were represented as well as a few atheists. I felt a powerful spiritual presence during that mass that I have never been able to find again, but not for lack of trying. The next morning was back to normal. .
We loaded up on a group of Hueys. After some time in the air we were landed into a hot LZ. As medic, I soon found myself running down a trail toward gunfire. Everybody else was running the other way. I quickly reached a clearing in the elephant grass. And found an FNG with a row of bullet holes across his belly. He was blond and baby faced and appeared to be about 19. I performed CPR on him with another medic for what seemed like hours. It was actually like 20 minutes. When we put him on the medevac chopper, he was still alive. He was dead when they got to the hospital. I didn't forget his name because I never knew it.

Sometime around New Year's we left for an indefinite mission in the mountains with resupply planned every three days. Eventually we came in contact with a sniper who was firing at us on a daily basis. It was during this time that I discovered that I could hide under a button. Either that or he was a very bad shot. He didn't hit anybody. But one of our guys eventually saw him crawl into a spider hole. A grenade quickly followed. What was left was hamburger. The guy who threw the grenade pulled out an ear. He salted it in a Baggie so he could send it home. Spent a few more days wandering around the jungle. Then on the morning of 1/9/68, I was picked up in a chopper to temporarily replace a medic in C company who was on R and R. It was the beginning of the longest chopper ride I had ever taken. I was sitting next to the platoon leader, a young lieutenant. He spent most of the trip talking about his wife and two baby daughters, one of whom he had never seen. We eventually arrived at what I much later learned was LZ West. The base had been under attack and we were to be reinforcements. A short while after we arrived I was called to the landing zone to see a crashed helicopter and a wounded soldier, two other medics were already on the scene. What I first saw was a geyser of blood pulsing out of his chest, apparently from a wound to a heart muscle, Then his left leg was totally mangled into pile of human hamburger. I helped with an IV, but it was waste of time. He was dead in minutes. It wasn't till it was all over that I recognized that the dead soldier was the lieutenant who told me all about his wife and daughters, one of whom he would never see. Later that night I was sharing a bunker with a guy I didn't know. I was woke up about 0200 to take watch. A short while later there was an explosion which I was not really aware of when it happened. I was unconscious. During the time I was unconscious, I had what has come to be known as a near death experience or an out of body experience. There was no bright light, no body waiting at the end of a long tunnel. Instead, I found myself in total darkness floating at some distance above my body. Total darkness like those dark nights in the jungle when you literally can't see your hand in front of your face. The other thing I became aware of was an entity many would call God. Then I remember telling that entity that I wasn't ready. I needed to stay. It was then that I woke. I seemed to become aware of many things at once. My right leg was gone. The front wall of the bunker was gone. Realized that the man with me was wounded. After a quick hands on assessment, I put tourniquets on both his legs below the knees. Then put one on my right leg high on my thigh. I gave the other guy a shot of morphine. Withheld the morphine from myself, after realizing that I needed to stay awake or we might both end up dead. Two other things, I became aware of the pain and put my hand through the remains of my leg. It was like hamburger with bits of shattered bone scattered throughout. No it wasn't like hamburger with bits of shattered bone, that is exactly what it was. We started to call for help, but soon became silent when small arms fire started to come in our direction. There was something else going on that really got me pissed. I could hear wounded soldiers calling for a medic and there wasn't a damn thing I could do about it. Eventually help arrived in the form of a couple of other medics. I passed out from the sudden intense pain when they pulled us out of the hole. Short while later I woke up in some kind of a shelter. A medic gave me a shot of morphine. I remember asking him if I could pass out. Which I did immediately upon receiving permission. I woke up three days later in a field hospital, but that is another story. When I woke up the next time I was in a country hospital and the first surgery. I then spent the next six months in hospital in Japan and the states. Was discharged from hospital in July 68 [*Bill Garbett, 1967–1968*[19]].

William E. Comrey, Jr., arrived shortly after Tet '68 and this is his memoir:

I arrived to 43rd Signal Bn HHD as a spanking new "Instant Speck 5[qm] (SP5) right out of my AIT training at Fort Lee, VA. I was drafted into the Army when I changed my college courses from a full time student to a part time student. My Draft Board took note of my college deferment change and drafted me within two months of that change. In fact I received my Draft notice on the day before Christmas in 1967. That was not a great Merry Christmas as I had been taking in all the drastic 6 o'clock news of the war raging in and around South Vietnam. As my basic training started at Fort Benning I took the usual aptitude tests and found that I was destined to AIT at Fort Polk for Infantry School. Although I was very familiar with hand guns, shotguns and rifles from hunting trips with my family since I was a kid, I knew that a weapon in my hand and an MOS of 11-Bravo–20 would put me out in the rice paddies or in the jungles of South Vietnam. Then a 1LT came to our unit and explained a program where the Army was looking for warm bodies to fill needs for certain jobs (MOS) that were needed ASAP in Vietnam. The Lieutenant said the men that selected the program would be expected to resign their 2 year Draft and immediately sign on for a 3 year regular Army enlistment. That brought a lot of grumblings from the 120 men in my C-3–1 basic training company on Sand Hill, Fort Benning, GA. Then the Lieutenant said the MOS's needed are considered "critical" and if the troops successfully complete the training they would be given the rank of SP4 from the first class and the top students from the first classes could be sent to another MOS school and be granted the rank of SP5 if

Bill Comrey (courtesy of Bill Comrey).

they complete the training. The two courses offered were for Supply guys needed with a specialty in Electronics and/or Aviation Repair Parts. Of our entire company only four guys stepped forward, and I was one. I wanted to avoid becoming a grunt from Fort Polk and going to Fort Lee, VA, was the ticket for me. I envisioned a supply guy would have a better chance to "come home" than a grunt. In 1966 and 1967 I received a few letters from my friends that joined the Army and Marines right out of high school, and they told me to do whatever I could to avoid going to Vietnam as an 11B grunt. One of my buddies was KIA near the DMZ working with the Marines and that fact had a big impact on my young teenage mind.

I arrived at the 43rd Signal Orderly Room on August 14, 1968, just 8 months after my first days at Fort Benning. I was supposed to set up an Aviation Parts Department for two Hueys that were supposed to be sent to Tropo Hill. But the 21st Signal Group decided to keep all the aviation equipment and troops with aviation MOS's at the Nha Trang Airbase. The First Sergeant told me to cool my heels and go to the Motor Pool to see if I could help the Supply Guy in the Motor Pool. The First Shirt said the Group would "cut" orders to send me to Nha Trang. That didn't happen for 4 months, which is true to form as the Army way of doing things.

After my first 5 or 6 weeks, the First Sergeant thought it would be good to have me serve as Sergeant of the Guard twice a week starting in October. I agreed, but was apprehensive. My first all night stint as Sgt. of the Guard was a doozy. I didn't really know what to do and of all things that night the sky was covered with clouds so there was no moonlight or star light to help me reference anything in what soon became the darkest and longest night in my life.

Nothing tragic happened, but my mind was working overtime to send a steady flow of fearful thoughts my way. Usually I was not fearful of the night, but that first night of Guard Duty was rather difficult, long and thoughtful. Walking the perimeter and checking on the men in my charge that night was uneventful, but at the time I was thinking of the worst things that could happen. I had to constantly think of what I'd have to do if Charlie decided to run through our wire on their way to the II Corp and MACV headquarters (which was right next to our unit on the west side of Tropo Hill).

Normally in the day time at the northern end of the down sloping north side of Tropo Hill was a peaceful Montagnard Village that was alive with oxen and children every day. But on that night of my first tour as Sgt. of the Guard, anything more than 100 feet beyond the Wire was total blackness. Not only could I not see anything, there was absolutely no sound coming from the Yards. With our M16s, M60s and M79s pointing their way … they had good reason to be silent and cautious from us and our hair triggered jittery perimeter troops.

The night went on and on and on. I shouldn't have kept an eye on my "Timex" watch, but I was. I was too young and stupid to realize that watching the time makes for a long endurance when you're doing something you either don't want to do, or are fearful of doing. The night was totally black, except for a few lights that were on top of the Tropo Towers (I always wondered if Charlie used the tower lights as beacon markers for them when they lobbed their mortars and 122mm rockets our way). I never expressed my fear of the darkness of that night. It was the first time in my life that I was ever so fearful of something that I could not control. I think it was a combination of the responsibility of the duty I was performing and the fact that I had great difficulty seeing so little that night.

After what I thought was the longest night of my life, a glimmer of light began to show itself behind the mountains of the east. As the minutes of the morning began to count off, the light became brighter and brighter. Finally the morning sun began to shimmer though the tropo towers. I looked at the sunrise and felt as if I had to get a picture of the sunrise … a sunrise that eased so much fear and drastic thoughts that now as I write this, seemed to be such a trivial thing, but at the time it was a big deal to me....

That's my "story" of being fearful of the dark night, and all was well and good when the sun arrived to burn off the fog of the night and any fear I had of my nights during my remaining tour during the Vietnam War. That was 1968, when we were all young and to a small degree, we were fearful and apprehensive [*Bill Comrey, 1968-1969*[20]].

Most would agree that Tet '68 was the decisive battle of the war. While the climax occurred in Tet of 1968, after that one of the best accounts of U.S. forces serving in the war is from Dante M. Puccetti's recollections during Tet 1969 seen here:

The 1969 Tet holiday (the Vietnamese New Year), if anything like the 1968 offensive, could prove to be more than just a memorable event. It started on February 4th. The powers that be decided to remove me from the relative safety of base camp and drive me directly into danger. I had driven convoys before, but on this particular holiday, driving a deuce and a half (similar in size to a moving van), my fear escalated to an unreasonable height. This particular vehicle had no top or back cover, leaving me completely exposed to the elements. The sun was a virtual fireball and the six inches of Vietnamese dust-covered road settled everywhere gravity allowed, as it ground into my every crease, making me sound and feel like a rusty robot with each movement. An enormous cloud camouflaged my truck from the enemy, but the engine noise would alert any North Vietnamese Army regulars who were nearby. Dehydrated and cursed by the oppressive grime and a cab that provided no defense from outside forces—i.e., the countryside stench, the miserable climate, gas attacks (both nerve and exhaust) and enemy activity. I knew my unit would never have owned an uncovered vehicle such as this.

Carrying a load of cordite explosives from the Artillery Hill ammo dump in Pleiku, I drove on Highway 19 to An Khe, through the treacherous Mang Yang Pass. Suddenly the convoy stopped. Shots rang out and a six-wheeled MP wagon sped past, heading towards the fabled pass. Upon restarting, the pungent odor of the nearby Montagnard hoochs mixed with the current stench of warfare overcame my grit-ravaged nostrils. I passed a tall, disoriented MP with a hand-drawn "Go Philly" crisscrossed Louisville Slugger logo on his flak vest. He guarded the area with an M-79 grenade launcher. His distressed face described this fucked-up mission. I wore my helmet, but my flak vest was safely tucked under my seat to protect the family jewels.

I left An Khe and drove west toward Highway 14, then north to Kontum to deliver the cargo. I hauled explosives around enemy territory, but not within a major offensive. I was becoming familiar with the rhythm of the bouncing seat, the deep potholes and the weird, triple-canopied jungle trees with huge root systems, vines that intertwined for miles, two-foot diameter leaves, a damaged jet wing that had been caught in the upper foliage forever. The soft mulch, which sank to your ankles when you walked on it, accentuated the lushness, eradicating my upstate New York sensibilities. I headed west toward Cambodia and Fire Base Maryann where I stayed with medic friends and the dispensary became my hotel. The great food and the bed were preferable to the cold C-rations and crashing in my cab.

Early the next morning, the empty convoy departed and proceeded to a desolate area that had been agent oranged. I waited until a shitload of flying crane helicopters delivered three batteries of 105mm artillery guns, one of which was slated for my truck. There was no way it would fit. I could tow the damn thing, but that sucker was too big. Impossible! The gun was cranked down as short as it would go, but it barely fit. And the two and a half ton springs sagged in complaint. I looked at this monstrosity, with the barrel protruding into the cab, just inches from my right ear. I smelled the cordite stench of death wafting from the worn muzzle, and I knew why the truck had no top.

I lost my bearings for a minute. Where was I? I was a sitting duck with a 10-ton artillery piece strapped to my back. I looked at the barrel and then glanced out the windshield up the jungle road. It was getting late—time to get out of here. Urgency was an understatement. Being stuck in Indian Country after dark with only my M-16 was not a wise idea. The jungle encroached onto the road, and the triple canopy covered it like a tunnel, concealing the stealthy VC and bamboo vipers, better known as two-steppers—one step to get bitten and a second step to die. The tunnel was never brighter than twilight and after sunset became blacker than Hitler's soul. I departed as the sun was heading toward the horizon. I followed the forward truck but I had a hard time staying on the road. I left the tunnel and drove on open fields and dust filled roads again. I whaled the hell out of the gas pedal, the gearshift, the clutch, but it was all I could do to keep the dust cloud in my line of vision; clouds obliterated all visibility, but without them I would be a vulnerable target to the enemy.

I wanted to be anywhere but here. My heart was racing as I charged toward my doom. I prayed fervently to avoid an ambush. As I sped up to keep the forward truck's cloud in view, I went wide around a curve causing my back wheels to hit a huge stump. Instantly the truck stopped squashing me into the windshield as I bounced off the barrel of the artillery piece. Recovering, I backed up and steered around the stump to catch up to the disappearing convoy. Using all my racing techniques, I steered the swaying truck the best I could as I approached a sharp curve and the truck spun out of control and once again slid off the road. My heart was now running the three-minute mile. I gained control of the truck and once again set out to find the security of the cloud of dust from the convoy. Sweat and dust was beginning to mound under my legs. Nam destroyed life in a cruel and ultra-unusual way. I wanted to turn north and drive over Ho Chi Minh, himself, at that moment.

When I finally caught the convoy, I decided to stick closer to the forward vehicle, staying in the tail end of the dust. I was completely covered with grit that if I knelt down, you couldn't tell me from a VC! Vision obscured, I missed a fork in the road and suddenly I was driving on the side of the hill on a 45 degree angle. The road and dust had vanished. I thought the truck would flip. What a kick in the ass surviving Nam for eight months just to be killed by a rolling truck. I instinctively turned down the hill to keep upright and slid to a stop. The other road went up and over the top. Where the hell was I? Where should I go—up or down? The wrong choice would be deadly.

Out of the windshield I saw the serene valley below. I felt scared shitless, but I was on this road now and I figured it was as good as any. I took my M-16 and laid it in my lap. I told myself, just keep on truckin' and deddi-moud [rushed] to catch the convoy. God was on my side. I finally caught the convoy at the bottom of the hill and we arrived at the newly-constructed forward firebase where we dropped off the 10-ton artillery gun. Relief! By this time it was dusk and I decided to stay here for the night, however, the officer in charge had other plans for us.

The empty trucks were to return that night to Firebase Maryann. That meant driving through unsecured territory during night, using blackout lights, in the middle of Tet. The blackout lights provided a low level of illumination for enemy spotters. Shit! I could hardly see the truck in front of me to know where I was going. I had to ride his ass hard throughout this night's mission. Periodically, the convoy stopped, and I would grab my weapon as I heard the deafening sounds of the quad 50s on the gun trucks open fire, spewing out doom to the enemy. The quad 50s were so loud that they over-powered the M-60 machine guns and the rapid fire of the small-arms M-16s. Thank the Lord they weren't shooting at me! Once my lead truck went off the road, I followed. I was thrown all over the seat as I plowed through stumps outside of an old village. The Montagnards built their huts on this kind of stump to stay dry during the monsoon season. What in the hell is going on here? Am I driving right through a Montagnard ville? I hope I'm not killing anyone; I never heard any shouts or screams. How the fuck can I find the convoy? I thought we both were lost.

Crashing through trees and God knows what else, as though driving through snow and ice, nothing was going to make me stop. I cut the wheel, slammed on the gas, shifted to second and cut the wheel back again—over and over. I followed the bouncing red lights. I turned hard right; trucks appeared and I felt relief. A miracle! I may make it through the night.

I made it back to Firebase Maryann late that night. I was exhausted, a state with which I was well acquainted in Nam. I crashed in the truck. There was always one more sand bag to fill, one more magazine to load, one more hour awake, shit to burn, hill to hump, weapon to clean, fire mission, ambush, grenade to toss, one more round to fire, horizon to scan, another radio check, mosquito to slap, 100 round ammo belts to hump, one more sound to agonize about, one more thing I had to do to get home. I've worked more in my time in Nam than most silyvison's [civilians] in peace. Fuck this hole!

One more thing—will I ever leave? The next day I convoyed back to Camp Enari to some unit's Motor Pool that formed this convoy. I found the reason I spun; when I hit the stump, I bent the foreword of the two duel-rear axial all to hell, so I parked the truck so no one could see the damaged front bumper or the bent wheels. Wearily, I hopped a ride back to my battery because: There was one more thing I had to do— [*Danté M. Puccetti, 1969*[21]].

FOUR

The Home Front

Connecting the dots to describe the home front during the Vietnam War and its effect on the war is difficult. One can only summarize the many events that were going on at that time and their effect on the war that forced our early withdrawal. A flashback of a hundred years may be useful.

The eight years in America from 1860 to 1868 uprooted institutions that were centuries old, changed politics of a people, transformed the social life of half of the country, and wrought so profoundly upon the entire National character that the influence cannot be measured short of two or three generations [Mark Twain, 1873].

The same can be said one hundred years later about the 1960s.

Jack Harrigan was assigned to the Pentagon during the Kennedy administration before the Vietnam buildup and tells us of activities there at that time:

I was in the service between 1961 and 1964 and stationed at the Pentagon. Our first big shakeup at the Pentagon came when it was discovered that General Lucien Coverdale had been compromised by his chauffeur, Sgt. Jack Edward Dunlap. Dunlap had been taking big bucks from the Soviets in return for information about what was going on in Coverdale's world. Needless to say, Coverdale retired in disgrace and Dunlap eventually ended up dead in his Cadillac from carbon monoxide poisoning. I always wondered whether Dunlap's death was a suicide or was assisted by some agency. KGB? CIA? Who knows?

Another event that rattled our cage was the Berlin Airlift. After the Soviets sealed off East Germany things got very tense and there was some talk that members of our unit might be airlifted off to Berlin as well. That was followed by the Cuban Missile Crisis. We were almost sure that was going to precipitate a shooting war between us and Cuba and Russia and that our unit was going to be moving to either Florida or Cuba but that never happened.

We had an opportunity to witness some historic events around the Washington, D.C., area. One evening around 4:30 p.m. we were at the Washington Monument and the curator got a telephone call from the White House helicopter pilot. He had the President on board and wanted the curator to turn on the lights because he was preparing to land the President on the White House lawn. Barb and I were standing near the fence one day and here came Caroline and John-John and their pony, Macaroni, whizzing by. I caught a very blurry shot of Caroline in her green jumper—green because it was March 17, 1963. Some of their cousins were out there playing with them. JFK and Jackie

Barb and Jack Harrigan (courtesy of Jack Harrigan).

and, I believe, Robert and Ethel were standing up by the White House door. I've always wished I had a telephoto lens at that time.

One night Barb and I were driving around in the vicinity of the Lincoln Memorial, which was well-lighted because the Shah of Iran was in town. And who should drive by at that moment but JFK and the Shah of Iran in the White House stretch limo. It seems a bit oxymoronic that the Shah of Iran, a despot who had just been deposed in his home country for outrageous cruelties to his people, should be paying homage to Abraham Lincoln who stood for all those things that the Shah did not. But, as someone said when they asked the President why he'd support such an asshole, the President said, "Yes, but he's our asshole." The Shah was in the U.S. for treatment of a very dangerous cancer which later killed him. I read later, possibly in one of Gore Vidal's books, that it was the Shah's own celebrity that probably caused his death. He was given a special floor in a top-notch hospital and assigned the best surgeons in the world. But the author said he would have been better off if he had been admitted as a plain citizen in a regular hospital because they would have felt free to try some of the new break-through treatments on him that would have saved his life. But since he was such a high-priority patient nobody would take chances on his treatment so they stuck to conventional methods which were ineffective at the time.

During November, 1963, after Kennedy had been shot in Dallas, our Army Intelligence unit got word that they had arrested Lee Harvey Oswald in connection with the shooting. Our lieutenant went to the files and right away pulled out a thick folder on Oswald. Apparently he was no stranger to U.S. Army Intelligence. I remember standing on Constitution Avenue and watching JFK's flag-draped funeral bier pass by. Seems to me there was a lone horse named Blackjack clomping by, too. A pair of boots were mounted backward in the stirrups as Blackjack made his way slowly to Arlington National Cemetery. Following the funeral cortege on foot was an entire platoon of world leaders, among them Charles de Gaulle. I always thought it was quite a security risk to have all these potentates marching down Constitution Avenue only a short time after our own world leader had just been assassinated in Dallas. What an opportunity that would have been for a bomb-throwing terrorist.

We also used to discuss in our unit the possibility of some terrorists eventually attacking the Pentagon and the possibility of someone actually flying a plane into the building was seriously considered. I guess they predicted that one correctly. There was also consensus even as early as 1963 that there would be increasing acts of terrorism worldwide in future years as we approached the turn of the century.

The March on Washington. A lot of people viewed this event as a great moment in the advance of freedom for all people, especially blacks. Still more viewed it as a great entertainment opportunity. The Army took a somewhat different look at what they considered a very disruptive, rebellious, potentially explosive exercise in civil disobedience. We were told to go home, lock our doors, and don't by any means go near this demonstration which could turn violent at any time. Both viewpoints had merit because anything could have happened. However, my sister, Ruth, wouldn't miss it for the world and came to Washington just to participate, to hear the speeches and enjoy the music.

A month or two after JFK was buried, President Lyndon Johnson paid a visit to the Pentagon. Our superiors rounded up all us Intelligence people, issued us .38's and told us to go out and patrol the corridors. The Secret Service issued us special lapel pins to wear so they could tell whether we were good guys or bad guys. I don't recall that we were issued any bullets so I don't know what us Barney Fife's were supposed to do with those .38's in a firefight. I suppose they would have caused just as much damage if we threw them as if we fired them since you can't hit anything with a snub-nosed .38 anyway [*Jack Harrigan 1961–1964*[1]].

Perhaps the greatest problem on the home front was that none of the administrations could adequately explain to the American people why we were in Vietnam and what was going on. It was very difficult for parents of a son just killed in action to understand how the domino theory explained why their son died. The American people watched the news every night and it was fascinating getting daily video from the battlefield. It was sort of like watching the Super Bowl, but of course there was no winner. When they saw the coverage of dead U.S. soldiers, could anyone blame them for asking, "What in the hell are we doing there?" As their son's body was being shipped back to the States they were told that we were fighting to defend our Cold War "credibility."[2] There is no evidence that Moscow or Beijing shared that view.[3] Media coverage of the war in Vietnam is the subject of many articles and books, but the point is that the U.S. government failed its people.

The Presidency

There was a saying during the war that the last domino to fall would be the U.S. president. In a sense this was true, and after JFK presidents made sure that they manipulated the war to assure their reelection. LBJ and the 1964 presidential election is a good example. LBJ was faced by Republican hawks led by Barry Goldwater. Goldwater accused LBJ of being "soft" on communism.[4] LBJ countered by painting Goldwater as an extremist. The passage of the Tonkin Gulf Resolution in August 1964 granted LBJ the authority to counter Hanoi's aggression and this undermined Goldwater's claim that LBJ was soft on communism. LBJ won by a landslide over Goldwater.

Welcome Home

When veterans got home, they were greeted by baby boomers (those born after World War II). Some veterans were unhappy because they did not get a parade when they got home, but most of us only wanted to be treated decently and not be attacked by crazy anti-war demonstrators. We were often disappointed. Here are a few accounts of veterans returning:

> One of the worst days of my life, Monday, 24 Aug 70, early morning after four anti-war extremists/cowards fertilizer-fuel oil bombed Sterling Hall, housing the Army Mathematics Research Center, their purported target. As I came upon the scene and sat down on a grassy knoll next to the hall, and the remains of Robert Fassnacht, a physics research assistant, were being removed—my eyes welled. There was evil in my country, no different than the evil I experienced in South Vietnam. Anti-war groups stated he was a casualty of political necessity. Tell it to his widow and three orphaned children [*James Allan Long, 1968–1969*[5]].

When I got back to the States at the end of my first tour in Vietnam I was in bad shape suffering from malaria. This was unusual since I had always taken my malaria pills, but these sorts of preventive measures are never 100 percent effective against all strains of malaria. I traveled a great deal during my first tour and had the bad luck of getting bitten by a mosquito that did not care if I had taken my malaria pills and it had a strain that nailed me. The medics diagnosed this as "Fever of Unknown Origin." So in November 1966 I was back in the States with a bunch of medals that I thought would impress all of the hometown people. I could not have been more out of touch with the reality of what was going on in the States at that time. I had a former girlfriend named Sandy whom I visited when I returned to Saint Paul after my first tour in Vietnam in 1966. She proudly informed me that her father had arranged to get her brother out of the draft. Daddy had it set so that Junior would claim that he was deaf at his physical. It worked of course, since daddy was wealthy and connected. I was shocked. These baby boomers like most of the others, did not get it. You cannot lie, cheat and steal just to preserve your lifestyle. What really bothered me was that she was so self-focused that she just rattled on like an airhead without considering the fact that two weeks earlier I was in Vietnam. I never saw her again. I later learned that she married a lawyer and is still enjoying the good life while others are dying to preserve it today in places such as Afghanistan. About the same time, I laughed when I got a letter from my local draft board to warn me that I had not registered for the draft and there would be severe consequences if I did not register. Apparently there were so many cheaters that they had trouble meeting quotas. The draft board was casting a large net to perhaps thousands of people with a form letter without regard to the individual circumstances. I had registered for the draft ten years earlier before I went to West Point and had my draft card. I got back to the draft board telling them that I had just returned from Vietnam and would be going back for a second tour. Did "severe consequences" mean that I might get shipped to Vietnam? I never got an answer. The bureaucrats were obviously not amused, nor was I.

It got worse. Between my two tours in Vietnam I decided to apply to study for a graduate degree at Columbia University, but for some reason, I had to wear my uniform. I arrived in the middle of a student demonstration. There were all of these dirty, bearded students who smelled bad and they were between me and the Columbia building where I needed to apply. I decided to go straight to the building through the smelly crowd. A weird event followed. As I approached the crowd they were yelling, "Hell no, we won't go," or something like that. People on the edge saw me coming in uniform and they pulled back to provide me a path to the building. The chanting stopped. It was very strange. They just stepped back and made a path for me to get to the admin building. I got to the entrance and one of the university people said they could not enroll me in graduate school (for obvious reasons) and would I care to escape through a back entrance of the building. I said, "No, thanks." What he did not know but what I sensed was that it was instant empathy between me and the crowd, although only a few on the fringes saw me. These students were in their twenties, as old as or older than I. They had no big grudge with me as a person, nor I with them. A path opened and I went back the way I came. As I left, the chanting continued and the mob later stormed and occupied campus buildings and what followed was a long negotiation to get the mob out of the buildings.

It got much worse. On one occasion I had to talk to people about the war in Vietnam, so I was in uniform. This was common during the late 1960s. It was an attempt to educate the U.S. people about the war in Vietnam. I had to stop for gas, and as the attendant topped up the tank and I got money out to pay him a group of four people arrived behind me in an auto and saw my uniform. They started heckling and gave me the finger and that sort of thing. I got in my auto and they decided to pursue. I guess their objective was to stop my car and beat me up just because I was a U.S. soldier. I had the better car and in my rearview mirror I watched them disappear. It occurred to me at that time that at least in Vietnam I had a rifle to defend myself when I was attacked. My thought was that many soldiers who returned from Vietnam observed the same thing. They were called "Baby Killers" and things like that by members of a self-focused society who only cared about their creature comforts. I suppose many soldiers reenlisted to return to Vietnam in order to escape this society. I also did that (*Mike Eggleston, 1966*[6]).

One veteran related that he left for Vietnam at age nineteen and returned a year later. He met with his girlfriend and her mother. Her mother objected and told her that this man looked to be in his mid-thirties and could not be the same man she had farewelled a year earlier. She assured her mother that he was the same man, and they married.

Philip Caputo summarized in his book *A Rumor of War*:

> Beyond adding a few more corpses to the weekly body count, none of these encounters achieved anything; none will ever appear in military histories or be studied by cadets at West Point. Still, they changed us and taught us, the men who fought in them; in those obscure skirmishes we learned the old lessons about fear, cowardice, courage, suffering, cruelty, and comradeship. Most of all, we learned about death at an age when it is common to think of oneself as immortal. Everyone loses that illusion eventually, but in civilian life it is lost in installments over the years. We lost it all at once and, in the span of months, passed from boyhood through manhood to a premature middle age. The knowledge of death, of the implacable limits placed on a man's existence, severed us from our youth as irrevocably as a surgeon's scissors had once severed us from the womb. And yet, few of us were past twenty-five.[7]

The average age of soldiers who served in Vietnam was much younger than those in World War II because of the nature of the draft in place during the Vietnam War. When my wife, Margaret, who is also an author, mother of many kids, and the world's best editor, reviewed the draft of this book she remarked: "I never realized that you were ever that skinny." I must have weighed in the range of 130 pounds in the 1966 photos. My boxing weight in college was 147 pounds. My reply was: "Sure, I was young, had malaria and dysentery, and that does have an effect." Her reply as she reviewed the photos of the Vietnam soldiers was, "My God these were kids." My reply was that we started out that way going to Vietnam, but when we came back we had aged a lot (*Mike Eggleston, 2013*[8]).

Philip Duncan Hoffmann described his return from Vietnam as follows:

> Brothers Steve and Tom picked me up at the St. Louis airport and we headed straight for the nearest airport bar to celebrate my return. It was there I had my first encounter with a civilian who showed bias against veterans in uniform. A surly waitress carded me and then refused to accept my military I.D. She insisted on a driver's license, which I didn't have. The conversation heated after my brothers got involved, and only when the bar manager stepped in did things quiet down. He apologized to me and made things right.[9]

Today it is apparent that many aging members of the "Me Generation" never understood what was going on. They watched the evening news and saw the bloodshed and worried about where their tax dollars were going and how to help their sons or brothers flee to Canada or fake illness to evade the draft.[10] They blamed the U.S. soldiers who were assigned there. The more important point is that many of the members of this generation volunteered for Vietnam or were drafted and served faithfully. The conduct of the "surly waitress" seen previously was repeated thousands of times. If you had to be in uniform for some reason during this period, you could expect a hard time. Being called a "Baby Killer" was common, but having a drink thrown in your face by a waitress was less common. Most members of the "Me Generation," for example those who fled to Canada or faked illness to avoid the draft, will tell you that the veterans returned with a chip on their shoulders, which was not true. Another smear was that we were all psychos who would get a gun and kill everyone in sight as soon as we returned to the United States. It rarely happened. All that we wanted to do was put Vietnam behind us and get on with our lives. But when a waitress throws a drink in your face or four guys want to trap and beat the hell out of you simply because you are wearing your uniform, you get bitter and defensive.[11]

Welcome home.

The Civil Rights Movement

The United States in the 1960s was a cauldron of discontent starting to deal with long overdue issues. Perhaps hundreds or thousands of books and articles have been written about the civil rights movement during this period, but what is of interest in this book is how it influenced the war in Vietnam.

Vietnam coincided with the civil rights movement during 1960s America. While African Americans were discriminated against at home the effects of Black Power, the impact of the civil rights struggle and the resurgence of black sub-cultural style, expressed through dress, language and gesture, had been transferred to the war zone. Amidst increasing tension, black soldiers embraced Black Power: culturally and politically. Vietnam was America's first racially integrated conflict. Black soldiers had fought in a great deal of America's previous military encounters, but for the most part in segregated units. One million African Americans had served in the Second World War and returned home imbued with the desire to possess the full rights of citizenship so long denied them. In previous wars also, African Americans had fought not only for their emancipation but also due to their firm belief in democracy. When black servicemen returned victorious after having defeated Hitler and the threat of fascism in Europe in 1945, they soon realized that they were still denied basic human rights. Protest groups were formed such as the Congress of

Racial Equality (C.O.R.E.). Subsequently, demonstrations, sit-ins and boy-cotts pressured the authorities to integrate schools and other public buildings.

Martin Luther King opposed the Vietnam War and in a 1967 speech summarized:

> I am as deeply concerned about our own troops there as anything else. For it occurs to me that what we are submitting them to in Vietnam is not simply the brutalizing process that goes on in any war where armies face each other and seek to destroy. We are adding cynicism to the process of death, for they must know after a short period there that none of the things we claim to be fighting for are really involved. Before long they must know that their government has sent them into a struggle among Vietnamese, and the more sophisticated surely realize that we are on the side of the wealthy, and the secure, while we create a hell for the poor.
>
> Somehow this madness must cease. We must stop now. I speak as a child of God and brother to the suffering poor of Vietnam. I speak for those whose land is being laid waste, whose homes are being destroyed, whose culture is being subverted. I speak for the poor of America who are paying the double price of smashed hopes at home, and death and corruption in Vietnam. I speak as a citizen of the world, for the world as it stands aghast at the path we have taken. I speak as one who loves America, to the leaders of our own nation: The great initiative in this war is ours; the initiative to stop it must be ours.

African Americans also recalled the words of earlier civil rights leaders. They recalled the words of the legendary leader of the National Association for the Advancement of Colored People W. E. B. Du Bois when he advised during the beginning of World War I: "Let us, while the war lasts, forget our special grievances and close ranks shoulder to shoulder with our white fellow citizens ... fighting for democracy. We make no ordinary sacrifice, but we make it gladly and willingly."

These words in turn echoed the sentiment of former slave and early African American leader Frederick Douglass when describing the fundamental requirements and rights of American patriotism and therefore citizenship during the Civil War: "[F]or once let the Black man get up on his person the brass letters U.S.; let him get an eagle upon his button ... bullets in his pocket, and there is no power on earth ... which can deny that he has earned the right to citizenship in the United States."[12]

The Congress

In the words of Mark Twain, "Suppose you were an idiot, and suppose you were a member of Congress; but I repeat myself." Congress made the mistake of giving LBJ a blank check to wage a war without declaring war with the advice and consent of Congress (Public Law 88–408, dated 7 August 1964).[13] It was called the Gulf of Tonkin Resolution, based upon the attack by North Vietnamese gunboats on U.S. destroyers in the Gulf of Tonkin. LBJ used this to escalate U.S. involvement in the war in Vietnam. As U.S. casualties mounted and the corruption and incompetence of the South Vietnamese regime became obvious to everyone on the planet, Congress reduced its support for the war because of public pressure. The Gulf of Tonkin Resolution was finally repealed in 1970. It was a bit late: By that time thousands of U.S. servicepeople had been killed along with millions of Vietnamese people. As Congress continued efforts to limit President Nixon's power, other acts were passed such as the War Powers Act. Other acts followed that were designed to choke off any support to the corrupt Saigon regime. When Nixon resigned, Jerry Ford took over. Ford was faced with a hostile Congress that had successfully blocked any further funding for the war in Vietnam. Ford tried but failed to get any further funding for the Saigon regime. Meanwhile South Vietnamese President Thieu was complaining that the United States was not providing him with the funds for artillery shells that he needed to repel the invasion by the NVA. This is perhaps a very fascinating aspect of history. The United States had shipped thousands of tons of supplies, including spare parts and ammunition to South Vietnam and these were stored in warehouses, but there was no inventory control. The South Vietnamese did not know what they had and never bothered to check. While Thieu was weeping and crying about the betrayal by the United States, he was packing all of the gold that he had looted from his treasury so that he could fly to Taiwan and live in comfort. This was at the same time that he was vowing to fight to the end at his Saigon palace. Congress cut off all funding and the Saigon regime collapsed as everyone expected. Thieu later recanted his criticism of the United States so that he could get treatment for cancer in the United States, where he died.

Student Protests

Students were protesting because they did not want to be cannon fodder for the war and, in 1967, thirty thousand marched on the Pentagon.[14] Students also identified with the Vietnamese people and their sacrifices.[15] Bernardine Dohrn, a member of the Weathermen, also suggested that the protests would hasten the end of the war by raising its social cost.[16]

The college and university campuses were in turmoil. Prior to 1967 the sons of the white middle class had largely avoided the war through the escape of the college deferment. By 1967 the needs of the Green Machine were such that the draft had taken significant numbers of them as they graduated. The threat of being conscripted for a war that was the object of wide-spread moral revulsion made marchers and shouters out of young men who might have been less concerned over the victimization of an Asian people and the turning into cannon fodder of farm boys and the sons of the working class and the minorities. The appeal of the cause aroused women students in equal number and with equal passion.[17]

Richard Nixon later summarized the student protests. It was a statement of the unpopularity of the Vietnam War in the United States among students and others:

Today, many Americans remember the demonstrations against the war as flocks of flower children marching in orderly candlelight processions. But what we saw from the White House at the time was quite different. Until 1968, antiwar demonstrators were basically peaceful, seldom doing more than holding "teach-ins" and symbolically burning their draft cards. But that had changed by 1969. Students shot at firemen and policemen, held college administrators hostage at knifepoint, stormed university buildings with shotguns in hand, burned buildings, smashed windows, trashed offices, and bombed classrooms. In the academic year 1969–70, there were 1,800 demonstrations, 7,500 arrests, 247 arsons, 462 injuries—two-thirds of them to police—and 8 deaths. The violence was not limited to college campuses; it was a national epidemic. From January 1969 through February 1970, there were over 40,000 bombings, attempted bombings, or bomb threats, most of which were war related. These caused $21 million of property damage, hundreds of injuries, and 43 deaths. Violence was becoming the rule, not the exception, in campus protests. Following the announcement of the incursions into Cambodia, a new wave of violent protest swept the country. At the University of Maryland, fifty people were injured when students ransacked the ROTC building and skirmished with police. In Kent, Ohio, a crowd of hundreds of demonstrators watched as two young men threw lighted flares into the army ROTC building on the campus of Kent State University and burned it to the ground. Ohio's governor called in the National Guard. A few days later, a large crowd of students began throwing rocks and chunks of concrete at the guardsmen, forcing them up a small hill. At the top, the soldiers turned, and someone started shooting. Four people—two protesters and two bystanders—were killed.[18]

FIVE

The Disintegration of the U.S. Army in Vietnam—The Reluctant Warriors

It did not happen overnight. The decline in the ability of the U.S. Army to fight took place over a period of years. Between my two tours in Vietnam (1965–1966 and 1970–1971) important events occurred that would lead to the collapse of the U.S. Army. Martin Luther King was assassinated and the use of drugs mushroomed.

The United States Failed to Adequately Prosecute the War

This topic has been discussed for at least forty years. The thesis was that we went into the war without the willingness to fully prosecute the fight. If you were to believe General Curtis Lemay (sometimes called "Bombs Away Lemay"), former air force chief of staff: "We should bomb 'em back to the Stone Age."[1] We tried that, but it did not work.

Corporal John Musgrave, USMC, was a fighter, wounded four times during his tour, and he described his view of the war in 1967:

> There was no withdrawal. We were bombing the living shit out of the North, and were literally waiting for orders that would let us cross the Ben Hai River and get into North Vietnam and start kicking their ass. Take Uncle Ho by his inscrutable balls and lead him down the streets of Hanoi.[2]

Musgrave never got the order to invade the North.

Drugs

Over 25 percent of the soldiers in Vietnam were draftees.[3] They accepted their duty of serving their country rather than fleeing to Canada or trying to fake illness during their physical exam. The problem was that as time went on and anti-war sentiment in the United States continued to build, they arrived in Vietnam with an anti-war view of the world. Added to that was the permissive view of drugs in the United States that assured that many of the arriving soldiers in Vietnam had experimented with drugs or were in some cases addicts who would seek out drug sources. In 1965 forty-five servicemen in Vietnam were arrested or investigated for drugs. In 1970 the number was up to eleven thousand.[4] In 1971 10 to 15 percent were using heroin while an additional 40 percent used marijuana. A good example was the driver who was assigned to drive my jeep in early 1971. It did not take me very long to figure out that he was usually high as a kite. When we got ambushed (a fairly good bet), I would be quickly out of the jeep returning fire, while he stood a good chance of getting in the way and becoming another friendly-fire casualty.

At the time of my departure from my second tour in Vietnam in 1971, every soldier needed to be drug tested to make sure that they were drug free and not a threat to the U.S. society back home. As I was tested, I sort of broke up laughing. They were testing us to return to a drug-drenched society. In the words of Timothy Leary, the Harvard professor: "Turn on, tune in and drop out." The United States was then and still is today a population with an incredibly large number of drug abusers. These same U.S. drug abusers sent their sons to Vietnam. Today abusers finance the drug cartels with their drug habits. But there were many other problems that caused the demise of the U.S. Army in Vietnam.

The Draft

Most considered the inequality of the draft as a national disgrace. Nixon terminated college deferments in 1969 and conscription was ended in 1973, but by then for the United States the war was over and the damage had been done. Middle- and upper-class parents were sending their sons to college and these received a student deferment from the draft. Also, many of the wealthy parents whose sons could not get into college would influence their local draft boards to exempt their sons. A favorite scam was to fake illnesses such as deafness. Most black males had no student deferments, so they were quickly drafted, while many whites never served. While 11 percent of the U.S. population was black, 12.6 percent of U.S.

forces in Vietnam were black. Assignments were more important than percentages. Since the blacks did not have the educational opportunities of the whites, most blacks ended up in the infantry, which meant that they had a greater possibility of becoming casualties. So in this way, many of the wealthy Baby Boomers, also known as the "Me Generation" (for obvious reasons), were able to avoid any discomfort such as service in Vietnam.

Loss of Public Trust in Its Government

The U.S. public did not trust the government because they had been lied to too many times. The best quote from the period is from LBJ, who when commenting on a TV program by Walter Cronkite that was critical of the war stated, "If we have lost Cronkite, we have lost the American people." LBJ was correct: Too many lies had been fed to the U.S. public. Senator J. William Fulbright summarized what he learned: "The biggest lesson I learned from Vietnam is not to trust government statements."[5]

The Withdrawal Starts

By the time the U.S. Army started its withdrawal in late 1969, it was obvious to everyone in the field that our army was disintegrating. A senior brigade officer spoke more to the point when he said, behind the cloak of anonymity, "Nobody in the brigade gives a damn about this war anymore, including me. We will be happy to get home and when we do the enemy will march down out of the hills and take over." That senior officer's bitter statement was widely shared among the departing American soldiers. The Vietnam experience had carried U.S. armed forces to the point of disintegration. Said army captain Steve Adolph, a veteran of three tours, "When I came home, I didn't think the U.S. Army could whip the North Vietnamese Boy Scouts, and I wasn't sure about the Girl Scouts either." Brigadier General Theodore C. Mataxis, who had served as a II Corps advisor, brigade commander, and acting division commander, summed up the army's tortuous journey this way: "It's been the opposite of Korea. There we went in with a bad army and came out with a good one. In Vietnam we went in with a good army and came out with a bad one."[6]

General Bruce Palmer, Jr., who had commanded IIFFV in Vietnam and later became the acting U.S. Army chief of staff, summarized:

> American direction and conduct of the war and the operational performance of our armed forces, particularly during the 1962–69 period, generally were professional and commendable. Performance continued to be of a high quality

until the 1969–70 period, when dissent at home began to be reflected in troop attitudes and conduct in Vietnam. From 1969 until the last U.S. combat troops left in August a decline in performance set in; the discovery of widespread drug use in Vietnam in the spring of 1970 signaled that more morale and disciplinary troubles lay ahead, The so-called "fraggings" of leaders that began in 1969–70 were literally murderous indicators of poor morale and became a matter of deep concern. Extremely adverse environmental conditions and very trying circumstances contributed to this decline in performance. Particularly galling to our forces in the field were the widely publicized statements of highly placed U.S. officials, including senators, against American involvement. Such statements were perceived to support the enemy and badly damaged the morale of our troops. The deteriorating climate at home also affected the conduct of American prisoners of war (mostly airmen) held in North Vietnamese POW camps; this was reflected in the increasing number of men who were accused of collaborating with the enemy in the 1969–71 period, as compared to the very few during the earlier years of the war.[7]

There are many other factors not mentioned by General Palmer in detail that also had an effect on the fighting ability of the U.S. Army in Vietnam. Historian Keith William Nolan summarized:

> Virtually no draftee wants to be fighting in Vietnam anyway, and in return for his reluctant participation he demands, and gets, personal freedoms that would have driven a MacArthur or a Patton apoplectic. It is an Army in which all questions—including 'Why?"—are permissible. Alpha Company seethes with problems, and it has now fallen into chaos … the company commander's continuing problem is to find an effective compromise between his own professional dedication and his draftees' frank disinterest in anything that might cost an American life…. Grunt logic argues that since the U.S. has decided not to go out and win the war, there's no sense in being the last one to die.[8]

Ticket Punching

Career officers were encouraged to volunteer for Vietnam. For the future, service in combat was a ticket that needed to be punched if one wished to be promoted and get good jobs. Graduate school and command of a unit were others. Ticket punching led to practices that were detrimental to mission accomplishment. Unlike other wars where we served for the duration of the conflict, in Vietnam officers served a year and were then rotated back to the States. In this way, more officers would be able to serve in combat. A year is hardly enough time for an officer to learn the terrain and the enemy and understand his troops. The problem was made worse because a common practice was to allow only six months in command and the officer would then be rotated back to a staff job. He would be replaced by another officer who needed to get his command ticket punched. There were many other abuses identified in studies that followed the Peers Commission.

The Peers Commission was established to investigate the My Lai massacre and the commission report revealed problems with army leadership and practices and attitudes that had developed over time, which caused the army to self-destruct in Vietnam. Army studies followed and one summed up the problem:

> Officers [interviewed] saw a system that rewarded selfishness, incompetence and dishonesty. Commanders sought transitory, ephemeral gains at the expense of enduring benefits and replaced substance with statistics. Furthermore, senior commanders, as a result of their isolation (sometimes self-imposed) and absence of communication with subordinates, lacked any solid foundation from which to initiate necessary corrective action. The study found that "careerism" was running rampant in the army, that officers concerned themselves more with career advancement than with the performance of their duties. According to the report, many shared the feeling that "If you are going to be a good officer, you must compete to be chief of staff." To attain even to the rank of colonel or brigadier general, an officer was under the impression he had to have a variety of experiences, like a manager in a high-powered business who climbs the corporate ladder by moving from department to division to subsidiary, turning in an impressive performance while on each rung. For an army officer, this meant that he needed to command men, work in a staff position, obtain a "civilian" master's degree in some subject, and attend the military war college and Command and General Staff College. Said one colonel quoted in the report (speakers are identified by rank only): "The Army has made it clear that an individual has to have 'certain tickets.' Without these he is in trouble as far as promotions and assignments are concerned." Added a major: "The tendency in the Officer Corps today is to get the 'ticket punched' regardless of the cost." A lieutenant colonel put careerism in further perspective: "Command of a battalion is sought not to make a contribution to the Army, not to lead troops and improve their performance," he said, "but to fulfill a requirement for the advancement of one's career." In accumulating the "tickets" needed to become a well rounded "general" officer, a man had to perform flawlessly at each step, and this expectation led to inflated officer efficiency reports (OER). Unless an officer from the time of his initial lieutenant's job were rated by his superior as virtually "the best officer I have ever seen," he risked falling behind in his career to those who obtained such ratings. A malicious boss, or one seeking to shunt responsibility, could damage a subordinate's career with something less than a stellar report. "The military requires success in everything, so success is reported," said one colonel. Making a mistake at any time costs one's career.[9]

It was a numbers game as Eric Blaine Riker-Coleman explained:

In addition to complicating the task of instilling unit cohesion and training officers, rapid officer turnover could pressure officers to handle their units unprofessionally. Merely getting a command was the object of intense competition. The vast majority of the 3,300 or so lieutenant colonels in the Army sought battalion command because commanding a battalion was one of the unofficial but clear prerequisites for promotion to general; for these thousands of men, the Army had only 250 commands. The Army tried to alleviate the shortage of commands by instituting the six month command tour, but this created problems of its own. An officer lucky enough to be assigned to battalion command held his future in his hands: the performance of the unit in his six months of command could make or break the remainder of his career. In these circumstances, many officers sought to produce quantifiable short-term results rather than working to improve the unit's long-term performance—after all, any improvements that took more than six months to show results would only aid the unit's next commanding officer, the current leader's competitor for promotion. As Westmoreland observed in a 1972 report, the system had led officers to place "too much stress on short-term objectives rather than on making a lasting contribution to the job to which he is assigned. The result is a compulsive urge to establish an instant reputation in the unit to which he is assigned in spite of the turmoil that is left in his wake."[10]

Awards

The award system in Vietnam was less than fair. It was an effort to mass-produce awards to make sure that officers in Vietnam got another ticket punched to assure their promotion in the future. A fact not lost to the troops. Commanders were getting their awards "package"[11] whether they deserved the decorations or not. David Fulghum described the problem:

In 1966 the so-called "Impact" award system was instituted, authorizing division and separate brigade commanders to award decorations, up to the coveted Silver Star, in the immediate aftermath of a battle. Naturally they relied on the testimony of subordinate commanders and staff officers. The rationale for this system was that courageous soldiers were honored promptly, while the event was fresh in the minds of those who had been there. Soon, however, this innovation was corrupted; many a Silver Star was pinned to the shirt of a commander who gave orders from the relative safety of a helicopter during battle, landing only after the shooting had stopped. As medals began to festoon officers' chests, respect for the awards degenerated. Said one disgusted major in 1970, "The only current decorations I admire are the Distinguished Service Cross and the Medal of Honor. All others are tainted by too often being awarded to people who do not deserve them." A captain who had been a helicopter pilot in Vietnam agreed. "It's the biggest farce going," he said. "Commanders give themselves the medals.

They need the medals to advance their careers." Despite the widespread knowledge of medal inflation, however, an officer who did not receive such awards risked slipping a rung on the career ladder. As Brigadier General Peter Dawkins observed, "A general attitude develops that any officer who has served in the combat theater and has not received certain medals is presumed to have somehow performed inadequately."[12]

Those of us who were advisors or combat support people did not have to read any lies written about us in "impact awards" such as those written for infantry company commanders and above. Instead, we could expect an achievement award of an Army Commendation Medal or Bronze Star for achievement with no "V" for valor.[13] This was similar to achievement awards for those serving in Germany and elsewhere. It basically said: "Good job for all of your work." We were happy to get that recognition. The only valor award that I ever received was from the South Vietnamese for my actions during Operation Masher. It means more to me than a basket of achievement awards because it was an authentic valor award.

Valor awards for the troops were more difficult to get. The problem was that unlike the "impact" awards that were mass-produced for combat commanders, a valor award for a soldier had to be handwritten in the field and then reviewed by staff officers at the next higher headquarters who had more than enough to do taking care of daily business. It was easier for a staff officer in his air-conditioned office to downgrade or refuse the award than to fill out the paperwork to send it forward. A sergeant saved my life under heavy VC rocket fire when I was wounded. His recommendation was for a Bronze Star with "V," which I wrote up. It was turned down. Another of my soldiers saved a convoy when the driver took a round through the head that killed him instantly. The assistant driver grabbed the steering wheel and kept the truck going through a volley of fire so that the convoy would continue without getting trapped. The vehicle was riddled, but the assistant driver got through, as did the rest of the convoy. His recommendation for a Bronze Star with "V" was disapproved. It was amazing. Having rank made it much easier to get awards. One flagrant example follows:

> The devaluation of medals and the imaginative citations accompanying them turned scandalous in October 1970, when Brigadier General ... was awarded a Silver Star for his actions during the Cambodian incursion. The citation described how on June 9, 1970, while flying in his command helicopter, he directed ground troops in a firefight. Although his helicopter was under enemy fire, he continued to observe and adjust artillery fire. He then flew to the nearby firebase to collect more ammunition and returned to the scene where he kicked

out the supplies and evacuated the wounded.... "gallantry and leadership were deciding factors in turning a desperate situation into a defeat of a determined enemy force," the citation read. *The problem ... was that the actions cited never took place.* As angry enlisted men in the awards and decorations office complained in letters to the House Armed Services Committee and the *New York Times,* they had fabricated the tale on orders from their superiors who wanted to present the general with a medal before he left the division. The men had borrowed some items from a genuine Silver Star citation on file in their office and had added some stock phrases, and they chose June 9 because it was one of the men's birthday. After an investigation provoked by publicity, ... the Silver Star was rescinded, and [the person]who instigated the award, received a reprimand.[14]

It is somewhat amazing that the army awards system had no controls and it took an outside investigation to prompt action in this case. More important, an army general accepted an award he did not deserve that was based upon fraud.

Racial Conflict

Lack of racial equality in the United States led to discontent and efforts of the civil rights movement to correct it. Martin Luther King opposed the war in Vietnam and called it the "White Man's War." When King was murdered in 1968, black rioting erupted across the United States. From this environment young black inductees were arriving in Vietnam. American extremist groups such as the Black Panthers were highly visible and many blacks were sympathetic to their cause. This led to friction between whites and blacks. Black assaults on whites climbed. In 1969 half of the prisoners in Vietnam stockades were black. Many of these were for assaults on whites that accounted for 19.2 percent of the murders, 50 percent of the attempted murders, 43 percent of aggravated assaults and 71 percent of the robberies in Vietnam.[15]

Fraggings

Fraggings were efforts by soldiers to kill their officers or NCOs, usually with a fragmentation grenade. In 1969 when morale started to decline there were 126 cases. By 1971 the number of cases had risen to 333.[16] Fraggings extended. I was a battalion executive officer and my battalion commander got fragged by mistake. The fraggers who did this mistook the battalion commander for a lieutenant. The lieutenant in question had stolen personal property (a radio) while inventorying the property of a soldier who had just been killed in action. When I confronted this officer, he simply said that the dead soldier did not need the radio anymore and he could use it. When I tried to have the lieutenant court-martialed, our higher headquarters took no action. The troops found out and tried to frag the lieutenant but missed their target and instead hit my battalion commander, one of the best people I have known. I was now acting battalion commander. The next fragging that hit our battalion in 1970 was our company commander, who was trying to crack down on hard drugs in his unit at An Khe. He called me the night before he was fragged to report that he had identified the drug dealer in his company. The next morning after he got fragged I relocated to Camp Radcliff to help the situation as best I could. In some cases it was too inconvenient for higher headquarters to investigate a fragging, especially if the target was only slightly injured. For that reason, in many cases senior commanders did not report or push to find fraggers since this would reflect unfavorably upon their record in Vietnam.

Raymond N. Fraley described his experience with fraggings:

All of us were given a Commemorative Zippo which had been engraved with 278th Signal info on it when the unit deactivated but alas it was lost also, I am pretty sure I left it at a bowling alley just outside Colorado Springs one evening, The wife & I and another couple were there bowling and I noticed it gone after we got home. Went back next day after duty hours to see if it was turned in but no it was not. While at Camp Enari the 278th was across the Street from C. Co. 124th Sig. Bn, 4th I.D., I was assigned to that same unit at Ft. Carson.

I recall two incidents of some evil minded person attempting to Frag someone, Once on Dragon Mt. someone tossed a grenade on the roof of a Barracks, it was one of the 4th Div. C. Co. 124th Sig. Bn. I seem to recall it being in early evening but could be wrong. Memory is foggy these days, The other Fragging incident was when someone was out to harm either Top or Capt. Townsend, I seem to recall the attacker blew a hole in wall right beside Top's bunk, I guess he was not in bunk at time. Story I think went that Top was sitting in easy chair watching TV or something. It was late evening after dark, I heard that a string or wire or something was found stretched to other end of building so it was surmised that a grenade had been jammed in between barrels filled with sand bags and wall and the wire or string had been pulled from the other end of the building.

I am not sure if this is a true description of what occurred but that is the rumor we heard next day. A few people were questioned about it but I do not believe the attacker was identified. I never could understand the mindset of people who want to do harm to ones they are going to rely on for help if thrown into combat. Just don't make no sense at all.

Another tidbit, when on Dragon Mt. Sgt. Collins and I made the morning

Raymond N. Fraley, left, and his brother Merrill (courtesy of Raymond N. Fraley).

Maid run. On the way into Pleiku we saw a Jeep from 43rd. Bn. Sitting alongside of road, we figured the driver was over bank taking a leak or something. On way back after picking up maids we see the Jeep still sit there, so after checking it out for Booby traps Sgt. Collins hopped in, started it and drove it up on to Mt. After Lt. Long did some checking it turned out it was Bn. Commanders' Jeep and had been stolen the night before then abandoned by the one who stole it. It was abandoned at intersection where the road into Camp Enari meets road to Pleiku. Also while we were deactivating at Artillery Hill, there was an incident where two of our guys was arguing about something and one shot the other, Shootee survived, never did hear outcome of that, Then later in a permanent company next to us 2 guys were arguing and one shot and killed the other with a .45. Stuff like that just never made sense to me, I ain't anti-gun but some people just should not have them [*Raymond N. Fraley, 1970*[17]].

While the South Vietnamese, not the United States, lost the war, U.S. officers were trained to accomplish the mission and take care of their troops, but the unwritten mission statement was to get a good efficiency rating if you wanted to get promoted. Army Vice Chief of Staff General

Bruce Palmer during the period 1968–1972 provides one of the few honest assessments at that time:

> The army's senior generals were among the last to recognize these changes. General Bruce Palmer, Vice Chief of Staff during the army's most turbulent years, 1968–72, believed that it took approximately two years for knowledge of change in the field to filter up to leaders in Washington. It took roughly a year, according to Palmer, for events at the grassroots level, in small units, to come to the attention of the senior officers in a theater. This was probably because small-unit leaders (up to battalion commander) did not know how to react to the restlessness of the troops and hence did not report it. Then another year might elapse, Palmer felt, before the news of change in the theater reached Washington. The state of the army did not really come to the attention of the army's top leadership until the time of the Cambodian incursion in May 1970. "All of a sudden, you're blindsided," Palmer said. "But it wasn't sudden at all. It had probably been going on for a year, a year and a half. We were slow catching on."[18]

Apparently, no one was talking to the troops above small-unit level.

I do not believe everything that Palmer said, but at least he focused on the problem everyone knew from the bottom up: that the U.S. Army was failing miserably during the period of 1970 to 1972. The situation in the chain of command above company level is best represented by the three brass monkeys: See no evil, hear no evil and speak no evil. That way, you can get a good efficiency report, get your ticket punched and get back to the States for your next promotion. Cover your ass (CYA) at all costs. Somehow, the concept of duty, honor, country got misplaced. The best example of this is the My Lai massacre.

Stand-down and Boredom

Units were standing down and the troops had nothing to do in their hooches but write letters home, unless they had good leaders to motivate them to do something else.

In our battalion we developed a civic action program to help children at nearby orphanages. Our troops loved it. It was dangerous because the VC would occasionally attempt to ambush U.S. troops trying to help the South Vietnamese. Our Protestant chaplain organized this effort to help Catholic nuns take care of orphaned children. Religion had nothing to do with helping the needy. I wrote home asking for donations to buy food and clothing for the orphanage and the troops did the same. Checks poured in. It was an accountability nightmare. I simply endorsed the checks and mailed them to my bank in the States. I would then take an equal amount of my money in Military Payment Certificates (MPC)[19] out

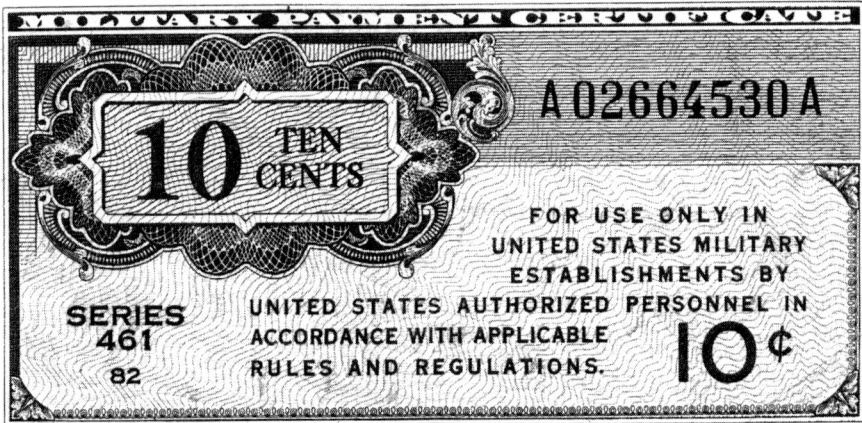

Military Payment Certificate (author's collection).

of my pocket and hand it over to the coordinator to go buy what was needed. After the nuns got the rice and clothing material, the next need was for construction material. I asked what the hell was going on? Were they building an annex to the orphanage? He said no, they needed to put in bunkers to defend the orphanage and provide protection for the orphans. I asked who would be manning the bunkers and what would the nuns use to protect the orphanage, holy water? The answer I got was: "The nuns will figure it out." My thought was since we were leaving to go back to the States very soon, maybe I could get some weapons for the orphanage. Many of the orphans were old enough to fight. The answer I got was: "Don't send weapons into the orphanage. It just gives the VC an incentive to overrun and kill everyone in the orphanage." I agreed.

Soon after that I got a call from a Catholic relief organization in Saigon. The individual wanted to know why we had an unauthorized relief effort in the Central Highlands (we were supporting more than just one orphanage). I said that they needed help and no one would help them so we were doing just that. He rambled on about proper channels and that we should not being doing this and I hung up on him and reflected that so it was with Vietnam: Bureaucracy trumps need and common sense, every time. We continued the program until we departed for the States and I have seen recent photos of the orphanages that indicate that they continued to survive (*Mike Eggleston, 1970*[20]).

There was also relief to the boredom. Lake Bien Ho was a small distance from Pleiku in the Central Highlands. Apparently, it was produced by an ancient volcano that collapsed and left a huge cavity in the ground

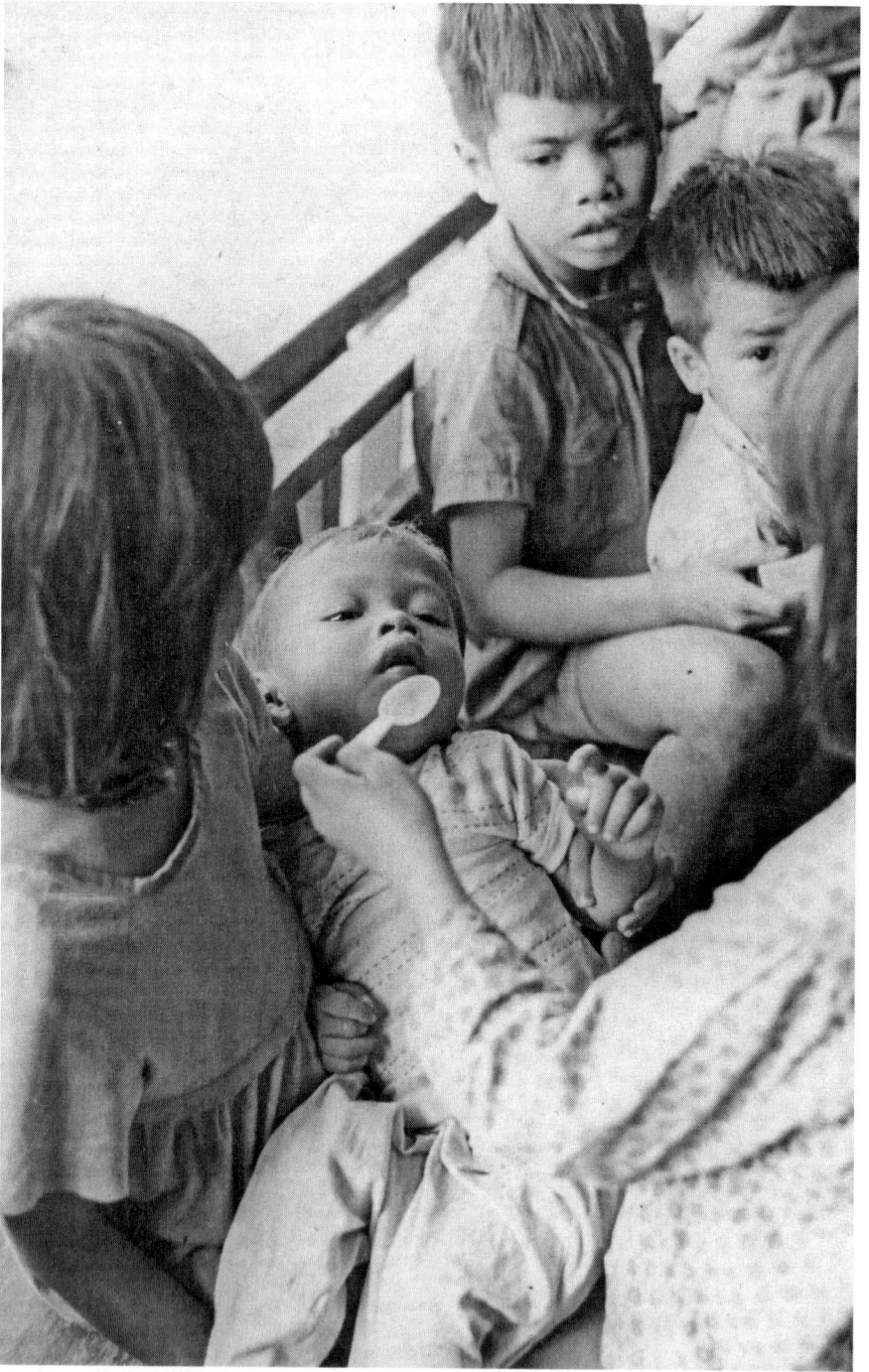

The orphans (author's collection).

that filled with water. It was a beautiful landscape, almost like Shangri-La, the mythical place made famous by author James Hilton.[21]

One went up a steep hill to get to the valley and looked down at a beautiful scene: a deep lake, surrounded by forested mountains and very quiet. I do not know of any other place like this in Vietnam. This was a perfect place to relax. When we could afford the time we went there to relax and swim. This was 1970 and my recollection is that it was a truce area. U.S. and RVNAF soldiers would use it in the daylight and the VC in the night.

I polled Vietnam veterans who confirmed my recollections and one offered a final twist to the story. It appears that unknown to me the United States had acquired a speedboat and water skis for use on the lake. A U.S. soldier was shot by the VC while water-skiing and that ended the truce. The first sergeant ordered that anyone going to the lake should go there fully armed.

As an epilogue, some of our veterans returned to the lake recently. It is the same except that much of the timber has been cut to meet the needs of the local Vietnamese. The lake was used as a water supply for Pleiku, but due to pollution it can no longer be used.

Lake Bien Ho (courtesy of Olen C. Phipps, Jr.).

Battles Lost and Search and Avoid

The Mary Ann affair[22] demonstrated that the U.S. Army had lost its fighting ability. Fire Support Base (FSB) Mary Ann was located in the westernmost part of the Americal Division's area of responsibility in Quang Tin Province located in the north of South Vietnam. It was scheduled to be handed over to the RVNAF. At Mary Ann security was lax, and the VC had been watching it for weeks. A carefully planned attack was launched against Mary Ann by about one hundred sappers on the night of 28 March 1971. They cut the wire and swarmed over Mary Ann. The result was very heavy losses for the U.S. battalion at Mary Ann. Thirty were killed and eighty-two were wounded. It was the heaviest loss for a U.S. unit in four years or so, one historian claimed. One medevac pilot described the scene: "It was the worst carnage I have ever seen.... Some [bodies were] burned to charcoal.... There were nine body bags full of bits and pieces of flesh."[23] An investigation followed and the report concluded:

The reduced level of combat activity and the increasing publicity by the news media focused upon ending of the war tend to create a great complacency among both the troops and their commanders. Coupled with this is the effect of anti–Vietnam and anti-military attitudes [in the United States] and the growth of permissiveness within the military establishment. All of these factors confront a commander in Vietnam today with a formidable task (challenge) of maintaining a high state of discipline and alertness among his troops.[24]

While Nixon and Kissinger were flirting with Hanoi to end the war and units were standing down to withdraw, the Pentagon had trouble shutting off the pipeline of people being shipped to Vietnam. As a consequence, in Pleiku in late 1970 we were in-processing some very bright people, many of whom had volunteered to go Vietnam. As a result we were overstaffed with lieutenants and I had to assign an officer to be an assistant mess officer, not a key job. Quite a letdown for a young officer who had volunteered to serve his country in Vietnam. For the soldiers it was a disaster. With little meaningful work to do on stand-down and drugs available, they dropped out, with disastrous consequences that they took home with them.[25]

A part of the problem was the new Army Chief of Staff Westmoreland's policy to send people home who had served the longest in Vietnam rather than sending units home.[26] Westmoreland overrode the objections of General Abrams and others. It is difficult to understand what Westmoreland was thinking. If you send home your most experienced people and replace them with new people, it is disruptive to the effectiveness of the unit before the unit itself goes home. At the unit level, we tried to cope with what can only be described as another stupid Westmoreland policy, but we also manipulated the system to get rid of idiots and druggies, as seen in the following chapters.

Of course the consequences of drug abuse in the field were equally disastrous. I recall one case at Camp Radcliff, An Khe. The troops in a bunker along the perimeter were shooting up with drugs as the VC sapper approached and tossed a satchel charge into the bunker. The troops inside were turned into paste on the walls of the bunker. The division commander decided that since the area around the twenty-one-kilometer perimeter was a free-fire zone, the troops on guard could fire their weapons all night long (to stay awake). The result was an insane all-night-long "mad minute"[27] of firing that kept us awake, but in time we learned that we could sleep through anything. The result of the lack of discipline was that many innocent water buffalo and other harmless creatures died an untimely death.

In other units the reverse was true. In one 25th Infantry Division unit, the company commander had a fraction of people authorized to do their jobs. He complained that he had only 50 or 60 riflemen to do their jobs.[28] It all depended upon your branch of service, where you were, and what the time frame was during the withdrawal.

As a result, as the war progressed the U.S. forces in Vietnam were faced with multiple problems. The demonstrations at home against the war generated disrespect for authority and this influenced the attitude of the troops. The system of rotation, especially the rotation of the officers to get their tickets punched, produced a less than competent force. Drugs, pills and alcohol were plentiful and cheap. We thought at the time that the VC were distributing the drugs to our troops through middle agents, and this was probably true. Jeremy Kuzmarov disputes this in his book *The Myth of the Addicted Army: Vietnam and the Modern War on Drugs.*[29] He discusses pills and alcohol and how these factors were used by the counterculture and other opponents of the war to portray the image of an addicted army. He raises good points, as seen in this chapter, but he was not in Vietnam. Those who were there such as this author do not agree with Kurzmarov. Other commanders and historians also dispute Kuzmarov's view.[30] The unfairness of the draft system that sent young blacks to war while wealthy whites got student deferments was a national disgrace. Racial unrest in the United States caused by such events as the murder of Martin Luther King influenced the attitude of many blacks toward authority. Senseless Westmoreland policies such as "body count" that killed many innocent civilians by mistake did nothing but infuriate the Vietnamese and add to the ranks of the VC. All of these factors produced atrocities by those with no moral compass, such as William Calley, and that led to the massacre at My Lai. War crimes by U.S. forces added to war protests at home and provided the enemy with propaganda that was used very effectively. In a strange twist of fate, Westmoreland while commanding forces in Vietnam commended Calley's unit for the high body count at My Lai. Later, as army chief of staff, Westmoreland moved to court-martial Calley and others for the murders at My Lai. By 1970 the U.S. Army in Vietnam was disintegrating. Those of us in Vietnam at that time realized the U.S. Army was no longer an effective fighting force.

The result was that by 1970 we all realized that our total effort should be in getting our troops home safely. For the infantry, it became an exercise of "search and avoid" rather than engaging the enemy.[31] We all realized that this war was a lost cause. The corrupt regime in Saigon under President Thieu could never hope to win without U.S. forces and the U.S. Army was disintegrating due to lack of discipline, drugs, racial problems and opposition to the war on the home front. While there are many examples of valor by South Vietnamese units and their leaders, they were operating in a sea of incompetence that started in Saigon.

Napoléon is said to have remarked that a strategy of defense is deferred suicide, and we followed that strategy during unit stand-downs. Firebase Ripcord is a good example. The 101st Airborne Division established the firebase in April 1970. The purpose of Ripcord is not clear, but the NVA moved in to attack the firebase in July 1970 and bombarded the firebase to the point that the army decided to withdraw the troops. Over a three-week period, the 101st lost 61 killed and 345 wounded.[32] Things got worse shortly after Mary Ann. Firebase Charlie 2 near the DMZ was attacked during mealtime. The troops scattered to a nearby bunker and a delayed-fuse round penetrated six feet of bunker protection, killing twenty-nine soldiers.[33]

A similar thing happened to my battalion at Pleiku during the same time period. When the first 122mm rockets hit, we scattered to our bunkers. We got word that a rocket had hit our mess hall and people were inside when it hit. The battalion chaplain and I left our bunker to provide help to the people in the mess hall. As we ran, a rocket exploded nearby and both of us became airborne. The chaplain landed with a concussion and I was out cold for a good deal of time. One of our NCOs left the nearby bunker and dragged us both to his bunker. He was recommended for the Bronze Star for his valor and the chaplain got a Purple Heart which may have been one of the few Purple Hearts awarded to chaplains. We lucked out. The 122m rocket that hit the mess hall exploded on contact with the roof, which collapsed on the mess hall. The troops had dodged under the mess hall tables and no one was hurt.

The defensive policy had tragic consequences.

At Pleiku in 1970, the VC fired rockets at our compound and we all rushed to bunkers and manned our firing positions waiting for a VC attack that did not arrive. We had no reaction force to counterattack since the drawdown had left nothing behind that could be used for that purpose. There were no patrols out or search-and-destroy operations in that area. We were not attacked, but I looked across a small valley that separated us from an ARVN ranger camp perhaps a mile away. The ARVN rangers were perhaps the best units in the ARVN and the VC of course knew that and decided to hit the ranger camp. The ARVN rangers were out on an operation and left a small security force behind to protect the camp, which was easily overrun by the VC. The VC proceeded to murder every woman and child left behind, tossing their bodies into burning hooches in order to send a message to the rangers. We were too far away to do anything but watch. It was horrible (*Mike Eggleston, 1970*[34]).

The boredom of the defense was occasionally interrupted by unexpected events like the night I met Martha Raye.

It all depended upon your mission and where you were. I was base-camped near Pleiku and involved in maintaining and defending the perimeter. It was a bad night.[35] There were a few near misses by VC rockets that hit close by and damn near blew out my eardrums, so I was shaken a bit and not in a good mood, but we had it easy compared to the infantry involved in combat operations in this area. I needed a drink, and when I finally went off duty I went to the bar. A bar was a luxury that only air force pilots and army advisors could afford. I was rattled. I sat down all sweaty, filthy dirty, shaking a bit, and ordered a triple scotch. The bartender put the drink in front of me and said someone would "pick up the tab." I do not like people paying my bar bill unless I know them. I turned to find out who had volunteered. It was Martha Raye (1916–1994), a great entertainer who participated in many USO shows in Vietnam. Somehow, our time in Vietnam intersected. She was on a tour to entertain our soldiers. She realized that I was temporarily hearing impaired, so she would repeat what she said until I nodded and replied. This was so incredibly kind of her, to chat with a soldier. That was Martha Raye. As we chatted, my shaking subsided and I settled down with the aid of a few more scotches that she paid for. Goddamn, she was so cool. She liked to play poker and I think that we did that, which was a big mistake. If you were playing poker with Martha Raye, you would lose. She served in three wars playing poker with GIs and she knew how to win. As the sun rose over the bar, I went on with my duties and she went on with her USO tour. It was like two ships passing in the night. You never know what is going on on the other ship. I have always thought since then that she had an incredible ability to read people and understand how to help them deal with problems. She is one of my heroes. There have been many tributes to Martha Raye, called "Colonel Maggie." She served as an entertainer in World War II, Korea, and Vietnam. No history of Vietnam would be complete without a mention of Martha Raye. Incredibly, she had a fear of flying but overcame it in order to do her USO tours. Few people knew that. The following are perhaps the greatest tributes to Martha Raye. A pilot wrote:

> I was the pilot of that "slick" which had received major damage to the tail-rotor drive shaft from a lucky enemy rifle shot. The maintenance team at the staging area inspected, and determined that a one-time flight back to base camp would be okay but grounded the aircraft after that. Upon arriving back at Soc Trang, I informed Martha (she came right up to us and asked how things were going) that we had a gunship down in the combat area and additional efforts were being made to extract the crew. I don't recall if we had received word of the death of the pilot at that time. Martha stated that she and her troupe would remain until everyone returned from the mission. As there were no replacements, the servicemen could not return to the mission. While the servicemen waited, Raye played poker with them and helped to keep everyone's spirits up. I enjoyed playing cards with Martha but regretted it somewhat. It appears that she had plenty of practice playing poker with GIs during her USO service in multiple wars. But I still love her for who she was and what she did. When the mission was completed, which had resulted in the loss of a helicopter, gunship and a Viking pilot, there was also an officer, the major who was in command of the Vikings, who had been wounded when the ship went down. He was flying pilot position but was not in control of the ship when the command pilot, a warrant officer, was shot. When he and the two remaining crewmen were returned to Soc Trang, Raye volunteered to assist the doctor in treating the wounded flier. When all had been completed, Raye waited until everybody was available and then put on her show. Everyone involved appreciated her as an outstanding trouper and a caring person. During the Vietnam War, she was made an honorary Green Beret because she visited United States Army Special Forces in Vietnam without fanfare, and she helped out when things got bad in Special Forces A-camps. As a result, she came to be known affectionately by the Green Berets as "Colonel Maggie." She was buried at Fort Bragg.

On November 2, 1993, she was awarded the Presidential Medal of Freedom by President Bill Clinton for her service to her country. The citation reads:

A talented performer whose career spans the better part of a century, Martha Raye has delighted audiences and uplifted spirits around the globe. She brought her tremendous comedic and musical skills to her work in film, stage and television, helping to shape American entertainment. The great courage, kindness, and patriotism she showed in her many tours during World War II, the Korean conflict and the Vietnam conflict earned her the nickname "Colonel Maggie." The American people honor Martha Raye, a woman who has tirelessly used her gifts to benefit the lives of her fellow Americans.[36]

The Fight for Pleiku

Jim Lovins tells this story:

Christmas dinner 1970 sucked. We had cold cuts for supper. Would rather have had turkey, obviously. But C-Rations would have been better than cold cuts. We saw all those turkeys being unloaded on TV at Cam Rahn Bay. You can imagine how mad we all were not to have a turkey dinner. To top the cold cuts off for supper, 150 of us got food poisoning. Oh well, the joys of being in the Army [*Jim Lovins, 1970*[37]].

Food was always a major topic on our minds. Garrison food was tolerable but somewhat less than gourmet. I recall that occasionally we got cut off and the only way to get supplies in was via air. This challenged the skills of the mess sergeant, so he would cook up captured VC rice, sometimes the only item on the menu. I recall standing in line with my mess tray behind a new guy who made the mistake of asking what those tiny black things were in the rice as a huge amount of rice was plopped on his tray. The mess sergeant replied that those were the bugs: good source of protein. The new guy turned green and left the mess hall in a rush headed for the latrine.

Field rations were a different story. These were boxed canned goods, many packaged during World War II. They were called C rations or C rats. Some were pretty good; others were horrible. The worst was ham and lima beans. The troops called these ham and motherf—s. They were almost universally hated, although I did find one soldier who said that he liked them. When a soldier got a case a C rats, he would flip it over and open from the bottom. That way he did not know what was in the package until he pulled out the can. It was like opening presents at Christmas: a sort of Christmas present from Uncle Sam. If you were unlucky enough to get ham and lima beans, then it was your problem to bribe someone to swap with you or go hungry (*Mike Eggleston, 1966*[38]).

By early 1971, most U.S. Forces had been withdrawn from II Corps, but the 43rd Signal Battalion remained and was deployed around the 71st

Evac to defend the hospital in case of attack. In March 1971, the VC mounted a full-scale attack to overrun U.S. positions at Pleiku and at the same time Pleiku Airbase was attacked.

My last day in Vietnam in March 1971 was not a good day. I had my bags packed and ready to go. At around midnight the VC attacked our compound and the nearby Pleiku Airbase with a ground and rocket attack. They did the usual VC thing: blow up aircraft. My "Freedom Bird" out of Vietnam was at Pleiku Airbase and it was my ticket out of this place.

At our 43rd Signal Battalion compound we took a lot of rocket hits and people got hurt. We manned the defensive positions and there was much fighting that night. I remember at one point I got a call on the radio saying that the VC may have penetrated our perimeter. I mounted a reaction team to plug the gap and was about to move around the inside of the perimeter to counter the breakthrough when I got an order to stand down. It was pitch-black and our own troops might have fired on us. Stand-down sounded good to me. It was better than death by friendly fire and we returned to our defensive positions and fought all night long (*Mike Eggleston, Vietnam, 1971*[39]).

Jim Lovins of the 43rd was also in the fight that night. He recalled:

I slept in barracks underneath the large [tropo] towers when I first got there in 1970. Every time that artillery was fired south, which was in the direction of the towers, the sound would ricochet downward and would physically knock us out of bed. That's one reason why in early 1971, we moved to the 71st Eva Hospital compound. The second reason was they thought we would be safer from mortar and rocket attacks since we were right near the hospital. That proved to be wrong, but we did have peaceful nights from then on when artillery hill fired south. With one exception. They had a habit of firing huge flares at night right over us. We continued to get rocket and mortar attacks. We even got overrun in, I believe, March of 1971, along with Tropo Hill and the airbase. One of our guys on guard duty was killed that night.

Tropo Hill and the Pleiku Airbase were the primary targets. SSDP (Signal Support Detachment Pleiku) happened to be right in the middle of both. I will never forget that night, as about 12 to 16 guys were in the bunker with me. About half had their M16's, *but no ammo.* We heard AK47's firing all around our bunker, along with satchel charges. (You could not help but recognize the cah ching of an AK47 going off all around you.) I asked "what are we going to do if one of the sappers came into our bunker," and somebody said, "I guess we will just throw our M16's at him." If you remember, there was a race war going on during that time because some white guy shot a black guy at an EM Club, and another black guy shot the white guy. So, some idiot decided to take away everyone's ammo, and only hand out some for those on guard duty. Ours was locked up in a supply room. Only two guys had a key to the supply room, the 1st

Sgt. & SP5 Gil Wall, who was and continues to be a great friend of mine. Gil was working at the Communications Center that night, and was on the roof defending it from the VC. SP5 Wall received a Bronze Star for his efforts that night. The 1st Sgt. was in Cam Ranh Bay during the attack.

Another time, I also remember a specific 122mm rocket and mortar attack on MACV Headquarters, and the Communications Center which was nearby. I was working in the Comm. Ctr. that day. I remember seeing guys on stretchers, one with his guts dragging the ground, being carried off. This Air Force soldier happened to have just left the window at the Comm. Ctr. where he dropped off some bombing coordinates to me that we were to be telegraphed out. I don't know if he made it or not, but I doubt it with him being in the condition that he was in (*Jim Lovins, Vietnam, 1971*[40]).

Jim Lovins (courtesy of Jim Lovins).

We beat off the VC attack, and as the sun rose most of us went back to our billets to reload and clean up. We were not sure if there would be another attack, but if so we would be prepared. There was not another attack that day.

I was in the middle of changing clothes when I saw that goddamn rat again. At night I could hear him scratching around snatching tiny morsels of food (leftover from packages that I got from home). This was no problem, because that's what rats do, but rats have a dark side. They are disease carriers (the Black Death in the Middle Ages). Also, they have some very nasty habits. In Vietnam some were as a large as a pussycat, but a rat is one creature you do not want to pet. Rule one in Vietnam was to keep your hands inside the mosquito netting. If your hand flopped on the floor, it was lunch for a rat and you might wake up in a great deal of pain. They have big teeth.

After all of the action and wounded the night before, I think I went psycho. This rat had been running around my hooch stealing food for a long time and I decided that this was *his time to die.* I figured that there was so much going on that no one would be upset by the gunshots coming from my hooch, but my driver was waiting outside and probably figured out what was going on and said to himself, "He's going after that goddamn rat again." I stood in my hooch, .45 pistol in hand, blasting at the goddamn rat as he circled inside the bunker. Rats are smart; they circle around against the walls at full speed when threatened. He kept looking at me with those small beady eyes and I swear he was laughing and saying, "Catch me if you can." Of course I missed. They are very clever and move too fast. I am sure that his descendants are still there stealing food.

The driver was waiting outside and asked, "How are your nerves?" My answer was, "My nerves are fine, but I am getting too old for this shit." He drove me to the airport to see if there were any aircraft left standing, with one stop along the way to visit our wounded in the 71st Evac Hospital. We had one guy in bad shape. He had been sprayed with shrapnel. I think that it was from a 122mm rocket. I do not know his name and I do not know if he survived. Things were happening fast and there was not much time to chat. When we arrived at Pleiku Airbase there were a few aircraft standing, but not my "Freedom Bird." The VC had destroyed the aircraft on the runway parking area with explosive charges. It was an amazing sight. There were piles of smoking rubble, and in the center of each was a propeller pointing skyward. My thought at the time was that the propellers must be made of better metal than the rest of the aircraft (they were). I chatted with the driver about the redeployment of the remainder of the battalion and then he had to get back to work. I never saw him again. When I looked back at things when the war was not going well, I see that our Sergeant Major made it his personal mission to organize an effort to dig in. He obtained supplies such as PSP, sandbags, plywood, and many other materials needed to fortify a position and then supervised the construction. More than any other person in the 43rd, he saved lives.

After the driver left I had time to think a bit while I waited for the aircraft. I had extended once during this tour and it was time for me to go home. My replacement was onboard and if I stayed around any longer I would be just getting in the way. During my first tour at Pleiku in 1965–1966, to the best of my recollection, we never had to fight off a ground attack or got mortared. There were ambushes on Highway 19, but we all survived this and if it got bad the road was closed and we were resupplied by air. Everything was different at Pleiku in 1970–1971. There were frequent 122mm rocket and mortar attacks as well as some ground attacks. In spite of what Nixon and the Pentagon were saying, to me it was clear that we were losing this war.

I flopped by the side of the runway with my head on my duffel bag baking in the hot sun while waiting for a replacement aircraft from Saigon to pick us up. A young corporal flopped next to me and put his head on his duffel bag. I looked over at him and his uniform. I figured that his first sergeant had done a great job in getting him ready to go home. His uniform was in great shape (better than mine). I checked out his ribbons. As I recall, he had a Silver Star and perhaps other valor awards along with other stuff like at least one Purple Heart. I thought that this guy was an authentic hero. If you see an enlisted soldier with valor awards like that, you can rest assured that he earned them. I asked him if he was okay and he simply said, "I'm okay now." I noticed that he limped some when the aircraft arrived from Saigon to start us on the first leg of our voyage home (*Mike Eggleston, Vietnam, 1971*[41]).

The Peers Commission

While the process of Vietnamization was in full swing, the story of the massacre of Vietnamese civilians at a village in South Vietnam called My Lai by members of the U.S. Americal Division (also known as the 23rd Infantry Division) hit the press. The Americal Division was later disbanded. As many as four hundred unarmed South Vietnamese men, women and children were murdered by U.S. soldiers. The battalion report noted that three weapons were recovered. This should have been a large warning light for anyone who reviewed the report, but it was ignored. No one in the chain of command questioned the large body count and small number of weapons captured. Everyone was delighted with the large body count and the concept of see no evil, hear no evil and speak no evil reigned. General Westmoreland sent a letter of congratulations to the men of the unit who had murdered unarmed civilians.[42]

Lieutenant General William R. Peers was assigned to investigate. Lieutenant William L. Calley, Jr., was eventually charged with the murder of 107 civilians and was convicted. Peers investigated allegations that there had been a cover-up of the massacre. Colonel Oran Henderson, who was in a helicopter flying overhead when the massacre occurred, was the only senior officer tried for dereliction of duty and he was found not guilty. The division commander, Sam Koster, was reduced in grade and subsequently retired from the army.

General Peers summarized the panel's findings, writing:

The My Lai incident was a black mark in the annals of American military history. In analyzing the entire episode we found that the principal breakdown was in leadership. Failures occurred at every level within the chain of command, from individual non-commissioned-officer squad leaders to the command group of the division. It was an illegal operation in violation of military regulations and of human rights, starting with the planning, continuing through the brutal, destructive acts of many of the men who were involved, and culminating in aborted efforts to investigate and, finally, the suppression of the truth.[43]

The Body Count

Body count was a policy pursued by General William C. Westmoreland, the commander in Vietnam. The priority was to count the enemy bodies after an encounter and report these to higher headquarters. It was a metric designed to show progress in the war. As most knew except Westmoreland, for every enemy killed there were several more coming down the Ho Chi Minh Trail to replace them. Hanoi had resources to enlist more people and send them south. Further, Hanoi could enlist more troops from their allies in Indochina such as Laos and send them south. Worse, when we killed innocent civilians such as at My Lai (and included them in our body count) the ranks of the VC swelled with those who joined the enemy effort because their relatives had been killed. The problem was that unprincipled commanders would count innocent civilians killed by mistake in the tally and abuses occurred, as seen in the Peers Commission report. The popular refrain of the day was, "Hey, hey, LBJ. How many babies did you kill today?"

Westmoreland in his autobiography was very blasé about the body count issue and blamed McNamara. It was a blame game. Westmoreland was clearly blaming everyone he could think of for the disaster of the body count policy that he vigorously pursued. For example, he says that his predecessor started it, as seen here:

Statistics were, admittedly, an imperfect gauge of progress, yet in the absence of conventional front lines, how else to measure it? Furthermore, Secretary McNamara and his Assistant Secretary of Defense for Systems Analysis, Alain Enthoven, constantly prodded for more and more statistics. How else, too, to judge whether we were meeting the essentially statistical goals that Washington officials had set at the Honolulu conference of 1966? The most controversial of the statistics was the number of enemy killed, which was based on tally in the field and known as "body count." I abhorred the term. A WAC secretary in my Saigon office, Sergeant Betty Reed, told me years later that the only time during several years in my office she ever heard me swear was when somebody mentioned "body count." Yet the term was already so firmly established in the lexicon of the war by the time I arrived that there seemed little point in trying to change it. It had been introduced in the early 1960s to appease the American press whose members were questioning the validity of casualty reports, but it subsequently became a favorite whipping boy of the press. Since conditions permitting count of enemy dead varied, it was hard to determine exactly how accurate the tally was. Because the press constantly questioned its accuracy, I directed several detailed studies which determined as well as anybody could that the count probably erred on the side of caution. Seldom, for example, were figures included on enemy killed by long-range artillery fire or air strikes, nor was there any way to determine how many later died of wounds. The best estimate of enemy wounded was that for every man killed, probably 1.5 were seriously wounded. A year after my departure from South Vietnam, North Vietnam's General Giap told an Italian news correspondent, Oriana Fallaci, that to that time the North Vietnamese had lost half a million men killed, a figure that squared well with our estimates.[44]

Even the master number-cruncher former Secretary of Defense Robert McNamara had lost faith in Westmoreland's body counts and other statistics. When testifying in court in Westmoreland's 1984 libel suit against CBS McNamara stated:

> By 1967 we had a lot of information on the number of men who had infiltrated, the number killed (from the body count) and current enemy strength. By then it was clear to me that the figures did not add up; if the body count was correct, then the figures were wrong. That's why I was losing confidence in the figures and in the optimistic military reports. My whole point was: Don't let's kid ourselves that we are making progress.[45]

The best summary is provided by author Eric Blaine Riker-Coleman:

> The body count's importance to senior officers led subordinates to concentrate on producing enemy corpses and claiming credit for them, even at the risk of their own men. More ominously, the focus on enemy casualties created a casual attitude towards Vietnamese lives that contributed to the My Lai slaughter and countless other less dramatic incidents of civilian casualties.[46]

There were efforts to verify body counts. When questioned how a body count was established, one marine replied, "Oh, I guess someone just counted up the arms and legs and divided by four."[47]

Six

Vietnamization

The myth of Vietnamization started in March 1969. As I told one graduate Vietnam history class in 2011, "Vietnamization was a fig leaf used to cover our bugout from Vietnam." We had no choice. A disintegrating U.S. Army in Vietnam coupled with mounting opposition to the war at home and an incompetent U.S. bureaucracy meant that we needed to get out of Vietnam, quickly. As seen in Chapter 4, the nation was unable to cope and the majority would not continue to support the war. There were many other problems that forced our withdrawal as early as possible. The United States of course did not have an unlimited budget and paying for the war was at the expense of other things. Vietnam had already cost LBJ his program called "the Great Society." Add to that a recalcitrant corrupt regime in Saigon under President Thieu, which had not won the hearts and minds of its people and never would. As correspondent Morley Safer noted in his book about Vietnam, as Thieu was running to an aircraft (after he had vowed to fight to the end) to save his life as the NVA took over Saigon in 1975 he had an entourage of assistants running after him with bags full of clanking gold bars to secure his comfortable exile.[1]

As we were disintegrating, the North Vietnamese with the help of their allies were becoming much stronger and more capable of overwhelming South Vietnam. Vietnamization was a foreign policy disaster. As Henry Kissinger was trying to negotiate a peace treaty for Vietnam, we gave away his biggest bargaining chip: U.S. forces were withdrawing from Vietnam. Why would North Vietnam want to negotiate a treaty when the United States was leaving Vietnam and the corrupt South Vietnam regime was incapable of defending anything? At the time, most on the ground concluded that Thieu was incapable of leading a squad through a tunnel, and subsequent events after the United States departed would prove this to be true.

The Vietnamization concept was simple: Turn the war over to the South Vietnamese. It started in 1969:

> Laird [the Secretary of Defense] coined the term *Vietnamization* as an improvement on *de-Americanization,* the more straightforward word for unilateral withdrawal then in use. Recognizing Laird's invention as a stroke of public-relations genius, Nixon immediately adopted the euphemism as official terminology ... everyone present understood that Vietnamization was designed to mollify American critics of the war, not a policy for the effective defense of South Vietnam.[2]

The withdrawal would be conducted in three phases. First, the ground war would be turned over to the South Vietnamese. Second, the South Vietnamese would develop their own combat support capability, and third and finally, the U.S. presence would revert to an advisory role, where we had started over ten years earlier. I do not think that anyone could believe that this was progress since the North Vietnamese were winning the war.

The heart of Vietnamization was a "buddy-up" concept that allowed U.S. units to work with their Vietnamese counterpart units to help equip, train, and hand over responsibility to the RVNAF. Numbers defeated the concept. In July 1969, the United States started its withdrawal and had about 544,000 troops in South Vietnam. This number was down to about 27,000 by November 1972.[3] This meant that over half a million U.S. troops left, but the RVNAF only increased strength by about 300,000 and this number is suspect.[4] Meanwhile, Hanoi was increasing troop strength in South Vietnam. As an example, sapper battalions were increased from thirty-nine in 1969 to sixty-five a year later.[5]

Hanoi had a strategy to counter Vietnamization, but it appeared to more political jargon than actual strategy:

> To attack U.S. forces vigorously and cause them losses and difficulties as to deny them the chances to "clear and hold" and to implement the step-by-step de-escalation in strength. The goal to be achieved through these attacks was to force the U.S. to withdraw completely.
>
> To attack the RVNAF vigorously so that they would be unable to replace U.S. forces and unable to consolidate, and therefore would have to crumble.
>
> To build up forces and to wrest back the right to become master of large rural areas strategic bases in jungles and mountains, and strategic lines of communication.[6]

Vietnamization was to be done in about two years. It was an impossible schedule and would take longer. Some things were doable, such as training ARVN infantry troops and tankers who already had the weapons of their trade and had been using them for years. Training RVNAF combat support troops was far more difficult. Combat support was the Achilles' heel of the Vietnamization concept. It takes years to develop a training structure to produce troops capable of maintaining complex equipment such as a helicopter and establishing inventory control over weapons and spare parts.

Horror stories started to appear. During the so-called Cambodian incursion in May 1970, RVNAF major general Nguyen Viet Thanh was killed in an aircraft collision. Was it because the RVNAF pilots had not had adequate training? No one can say. Lieutenant General Do Cao Tri was considered by many to be the best fighting general the South Vietnamese had. He was killed when his helicopter crashed shortly after take-off. The crash was attributed to mechanical failure. Since a *Newsweek* correspondent, François Sully, had also been killed in the crash, Ed Behr of *Newsweek* was sent to investigate the air-worthiness of the now South Vietnamese helicopter fleet. Here is part of his report:

> At Bien Hoa, SFC John Keith had been a helicopter maintenance man for eight of his eighteen years in the U.S. Army. Keith showed him row after row of Hueys with serious maintenance deficiencies—oil and fuel leaks, engine filters and compressor blades caked with dirt, and missing rivets. Keith and other advisers revealed that Vietnamese never flushed engines with water and solvent, a routine item of maintenance required for every twenty-five hours of operation. Over U.S. objections, many of the helicopters had nevertheless been rated fit to fly by the Vietnamese maintenance men. One chopper, with a torque so low that the advisers called it a "potential crash just waiting to happen," had been rated unfit to fly early one day, but a Vietnamese technician later blithely gave the chopper a "positive checkout" and certified it as ready to fly. Taking the machine up, Sergeant Keith said, would be "tantamount to suicide."[7]

The U.S. Army's 43rd Signal Battalion was spread throughout the II CTZ, with headquarters at Pleiku. The ARVN 620th Signal Battalion was the counterpart to the 43rd and located at many of the same locations. During my second tour in Vietnam the focus in 1970 was on Vietnamization and transferring equipment and responsibility to RVNAF signal units.

Equipment

The United States was flooding the RVNAF with large quantities of all sorts of equipment. Author Neil Sheehan identified hundreds of tanks, squadrons of jet fighter-bombers, and over 500 Hueys and Chinook helicopters.[8] How the South Vietnamese were expected to operate and maintain this extravagant flood of equipment is anyone's guess. Transferring signal equipment was more complicated than transferring other items such as rifles and artillery that the RVNAF already had in large quantities. Some of the 43rd equipment was new and had not been used by the RVNAF.

I had spent a few years training U.S. troops in the operation and maintenance of U.S. signal equipment such as radios and satellites. This takes months of training time with English-speaking people using manuals written in English. We had none of these luxuries during the period of Vietnamization.

Training

As stated earlier, for signal units equipment training was extremely important, because the RVNAF had no experience with some of the items that we would transfer to them. The job was made more difficult because there were no operator or maintenance manuals written in Vietnamese. Nevertheless, most of the RVNAF officers spoke some English, so we made it work. There were exceptions. Some of the signal equipment was so huge and complex that there was no way training could be accomplished. For these sites, such as the tropo communications complex at Pleiku, the army turned to the U.S. private sector to run them, and Federal Electric took over the Pleiku complex. The contractors were Americans for the most part, but Federal Electric tried to hire Vietnamese and would train the South Vietnamese to take over the Pleiku complex.[9] Federal Electric was still in place long after we departed. General Rienzi, the senior signal officer in Vietnam, simply said that it was too difficult to disassemble some of the complex signal equipment such as the huge tropo dishes at Pleiku, so we left them behind. Years after the war, these tropo dishes had disappeared and the sites were overgrown with weeds.

There were some training disasters. Toward the end of the war, most South Vietnamese aircraft were grounded due to the inability to locate needed parts. There were warehouses full of parts, but apparently no one trained the South Vietnamese on how to locate the parts in the warehouses. There was very little inventory control. Although the United States attempted to train some Vietnamese civilians, the RVNAF officers had no interest in that.[10]

John Paul Vann

John Paul Vann left the army and returned as a U.S. senior civilian employee by mid–1970. His civilian rank was the equivalent of a two-star general. Vann was located in II CTZ, which included most of the Central Highlands.[11] He traveled a great deal throughout II Corps. One night I received a call from Vann. He was at Hau Bon south of Pleiku. We had talked previously because we were both involved in Vietnamization. The 43rd had trained the RVNAF soldiers and transferred our equipment, and many of the 43rd troops were on their way home. Vann was not happy. He knew my troops that had been at Hau Bon (also called Cheo Reo) and they had done well. The 43rd always did a good job. The RVNAF soldiers went to sleep at their communications equipment as soon as the sun went down, and Vann had difficulty communicating with them and the outside world. He wanted me to send my troops back to take over. I refused. I think I told him to get hold of the local RVNAF lieutenant and tell him that his life depended upon keeping his troops awake. We could equip and train, but the third ingredient, leadership, was hard to find in the RVNAF. John and I both laughed and that was the last time that I spoke with him. He was killed several years later in a helicopter crash.

The Last Stand of the 43rd

A U.S. division was based at Camp Radcliff near An Khe in the Central Highlands. The division left for the States in December 1970. By the time they left, the use of drugs was widespread and the leadership in the division was less than stellar. This was the same division that I had greeted as an advisor when it arrived at Pleiku in 1966. By 1970 the division had the same problems as many others, as seen in Chapter 5.

I recall that the executive officer of one of the battalions departing Camp Radcliff told me that his battalion commander ordered that troops on the departing two-and-a-half-ton trucks should be armed with rocket launchers to fire back in case the convoy was ambushed in moving from An Khe to the port of Qui Non. I knew the battalion commander, who was a drunk and had not drawn a sober breath in Vietnam. Unfortunately, if anyone fired, the back blast from the launcher could wipe out many in the truck. I seem to recall that I later asked the executive officer how the withdrawal was going and he said something to the effect that it was going fine because the troops threw away the rocket launchers as they boarded the trucks. The troops were smarter (and more sober) than their battalion commander.

The 43rd had two companies at Camp Radcliff and these were the only units left behind at Radcliff after the division departed. With two companies to defend a twenty-one-kilometer perimeter, the first order of business was to establish a perimeter of a few hundred meters within

43rd Signal Battalion, Pleiku, 1970, the author third from the left, front row. Mike Cason is second from left, back row (author's collection).

Camp Radcliff that could be defended. We chose a slight rise in elevation that I named "Custer's Hill." The troops loved the name: more gallows humor. Next we dug in deep and ordered more weapons and ammunition than we could possibly use. It was choppered in and dumped.

This was not a happy time. Our battalion commander had been fragged and was temporarily disabled. I was acting battalion commander. Next one of our company commanders at Camp Radcliff was fragged and was medevaced back to the States. I sat down with Bruce, his senior lieutenant, and asked if he would step up and assume command of the company. Bruce was not a career officer and was serving in Vietnam because he believed that it was his duty. He would be discharged when he finished his tour in Vietnam. We both knew that if he commanded the company he would be the next target. The issue was our effort to crack down on hard drugs like heroin, which was so pervasive that the 43rd units at An

Khe, like the division (where they got their drugs), could hardly function. The U.S. Army drug dealers did not like it when the chain of command interfered with their trade and reacted as one might expect. In a scene that I will not forget, Bruce looked me in the eye and said, "I'll handle it," and so he did. I was very concerned and asked the sergeant major to go to work and make sure that the druggies did not get to Bruce. He did that.

Rather than Bruce, they went after me. It was a very clever booby trap.[12] Bruce walked up and simply said, "Sir, you need to see this." I saw it and said, "Call the EOD [Explosive Ordnance Disposal]." He said, "Why bother?" and in a hand action so fast that I barely saw it he disarmed the damned thing. By this time the departing division's Criminal Investigation Division (CID) decided it was time to put in a major effort to apprehend the drug dealers who were trying to kill the members of my chain of command and they were cracking down on hard-drug usage. The head of the local CID at An Khe checked in with me and said, "Sir, we will apprehend these people." They did just that. They figured out who the local "drug lord and assassination expert" was and had enough evidence to try him and get a conviction. The CID agent suggested that Bruce assemble all of our troops at Camp Radcliff and Bruce did just that. In front of all of the troops this pathetic guy was marched out of his hooch in handcuffs. This whining human being was weeping and crying like a tiny child. The effect on the drug dealers in the group was not lost. He was sentenced to serve in Leavenworth Prison in Kansas.

Pills were another problem. The friends at home sent a good supply of pills to our soldiers in Vietnam. The United States at that time was, and perhaps still, is a drug culture. One day, this guy came screaming at me. He was no big threat since he was unarmed. I simply grabbed him. I checked his eyes (dilated) and his mouth, which I can only describe as a pill fun house. I held on to him until others grabbed him and led him away. There was no harm done. Somehow, we managed to ship him back to the U.S. society that had produced him. After the division left Camp Radcliff, the situation improved because the major drug dealers had departed. Addicted 43rd soldiers rotated out (we made sure of that) and back to the States to continue their habit in a less trying environment. What remained was a very hard core of competent 43rd soldiers who would continue to perform their duty until we rotated out.

Due to drawdown, I think we had about a hundred people, and Bruce was commanding the residue of the two companies. I had to deal with the flag officers in Saigon. This was new to me because the battalion commander had always handled this, but he was temporarily disabled. Strange orders started to arrive. There were miles of water pipe at Camp Radcliff:

"dig up the pipe and ship it back to be used to water the golf course at Fort Huachuca." There were thousands of meters of multiwire multicolor communications cable: "Please take it down and ship back." "Please conduct a joint inventory of everything at Camp Radcliff and have a South Vietnamese officer sign for it." This was not feasible because by this time the VC had occupied most of Camp Radcliff and they entertained themselves by blowing up buildings at night. I think that it may have been a training exercise for them. We watched from Custer's Hill and called this our sound and light show. The VC never attacked us: Why bother risking sudden death from air strikes when they knew we were leaving and they would take over? The last order from Saigon kept us at Custer's Hill: "We are sending a deinstallation team to Camp Radcliff to take apart the dial telephone exchange and ship it back to the U.S.A. so it can be used elsewhere." This meant that we could not leave until the team had finished their work, which could take weeks. I told the team upon their arrival, "Better hurry up, because if the VC attack, you are the first to die." They finished their job in record time and left. Later we found out that after all that work and cost the equipment arrived in the U.S.A. worthless because of moisture and rust in the equipment, which one might expect in a tropical climate, even though these facilities had air-conditioning (something we all envied).

Everything worked out. Nobody wanted to leave Saigon to find out what we were doing at Camp Radcliff. Leaving Saigon and visiting the field was dangerous: A staff officer could get hurt. I recall a general (he was obese) who landed at Camp Radcliff after everyone had left except the 43rd. He kept his helicopter with rotors turning, which meant that this would not be a long stay for him. Camp Radcliff was a place where you could be up to your knees in mud and blinded by dust blowing into your eyes. While I was nearly blinded by the dust (from the helicopter rotors), he shook my hand, said, "Hang in there," and ran back to his helicopter and the safety in Saigon. "Hang in there" meant "get the job done and don't bother us, we don't want to return to Camp Radcliff: We might get hurt."

I turned to Bruce and simply said, "We need to get out of this place if it is the last thing that we ever do."[13] We did that. The general never got his water pipe to irrigate the golf course at Fort Huachuca, nor did we follow other orders like "take up all of the thousands of meters of communications cable." I knew by this time that the chain of command in Saigon was dysfunctional: They could not recall day-to-day what they had ordered and never followed up on anything. They would never leave the safety of Saigon to check on anything. It could be dangerous, but they did get their tickets punched for serving in Vietnam.

Signing for Camp Radcliff was easy. I knew a South Vietnamese colonel (my same friend from the FULRO incident a few years earlier) who would sign for anything after a few drinks at the bar. He signed my handwritten receipt at the bar that said: "The undersigned signs for one each base camp called Camp Radcliff." That was it. The note was sent to Saigon and I heard nothing back. We left An Khe for Pleiku without incident. The U.S. Air Force monitored our progress ready to provide air support if needed.

A few weeks after we left An Khe, I noticed Montagnards selling beautiful colorful woven baskets by the roadside and near our camp at Pleiku. We bought one from the Montagnards and discovered that it was woven from U.S. Army multicolor communications wires. I wish that I had purchased one for myself. It was the best epitaph to our involvement in Vietnam. At least someone got something out of this wretched war.

SEVEN

Lam Son 719—
The Test That We Failed

Background

At the end of 1970, U.S. force levels had dropped to 200,000 and more major reductions were scheduled for 1971.[1] Both President Richard M. Nixon and South Vietnamese President Thieu had elections coming up soon, and a military victory would fit nicely into their reelection plans. The Lam Son 719 operation into Laos in early 1971 was intended to demonstrate the success of Vietnamization, but it did not quite work out that way. Lam Son was the site of an ancient Vietnamese victory over the Chinese, 719 was based upon the year of the invasion (1971) and Route 9 was the entry point into Laos.

Early in the war, the Ho Chi Minh Trail was established to move men and material from North Vietnam to South Vietnam through Laos and Cambodia. Initially, it was footpaths used by porters and bicycles, but by 1971 it had expanded to a two-lane road. Fleets of trucks moved the material south in massive quantities. While there were efforts made to interdict the trail, they were largely ineffective. It was not just a single trail but a web that moved the material south. The total length of the web was 3,500 miles.[2] Incredibly, it included a fuel pipeline that ran south from North Vietnam to the Ashau Valley in the South.

Cambodian Invasion

The story of Lam Son 719 started nearly a year earlier when Nixon decided to launch an incursion into Cambodia from a number of points,

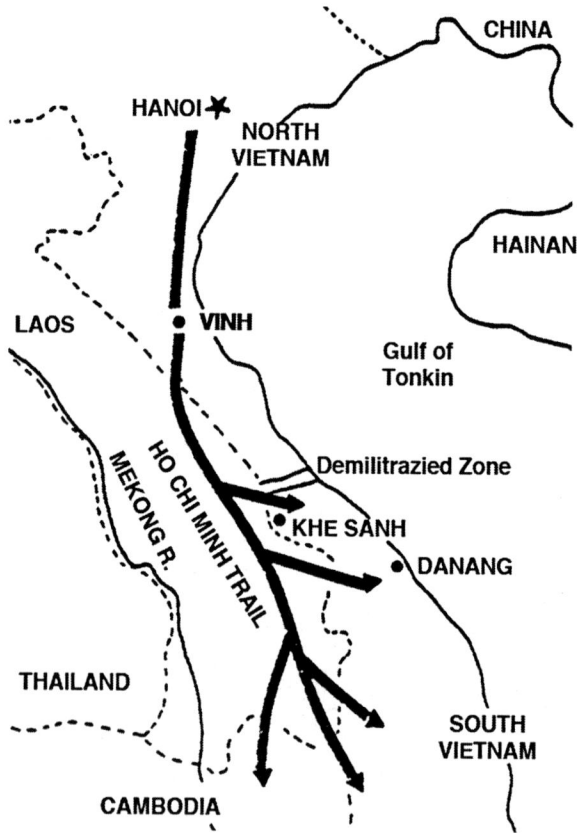

Ho Chi Minh Trail (courtesy of Nguyen Duy Hinh).

including II CTZ, moving west from Pleiku and other locations. The purpose was to destroy NVA supplies, cut the Ho Chi Minh Trail and capture NVA headquarters. It would be a combined operation including U.S. and RVNAF forces. This was spring of 1970, so by this time the drawdown of U.S. troops had left 330,000 U.S. Army and 55,000 Marines still in-country, but many of these were in stand-down and would not fight. As seen in Chapter 5, the forces remaining were of limited effectiveness because of the policies of the U.S. Army Chief of Staff, William Westmoreland. The story behind the invasion or "incursion," as it is frequently called, follows.

While Prince Sihanouk, the Cambodian head of state, was out of the country in March 1970, Cambodian general Lon Nol seized power and ordered the NVA out of Cambodia. It was a bold move, since Cambodian armed forces were few. On 18 March 1970, the closing of the port of

NORTH VIET-NAM

DEMARCATION LINE

QUANG TRI

KHE SANH
LAO BAO

HUE

1

A LUOI

A SHAU

NAM DONG

SOUTH CHINA SEA

DA NANG

HOI AN

QUANG NAM

TAM KY

A RO

CHU LAI

LAOS

14

QUANG NOAI

DAKTO

DO XA

KONTUM

1

LEIKU

19

QUI NHON

14

HAU SON

Border Areas (courtesy of Nguyen Duy Hinh).

Sihanoukville to Hanoi due to a Cambodian change of government made the Ho Chi Minh Trail more vital to Hanoi.[3]

Some called this Nixon's secret war into Cambodia, but it was not very secret aside from the secret Cambodian bombing campaign. The first thrust across the Cambodian border was on 29 April 1970. The next morning the press and Congress were clamoring for answers. Nixon was surprised by the violent reaction to the campaign and addressed the nation. He highlighted the fact that the Communist headquarters for South Vietnam (COSVN) was in the Fishhook area of Cambodia, the first target of the incursion.[4] Some blamed Laird and others for leaking it to the press, but it did not matter.[5] The operation was under way. After his press briefing Nixon met with the JCS, and his recollections are in a way an indictment of the way generals were trained and think. Nixon recalled:

> On May 1, I went to the Pentagon for a firsthand briefing. Colored pins on a map indicated the positions and movements of the various forces. As the briefers described the initial success of the operation, I noticed the map showed that four other areas besides the Parrot's Beak and Fishhook were occupied by Communist forces. I began wondering whether between South Vietnam's forces and our own we could mount offensives against the other sanctuaries as well. "Could we take out *all* the sanctuaries?" I asked. The Pentagon officials answered that although this was feasible, it had not been offered as an option because of the negative reaction that attacking more than two areas would have produced in the media and Congress. "Let me be the judge as far as the political reactions are concerned," I said. "The fact is that we have already taken the political heat for this particular operation. If we can substantially reduce the threat to our forces by wiping out the rest of the sanctuaries, now is the time to do it." I knew we would take just as much political heat for taking out two sanctuaries as we would for taking out six. I then made an on-the-spot decision: "I want to take out all of those sanctuaries. Make whatever plans are necessary, and then just do it. Knock them all out so that they can't be used against us again, ever." This was a textbook case of one of the most frustrating problems I had to deal with in conducting the war: the tendency of our armed forces to confuse *military* analysis with *political* analysis.[6]

At the start of my second tour in Vietnam in March of 1970, I traveled by jeep from An Khe to Pleiku. Along the way I noticed pipe along the road perhaps six to twelve inches in diameter. Nearly all of the pipe was twisted and disconnected, with scorched burn marks along the way. I asked the driver what had happened and he told me that the U.S. Army in Vietnam had decided to install a fuel pipeline from the port of Qui Nhon to points west. Obviously, as everyone knew, the VC ruled the night. Therefore, if the United States laid pipe during the day, the VC would blow it up at night. The next day U.S. soldiers (who could be ambushed) would repair the pipeline, and the next night the VC would blow up the pipes, and so it goes. This was a very expensive operation, needing U.S. troops and resources such as pumping stations. The VC also had their problems with this. U.S. teams could set up along the pipeline and wait for the VC to come out at night. At that time we had "starlight scopes," an early version of the night-vision goggles that are standard issue in the army today. U.S. snipers could pick these people off before they knew of the presence of a U.S. team. Somewhere along the line someone realized that we were standing down and did not need a large supply delivered to Pleiku. The pipeline was allowed to fall into disrepair. Fifty years later, some pipes may still be there left as monument to another failed army concept.

There are also monuments to French stupidity: For years when we landed at Hau Bon Airfield south of Pleiku we were greeted with a view of a riddled, rusting French armored car at the side of the runway. This was a sobering reminder for all of us who landed there. This relic and perhaps the French soldiers inside of it were incinerated during the French war in the early 1950s. The French never did learn how to avoid an ambush.

When Nixon decided to invade Cambodia in April 1970 prior planning was needed. I sat in on a logistics briefing and a general introduced his concept of a "rolling pipeline" of fuel going west from Qui Nhon to Pleiku. This meant that an endless convoy of fuel tankers would drive west to the Cambodia border. This beat the concept of a fuel pipeline. The convoys worked.

The battalion executive officer of one of the division's battalions stopped by to tell me that the division was moving into Cambodia and he wanted to make sure that my battalion would cover all of the communications responsibilities at Camp Radcliff. We had already done that. By this time the division had many heroin users and potheads who could not function. The troops of the 43rd kept doing their job while the division troops tripped out. The 43rd had a sector on the perimeter that we defended. I asked who would defend the rest of the perimeter while the division was gone. The answer that I got was that the division would leave behind less useful troops to defend Camp Radcliff. This meant that drunks, pill poppers, heroin users and potheads would be left behind to defend the perimeter without responsible adult supervision. As I recall, at that time there was a marijuana haze hanging over Camp Radcliff. You could not walk through the camp without getting high. This was okay but interfered with getting the job done. It is strange that unit histories seldom mention this period of the units at Camp Radcliff. This was not their moment of glory.

I figured that we needed a "Plan B." I asked Bruce to see me. We needed a fallback plan. If the division troops on the perimeter were attacked and caved in (a certainty), where should we fall back while the druggies were being slaughtered? He picked our spot and it was a matter of wait and see. We were not overrun, nor was Camp Radcliff.

The 43rd was not excluded from the Cambodian incursion. We had a photo detachment attached to the battalion and they were airlifted into

Cambodia. I went in on a separate chopper. On the way in, the chopper with our photographers exploded and the entire photo detachment of six people and helicopter crew were killed. By some miracle several cameras survived the explosion and crash. Film was rushed to a lab and developed to see if there was any indication on film of what caused the explosion. There was. Intelligence people stepped in and classified everything. It seems that as photographers do, they were constantly scanning landscape looking for a good shot. One photographer apparently saw a flash on the ground and photographed a surface-to-air missile as it headed for his helicopter. It was the last photo that he would ever take. No one ever told us what missile killed our people, but it was probably a Soviet Strela. I thought at the time, We are flying into all of this shit and the army has no clue of what we are up against. This would play an important part in Lam Son 719 the following year.

This was a big deal: An entire detachment was wiped out by a single missile. General Rienzi, the senior signal officer in Vietnam, flew in from Saigon to talk to the troops. Those who knew the photographers were devastated. Thomas Matthew Rienzi, whom I had known for many years, was very good talking with people. He sat down with me, we chatted, and then he went out to talk to the soldiers who wanted to see him. As I recall, his message was that these were very good people who had done their job and paid with their lives. We should all follow their example.

In Cambodia, Hanoi pulled back its troops when they learned of the U.S. invasion and as a result some of their supplies were destroyed. No headquarters were discovered and business resumed as usual on the Ho Chi Minh Trail as soon as the United States and RVNAF departed. The U.S. Congress and citizens were outraged by Nixon's war in Cambodia and intended to end it by prohibiting the U.S. Army from invading counties outside of the boundary of South Vietnam (the Cooper-Church Amendment). There were other amendments aimed at curbing Nixon's power and these were passed over Nixon's veto.[7] Nevertheless, polls taken at that time indicate that Nixon still enjoyed the support of the majority of the citizens.[8]

In his final report to the nation at the end of June, Nixon listed an impressive amount of NVA equipment captured or destroyed:

—22,892 individual weapons—enough to equip about 74 full-strength North Vietnamese infantry battalions, and 2,500 big crew-served weapons—enough to equip about 25 full strength North Vietnamese infantry battalions;

—more than 15 million rounds of ammunition or about what the enemy had fired in South Vietnam during the past year;

—14 million pounds of rice, enough to feed all the enemy combat battalions estimated to be in South Vietnam for about 4 months;

—143,000 rockets, mortars, and recoilless rifle rounds, about 14 months' expenditures in South Vietnam;

—over 199,552 antiaircraft rounds, 5,482 mines, 62,022 grenades, and 83,000 pounds of explosives, including 1,002 satchel charges;

—over 435 vehicles and destroyed over 11,688 bunkers and other military structures.[9]

Henry Kissinger, national security advisor, also provided a surprising assessment from two anti-war activists from the Senate Foreign Relations Committee who had visited Southeast Asia after the campaign, Richard Moose and James Lowenstein:

> It appeared to us that there is considerable support for the government of General Lon Nol among the youth and intellectuals, in marked contrast to the situation in South Vietnam, and among civil servants and members of the Senate and the Assembly.... There is an evident sense of national identity and purpose and a determination. Cambodians find it difficult to understand the complicated and involved elements of the American dilemma in Southeast Asia today. Looking back at the pattern of American behavior in Asia over the past two decades, they seem mystified by the signs of American hesitancy in arming them to defend against an invading force armed by China and the Soviet Union.[10]

The first result was that the U.S. Congress reduced aid to Cambodia and finally cut off all aid. The second result was that the United States assumed that if there were any further efforts to interdict the Ho Chi Minh Trail, such as a penetration into Laos the following year, the NVA would again flee.

The result of the Cambodian invasion was that many NVA supplies that had come down the Ho Chi Minh Trail were captured or destroyed. Apparently, it set back the North Vietnamese timetable for the capture of the South, but General Bruce Palmer had a more thoughtful view of the result. Palmer suggests that the Cambodian invasion ended any hope that South Vietnam would survive. Hanoi realized that the Ho Chi Minh Trail as it stood in 1970 was vulnerable, and so a major effort to expand the network of roads was launched. All-weather roads and way stations were established that could handle a larger volume of traffic and supply dumps were moved farther west out of harm's way. Anti-air capability was enhanced. When the NVA invaded the South in 1975, it had a first-class network of roads to move tanks and people. The major effort by Hanoi in Cambodia has been called the North Vietnamization of Cambodia.

Two weeks before Saigon fell, a victorious Pol Pot, the Cambodian Communist revolutionary, entered Phnom Penh and introduced wholesale murder of Cambodians on a scale perhaps not seen since the days of Hitler in Europe.[11]

The Effort to Delay the NVA Invasion of the South

From the standpoint of intelligence, planning, and execution, Lam Son 719, nearly a year after the Cambodian incursion, was a nightmare. General Abrams was the U.S. commander in Vietnam at that time, and so he was responsible for this monumental blunder. Further, he did not seem to comprehend what was going on as the battle continued.

At this time Hanoi was building up forces to invade South Vietnam and the United States was on an exit schedule that would be largely completed by 1972. A strike into Laos was needed to disrupt Hanoi's buildup, cut the Ho Chi Minh Trail, and buy time for the South Vietnamese to prepare for attack from the North.

On 31 January 1971, Hanoi's Van Tien Dung, Deputy Chairman of the Politburo's Central Military Party Committee and the chief of the General Staff, visited the front to address the troops. He made Hanoi's objectives clear to the troops:

> The coming engagement will be a strategically decisive battle. We will fight not only to retain control of the strategic transportation corridor, but also to annihilate a number of units of the enemy's strategic reserve forces, to … deal a significant defeat to a portion of the "Vietnamization plot," to advance our resistance effort to liberate South Vietnam and defend North Vietnam, to gloriously fulfill our international duty, and to hone our main force troops in the fires of combat. Our Army must certainly win this battle.[12]

To summarize Lam Son 719: Hanoi was committed to win with whatever resources were required. The United States would be on the sidelines watching the fight, since the Cooper-Church Amendment prohibited U.S. servicemen from entering Laos. U.S. air support was not prohibited by the amendment. Nixon was hopeful that Lam Son 719 would prove that Vietnamization was working and this would help him secure his 1972 reelection. Thieu wanted to minimize casualties in order to secure his reelection, but he was also concerned about committing his "palace guard," since they were insurance against a coup attempt.

Weather was a key factor in all of this. The dry season from November to March was prime time for the NVA to move supplies, stockpile, and prepare for an invasion of South Vietnam after the monsoon season passed.

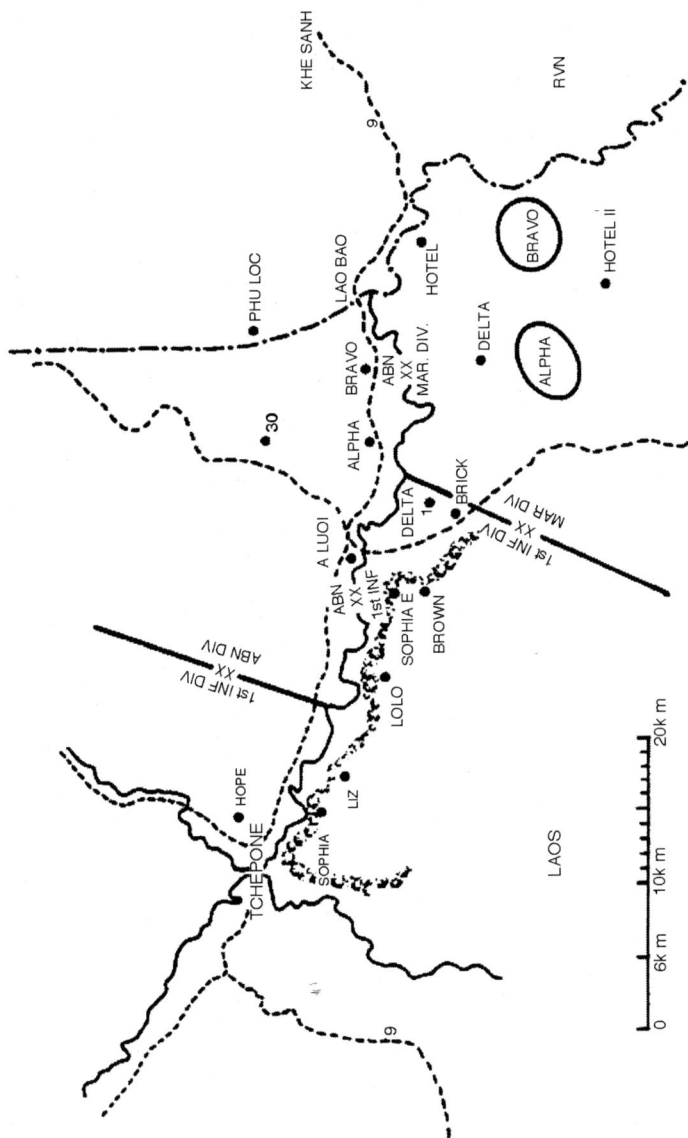

Tchepone (courtesy of Nguyen Duy Hinh).

The goal of the penetration into Laos was the town of Tchepone, about forty miles inside the Laotian border. Tchepone was a valuable target since it was a crossroad for the Ho Chi Minh Trail but slightly east of it. Thieu, in a rare moment of candor, ordered Lieutenant General Lam, the I Corps commander and operation commander: "You go in there just long enough to take a piss and then leave quickly." Major General Nguyen

Duy Hinh, an infantry division commander, put it more politely: "It was apparent that President Thieu had decided at the outset that once Tchepone had been entered by RVNAF, the withdrawal should begin without delay."[13]

It all came down to how fast the RVNAF could travel into Laos to reach Tchepone and how long it would take the RVNAF to escape back to the border with Vietnam without being destroyed by the NVA. Time … distance … and how much damage the U.S. Air Force and other U.S. assets could inflict on the NVA would be the deciding factor in making Nixon look good for his 1972 reelection campaign.

Doing any significant damage to the Ho Chi Minh Trail was no longer a priority. This was a political exercise designed to get votes and impress the public in the United States that Vietnamization was working.

It was hoped that this would delay the expected North Vietnamese offensive into South Vietnam. In a sense, it was a test of the Vietnamization policy of Nixon, since the RVNAF would engage the NVA without their U.S. advisors. This was a major disadvantage because the advisors provided a link to U.S. artillery firing from Vietnam and air support.

Lam Son 719 was planned as a six-week operation in February–March 1971 designed to disrupt the Ho Chi Minh Trail in Laos. With monsoon season approaching, it was thought that Hanoi would have great difficulty rebuilding supplies in the bad weather, and this would delay their invasion of South Vietnam scheduled for 1972.[14] Lam Son 719 followed an unprecedented bombing campaign against the trail ordered by Secretary of Defense Melvin Laird that started in mid–October 1970.[15] The air force claimed that twenty-five thousand trucks were destroyed on the trail between October 1970 and May 1971. Laird thought that the extensive bombing raid would not be enough to stop the NVA.[16] Laird asked the JCS for plans and was appalled to find that they recommended a strike into Laos by a joint U.S.–RVNAF force, which would be in direct violation of the Cooper-Church Amendment. Laird thought that Westmoreland[17] and Alexander M. Haig, Jr.,[18] were behind this plan. Laird quickly rejected the JCS plan and tasked Abrams to develop a plan involving RVNAF only with a three-month strike supported by U.S. air support.[19]

Kissinger had other thoughts. He initially supported another raid into Cambodia as had been done the previous year. Actually, a small RVNAF invasion into Cambodia was launched in 1971 and met with limited success. Private First Class Clyde Baker wrote to Nixon:

> In my opinion the Cambodian operation and this operation [Lam Son 719] are the 2 most intelligent moves we made since we have been in S. Vietnam. This operation may end the war and may save hundreds of lives in the long run, and

everyone here is putting out 100 percent. I'm sorry for the lousy handwriting, but I'm writing this letter down inside a tank.[20]

Kissinger's focus agreed with others: The Hanoi invasion of 1972 should be forestalled. Kissinger thought that an invasion of Cambodia would also stabilize the Lon Nol government.[21] He sent Haig to South Vietnam to "study prospects." Haig returned with the concept developed by Abrams that would become known as Lam Son 719. Nixon was determined that he would not stand "naked in front of his opponents" as had occurred after the Cambodian incursion. This time Nixon wanted his cabinet and the JCS to sign up to the plan, a sort of share-the-blame philosophy, and that was done.[22] Nixon gave his tentative approval to proceed.[23] Kissinger and his staff were able to get the consent of Laos to the invasion of their nation.[24]

Planning

The concept was to invade Laos to destroy NVA supplies, interdict the Ho Chi Minh Trail and delay the NVA invasion of South Vietnam until the United States could complete its withdrawal of troops the following year. (This is not what Nixon publically stated: He was glorifying Vietnamization and why the United States could exit.) This would be done with a quick thrust into Laos with four RVNAF divisions (Thieu later cut this to two divisions). None of the objectives could be achieved given forces and time allocated to the task. As early as October 1970, Hanoi had intelligence and began preparing to counter the RVNAF strike into Laos.[25] This was several months before General Abrams started planning the operation. The U.S. planning and execution of Lam Son 719 flowed from Nixon to Kissinger to Haig to Abrams. The JCS were occasionally consulted and required to endorse actions. That was the extent of Pentagon involvement.[26]

Abrams developed a very strange plan. He knew that two of the objectives could not be achieved because Thieu had reduced his invading force and ordered them out when they arrived at Tchepone. The objective was to interdict the Ho Chi Minh Trail, yet because of Thieu's orders the stay in Laos was so short there was no chance of doing that, since the Ho Chi Minh Trail was not just a single trail but a network of trails. Further, the Ho Chi Minh Trail network was a bit west of Tchepone, where the advance would stop. The possibility of destroying Hanoi's supplies was also slight given the short stay in Laos and the fact that supplies were located in the jungle and on mountaintops.[27] It would be difficult to find and destroy supplies in a rather short campaign, much of which would be spent trying to extract the RVNAF from Laos. Nevertheless, there were some very extraordinary unsubstantiated claims of tonnage destroyed by the RVNAF (see appendix C for details). Historians have not been able to confirm these claims, but there is a very important point: Most of the tonnage claimed was the result of B-52 strikes, but Nixon and others would claim this as proof of the fact that Vietnamization was working—an incredible sleight of hand and another deceit inflicted upon the American public.

An intensive bombing campaign in that region that was ongoing and could achieve the goals without putting boots on the ground (a very expensive solution in terms of men's lives), but U.S. Secretary of Defense Laird did not believe that it was entirely successful. This was the conclusion of Laird, pushed by Nixon. U.S. Air Force estimates of the NVA tonnage destroyed by bombing the Ho Chi Minh trail were amazing. If allowed to continue this could have delayed any invasion of South Vietnam by the NVA, but this would not provide Nixon with the proof that Vietnamization was working. The unanswered question is: If B-52 bombing had been allowed to continue would Lam Son 719 have been necessary?

The campaign would be conducted in four phases:

1) Reoccupy Khe Sanh and clear Route 9 to the border (this was called Dewey Canyon II)
2) D-day: enter Laos
3) Occupy Tchepone and destroy supplies
4) Withdrawal[28]

Weather was an important factor. Although the monsoon would not arrive until May, the weather during the operation was considered to be unpredictable and favorable for air operations only from 10:00 to 12:00 in the AM until mid-afternoon.[29] This was a very small window.

Most important, there was a lack of intelligence information about the deployment, capabilities, and intentions of the NVA. General Hinh later stated that the most significant failure was timely tactical intelligence.[30] This is quite unusual given the number of years that the United States had spent in developing its intelligence capabilities. Instead of solid intelligence, the plan was based upon questionable assessments that stated that the opposing forces were a small fraction of the NVA troops available (a rather ambiguous statement). This time, there would be no withdrawal by the NVA as found in Cambodia the previous year. Why bother? Most U.S. troops had been withdrawn and everyone knew that U.S. troops could not cross the border to support the operation. What mattered was getting our troops home. Of course, Nixon and Kissinger approved the plan.

It was a bad plan developed by MACV that was then handed to the South Vietnamese for execution. The MACV and RVNAF staff had only nine days to develop their plan. On January 7, U.S. Lieutenant General Sutherland in I Corps at Da Nang received the order from Abrams to develop a detailed plan for the invasion of Laos as indicated in the phasing outlined earlier. The operation would commence immediately after Tet in February and the plan was to be completed by 16 January. At the same time, General Lam, the RVNAF commander, received his orders from Saigon to do the same thing.[31]

Planning went forward at a feverish pace. The U.S. 1st Brigade of the 5th Mechanized Division would secure Khe Sanh, which would be the staging base, and clear Route 9 to the Laos border. The U.S. 101st Airborne Division would control and provide support to all army aviation elements that could be mustered for this operation. Security was important and made it difficult to plan and recon the operation. This slowed planning.

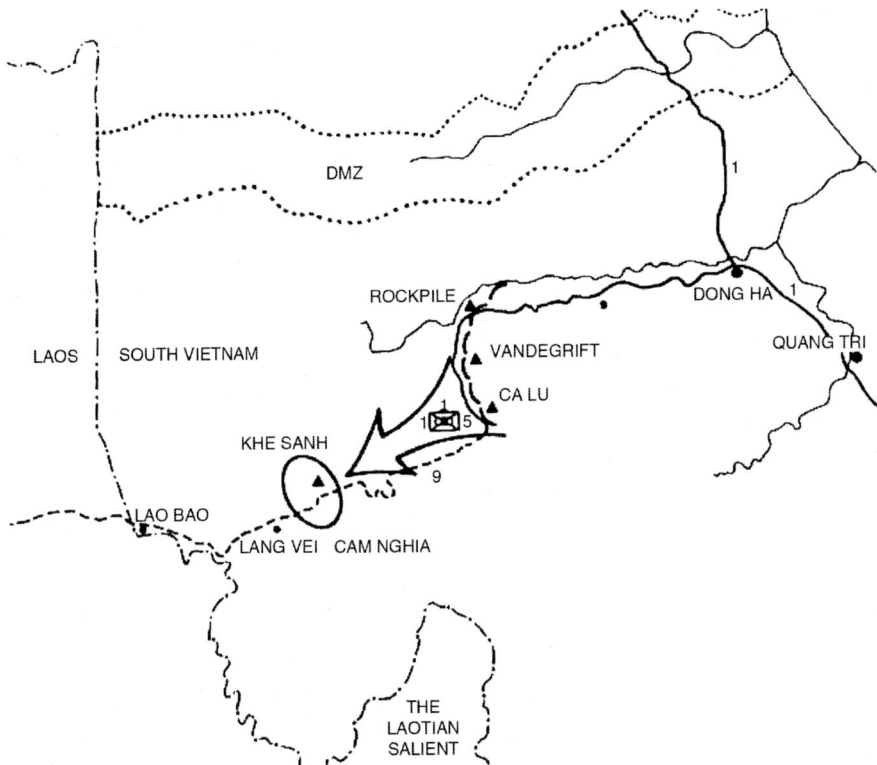

Dewey Canyon II (courtesy of Nguyen Duy Hinh).

It did not matter; the RVNAF in Saigon had already leaked details to Hanoi and the NVA was already concentrating troops to thwart the invasion of Laos.

Thieu enthusiastically accepted the plan but had inadequate time to prepare. To make sure that all in North Vietnam understood the plan, there were press leaks.[32] These allowed ample time for the NVA to reinforce. Some of the lift helicopter pilots would find NVA tanks on or near their landing zones. In a departure from reality that was common during this period, MACV intelligence estimated the NVA force at the point of the RVNAF assault to be no more than 3,000.[33] At the same time, the JCS estimated that the NVA had amassed 25,000 troops in the area.[34] Author A. J. Langguth summarized:

> Thieu estimated that the campaign would last two or three months. As always, however, the Communists had informants within RVNAF who deprived the South of any element of surprise. By now, the North Vietnamese had amassed 60,000 troops [in Laos], the largest concentration of men in their country's history.[35]

Thieu would send 16,000 men into Laos (later reinforced by 4,000 more), so the attacking force was outnumbered by nearly three to one.[36] This fact, alone, ensured a colossal defeat for the RVNAF. The United States supported the operation with the 10,000 U.S. support troops in Vietnam, 2,000 fixed-wing aircraft and 600 helicopters.[37] Kissinger summarized: "The operation, conceived in doubt and assailed by skepticism, proceeded in confusion."[38]

At this time I was south in An Khe trying to extract my troops. I received a letter from a World War II veteran who asked if SNAFU (Situation Normal, All F——d Up) was still in effect. I wrote back that SNAFU ruled and probably always would.[39] I still have his letter.

The RVNAF armored column would move from Khe Sanh to Tchepone via Route 9 and would link up with troops inserted by helicopters as they moved west. The MACV plan provided for the Vietnamese Airborne Division and marines to act as reserve and to move to support the attacking RVNAF forces in Laos. Thieu kept these units on a tight string. They were his "palace guard" and insurance against a coup attempt.[40] It was very unlikely that Thieu would allow these units to become bogged down in a campaign in Laos, but he did commit them to this operation. The United States grossly underestimated the opposing NVA forces. W. Pence, senior advisor to the RVNAF Airborne Division, noted:

> It was apparent at this time that United States Intelligence felt that the operation would be lightly opposed and that a two-day preparation of the area prior to D–

Day by tactical air would effectively neutralize the enemy anti-aircraft capability, although the enemy was credited with having 170 to 200 antiaircraft weapons of mixed caliber in the operational area. The tank threat was considered minimal and the reinforcement capability was listed as fourteen days for two divisions from north of the DMZ.[41]

Nothing could have been further from the truth. The NVA already had the U.S. plan and was concentrating NVA forces to attack the RVNAF air assault landing areas. Since this was an election year for Thieu, he (like Nixon) wanted reduced casualties and a nice victory that would assure reelection. Thieu decided that casualties in the operation should not exceed three thousand.[42] RVNAF commanders were expected to be conservative and avoid casualties. As a consequence, RVNAF commanders did not push far beyond their landing zones.

A march by a foot soldier (we do that) to the objective town of Tchepone in Laos, which was little more than twenty miles from the South Vietnamese border, would be the best approach, but instead many of the RVNAF forces were moved into Laos by truck and U.S. helicopters. More were extracted by helicopter at the end of the operation. Terrain favored the NVA: It was mountainous and there were few locations suitable for helicopter landings. The NVA staked out these potential landing zones and waited with troops, tanks and anti-air for helicopters trying to make their approach. In South Vietnam, U.S. Army engineers had repaired Highway 9 to the Laos border. Inside Laos it was a mess that stopped traffic when these soldiers should have been on foot. To make matters worse, Tchepone was at the precise point where the NVA could easily reinforce. Its strategic location made it possible for NVA forces to be moved from the north or from their forces in the south.

Kissinger provided, perhaps, the best assessment of the plan: "It soon became apparent that the plans on which we had been so eloquently and frequently briefed reflected staff exercises, not military reality."[43] He went on to assess the planning:

As for the American side, General Abrams was one of the ablest soldiers, greatest patriots, and finest human beings it has been my privilege to meet. But he was being given tasks beyond human capability and perhaps endurance. By 1971, our command in Saigon had concentrated for nearly two years on preventing disaster while redeploying forces. Indeed, in its role as redeployment headquarters, it was being asked to reduce its forces by 60,000 even while the Laos operation was going on. It simply could not adjust to performing both of its missions: withdrawal and offensive operations. It remained silent while the Vietnamese headquarters for the battle remained in a comfortable permanent base over fifty miles from Tchepone. It did not set up a special command structure for what was described to Washington as a "decisive" operation. It assumed that Vietnamese air controllers could replace American ones; too late we found out that many of the Vietnamese air controllers spoke no English. The untested Vietnamese divisions were thus deprived of much of the air support on which the original plan had counted to control the battle. The Laos operation had to compete for resources with all the other requirements for Indochina, including redeployment.[44]

The Kissinger assessment appears in line with others except for his comment about air controllers: The United States provided the air controllers needed to provide the support.

Execution

The Time Line[45]

Nixon go-ahead—3 February

Reoccupy Khe Sanh and clear Route 9 to the border

D day: enter Laos—8 February

Thieu halts the advance—12 February

First NVA counterattack—18 February

JCS briefing of Kissinger—23 February

Laird press conference—24 February

The destruction of FSB 31—25 February

The "taking" of Tchepone—9 March

Withdrawal—started 9 March

Nixon press conference: "Tonight I can report that Vietnamization has succeeded"[46]—7 April

Anti-Vietnam rally in Washington: 200,000 calling for the end of the war—24 April[47]

No U.S. forces were allowed to cross the border, but U.S. helicopters could provide lift and air support, as well as U.S. Air Force and Navy air. A sign at the border in red and white said: "Warning—No U.S. Personnel Beyond this point."[48] The first casualties were an RVNAF unit on 6 February that U.S. air support mistook for the NVA. Six were killed in this friendly fire incident.[49]

More problems: Two helicopters carrying correspondents and the RVNAF I Corps G-3 and G-4 were shot down with all hands killed. The bodies were not recovered. It was thought that the RVNAF onboard carried operational maps and codes that would be of great value to the NVA.

On the first day, 8 February 1971, as the RVNAF armored columns prepared to enter Laos airlift was meeting unexpected resistance. "We are fighting a conventional war out there,"[50] said a U.S. helicopter pilot who came under heavy anti-aircraft fire. The NVA had carefully planned their air defenses, which consisted of various flak guns, surface-to-air missiles (probably the Soviet-made Strela) and the deadly 12.7mm machine guns. Some of the guns were radar controlled. They were set up with interlocking fire so that if a helicopter received fire and turned to avoid it, another anti-aircraft gun would engage. From the NVA point of view it was a "turkey shoot."

This was a new phase of the war. Rather than fade away, the NVA would stand and fight as they did at Dien Bien Phu. Author David Fulghum summarized:

> The success of Lam Son 719 depended on many factors—coordination of ground troops, the tenacity of the North Vietnamese, the boldness and efficiency of the plan itself. But at the tactical level the operation was going to succeed or fail in large part because of the leadership of the officers and the skill of the RVNAF soldiers.
>
> The troops entering Laos remarked on the lush greenery of the jungle, so different from the ravaged Khe Sanh plateau where chemical defoliants and countless tons of bombs had denuded the red earth. When a convoy of armored vehicles halted, however, the soldiers noted that: no single bird chirped [a bad sign]. Perhaps the preparatory artillery strikes had chased away the birds, some suggested. There was virtually no resistance as the troops advanced, and that very absence of opposition was worrisome, A correspondent riding in the armored column reasoned the NVA patrols must surely be following and watching. But "with Cobra gunships firing rockets all around us," he wrote, "we advanced the next day 25 klicks into Laos [they did not get that far as seen in the following accounts]. There was no return fire and I felt it was an NVA tactic to draw us in deeper."[51]

This might well be an ambush on a grand scale not seen before and exceeding the Vietminh annihilation of the French Mobile Group 100 in the French war.[52] The only difference would be that the United States would provide an enormous amount of air support. B-52 bombing raids could disintegrate huge portions of landscape, including NVA troops.[53] Director of the Joint Staff Lieutenant General Vogt reminded the JCS Chairman, Admiral Moorer, that "General Abrams had said that he would welcome North Vietnamese reinforcements, because he would then be able to strike at them."[54] This may have been the key to any success of

Lam Son 719. While the RVNAF fled, U.S. air inflicted an enormous number of casualties on the NVA.

Inside Laos, progress slowed. On the first day in Laos, only nine kilometers were made by the RVNAF troops. This was caused by bad roads and slowdown due to fear of ambush: nine kilometers, only thirty-three to go to get to Tchepone. On the second day, things got worse. The rains came and everything bogged down. Route 9 turned into a quagmire.[55] On the third day, the RVNAF had reached the halfway point to Tchepone. At this point, time was no longer a factor. As the campaign progressed, the NVA increased efforts to ambush convoys and attack rear bases.

It was time for the NVA to move in and annihilate the RVNAF. This was not an easy task due to U.S. airpower, but the tactic was to move in close to the RVNAF unit; "grab him by the belt buckle" was the NVA expression. In that way, U.S. aircraft could not bomb for fear of hitting friendly troops.

There were monumental screwups by all sides. When a U.S. Forward Air Controller (FAC) over the RVNAF Fire Support Base (FSB) 31 in Laos saw a U.S. fighter hit and going down with the crew ejecting, he left his

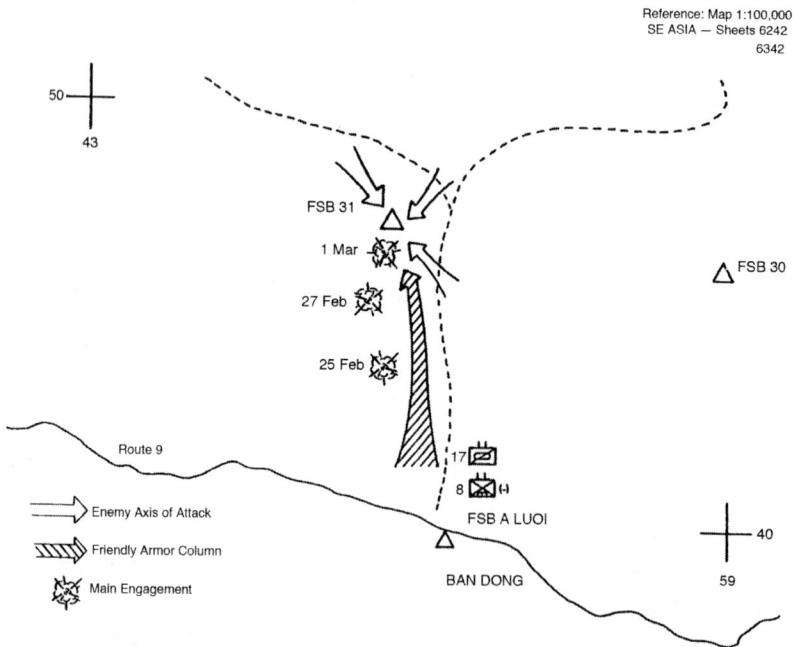

Reference: Map 1:100,000
SE ASIA — Sheets 6242
6342

Fire Support Base 31 (courtesy of Nguyen Duy Hinh).

post to follow them down in order to direct U.S. air rescue.[56] That meant that air support lacked direction for the crucial fight at FSB 31. The only defense at FSB 31 other than defensive bunkers was barbed wire. The NVA easily overran FSB 31 with heavy Soviet T34 tanks. The tanks rotated on the bunkers, grinding them into the mud. Nearly all ARVN at FSB 31 were killed, wounded or captured. Only a few escaped.[57] The concept of fixed FSBs in Laos did not work, as it had to some degree in South Vietnam.[58] What was needed was fast-moving fire support that could quickly set up, fire and move. The fixed FSBs in Laos allowed the NVA to surround and destroy them, as seen at FSB 31. First, the FSBs were isolated from helicopter support with NVA anti-air, next, superior heavier NVA guns pounded the FSB, and finally, an assault by heavy tanks would overrun the defenses, as seen at FSB 31.[59]

For some reason not explained, Thieu visited Lam on 12 February and ordered the RVNAF to hold at present positions. The hold was to last three to five days.[60] This does not appear to have been a good decision. The weather was getting worse and had already limited close air support on several days. Halting also meant that the NVA could concentrate more of their forces and in many cases destroy more RVNAF units. Thieu's halt in the operation may have been due to his edict that when casualties reached 3,000 the operation should stop.[61] Hanoi knew this and intended to maximize RVNAF casualties as early as possible so that Thieu would stop the advance. This would allow the NVA to concentrate their forces and destroy the RVNAF.[62] Some suggest that at this point Thieu had lost his nerve or that he wanted time to assess the situation before continuing to Tchepone.[63]

Nixon had a slightly different opinion from those on the ground. His thought was that the RVNAF stopped at Tchepone and withdrew because they had reached the 3,000 casualty limit imposed by Thieu, but other sources indicate the halt due to 3,000 casualties occurred much earlier. Nixon's view is provided here:

On February 8, the operation began. South Vietnamese troops fought
bravely and effectively, but some problems soon developed. Communist forces
put up stronger resistance than we had anticipated, and American military
commanders in Saigon failed to respond with a corresponding increase in air
cover. When South Vietnamese forces sustained large casualties about ten miles
into Laos, they made the mistake of temporarily digging in, which gave the
North Vietnamese a sitting target to hit. Thieu became overly cautious and
ordered his commanders to stop their offensive as soon as casualties reached
3,000. By the middle of March, soon after the South Vietnamese reached
Tchepone, their casualties hit Thieu's arbitrary ceiling, and they began to retreat

to the southeast along Route 914. American news-media reports presented a distorted picture of the operation by focusing almost exclusively on the failings of the South Vietnamese troops. Because of inadequate air support during the withdrawal, a few units took such a severe pounding from enemy artillery that they panicked. It took only a few televised films of soldiers clinging to the skids of our evacuation helicopters to reinforce the widespread misconception that South Vietnam's armed forces were incompetent and cowardly.[64]

Kissinger was not happy with the delay and asked for a briefing by the JCS. Since the Chairman, Admiral Moorer, was out of town, General Westmoreland, the Army Chief of Staff, was acting chairman. Kissinger wanted Westmoreland's assessment, but Kissinger's understanding of what was going on indicated that he had a better grip than the military on the situation:

On February 23, Moorer was absent from Washington, which made General Westmoreland Acting Chairman of the JCS on the basis of seniority. I used the occasion to ask for a briefing; in reality, I wanted Westmoreland's assessment. According to the protocol of the Joint Chiefs, the White House was supposed to deal with the Chairman, not individual chiefs. Westmoreland looked like the beau ideal of an American officer: straight as an arrow, handsome, serious. Like so many of his colleagues, he had launched himself into Vietnam with self-confident optimism only to withdraw in bewilderment and frustration. Saddled with restrictions for which there was no precedent in manuals, confronted with an enemy following a strategy not taught in command colleges, he soon fell into a trap that has been characteristic of American commanders since the Civil War: substitution of logistics for strategy. With rare and conspicuous exceptions like Douglas MacArthur or George Patton, America's modern generals have preferred to wear down the enemy through the weight of materiel rather than the bold stroke, through superior resources rather than superior maneuvers. In this, they reflected the biases of a nonmilitary, technologically oriented society. But wars of attrition cannot be won against an enemy who refuses to fight except on his own terms. The Vietnam terrain, the nature of guerrilla warfare, the existence of sanctuaries—all combined to make it impossible for Westmoreland to wear down his adversary as he sought. Instead, the North Vietnamese hiding in the population and able to choose their moment for attack wore *us* down. And then the 1968 Tet offensive, though a massive North Vietnamese military defeat, turned into a psychological triumph by starting America on the road to withdrawal. (In fairness, it must be stressed that Westmoreland labored under political restrictions that barred any of the major maneuvers that might have proved decisive—sealing off the Ho Chi Minh Trail in 1968, for example.) Whatever the reason for the failure, Westmoreland lived through the neglect suffered by those who have teetered on the edge of popular acclaim and whom the public then punishes for not living up to their assigned roles. Whoever is at fault, they are consigned to an oblivion all the more bitter for having been just one step away from being cast as hero.

Westmoreland sat in the sumptuous office of the Army Chief of Staff, deliberating over weapons procurement, enjoying the deference of the uniformed service due to his position, but ignored by the policymakers. He was almost never consulted about the war he had conducted with gallantry, if not always ultimate success. His advice had not been sought individually about the proposed assault on Tchepone, though we were told that he had endorsed it together with the other Joint Chiefs of Staff. When I saw Westmoreland on February 23, his assessment was bleak. He did not think that the forces assigned to the Laos operation were adequate; he himself had considered that four American divisions would be needed to seize and hold Tchepone; the South Vietnamese had allotted less than two to the operation. Nor did he think a frontal assault the best way to interrupt the trail system. He recommended hit-and-run raids by air-mobile units out of Khe Sanh to cut the trails at various points. This would throw the Communist supply system into a maximum of turmoil and achieve our objectives at much less risk. Even allowing for a natural bias against his successors, Westmoreland's comments made a great deal of sense.[65]

By this time the press smelled a disaster, and Laird held a news conference on 24 February. Lieutenant General Vogt, the Director of the Joint Staff, explained the objectives of Lam Son 719 and showed a piece of pipe, explaining that this was a part of the pipeline that carried fuel south to NVA forces. Vogt left the impression that this piece of pipe was fresh from the battlefield, which it was not. It had been collected months earlier during a Special Forces raid. Abrams called Laird, reminding him that bad information had been given to the press, and Laird held another press conference to correct the record. The press had a field day. Humorist Art Buchwald wrote an imaginative story that had Laird showing rifles from Custer's Last Stand, chickens from World War I, sandbags from Iwo Jima, etc.[66] The point of all of this was that the credibility of the U.S. government was never high and continued to decline. Laird was concerned that the press would turn a military victory into a defeat as had been done after Tet in 1968, but at this point no one knew the outcome of Lam Son 719 and Laird could not know that it would be a disastrous defeat.

Abrams was frustrated by the delays. He blamed it on RVNAF lack of aggressiveness and leadership. To a friend he said, "I think tomorrow I'm going to go up there, just me and a radio operator, and I don't give a damn if the bastards kill me. Those soldiers [RVNAF] deserve better leadership than what they are getting."[67] This was a curious statement given the fact that Abrams had developed the bad plan that could not be washed away by claims of bad RVNAF leadership. During the battle, finger-pointing like that of Abrams had already started. The RVNAF blamed lack of U.S. air support for their failure, which seems unproven given U.S. air losses during the fight and the fact that there were limited forces available due to the drawdown.

By late March, panic had set in among the RVNAF in Laos. While there were accounts of RVNAF bravery, (perhaps exaggerated for political reasons in the Saigon regime and the United States), the RVNAF fled in panic. Images of healthy RVNAF soldiers pushing their way through waiting wounded to invade waiting helicopters were the order of the day, as well as dozens of panicked RVNAFs hanging on to the helicopter skids in order to escape with their lives.

The whole debacle proved beyond any doubt that the RVNAF command structure was flawed and could not fight. RVNAF leadership was, at best, poor. This lesson was learned by Hanoi, and it was clear to Giap that the RVNAF could be easily defeated once the United States departed. For Hanoi, it became a waiting game for the United States to depart and then they would invade South Vietnam, which is exactly what happened in 1972 and later in 1975. President Thieu realized the incompetence of his commander in the North, General Lam, and ordered that he be replaced. Unfortunately, his replacement, one of RVNAF's best generals, Do Cao Tri, was killed in a helicopter crash (apparently caused by bad RVNAF maintenance: another example of the failure of Vietnamization), so Lam continued in charge of the debacle.

The battle of Lam Son 719 was a disaster. While Thieu, Abrams and Nixon were publically proclaiming that it was an RVNAF victory and a proof that Vietnamization was working, a monumental lie, the battle, which was supposed to set back the Hanoi plan to invade South Vietnam in 1972, did not do that. Kissinger stated that it was hoped that the operation would delay the NVA invasion of 1972,[68] but the NVA moved forward into Vietnam on 30 March 1972. Author David Fulghum described the "taking" of Tchepone:

> On March 6 an armada of 120 Huey helicopters, protected on all sides by Cobra gunships and fighter planes, lifted the 2d and 3d Battalions of the 2d Regiment from Khe Sanh to Tchepone—the largest, longest helicopter assault of the war. Losing only 1 helicopter to antiaircraft fire enroute, the fleet set down the troops amid sporadic gunfire at LZ Hope, four kilometers northeast of Tchepone. Thanks to intensive B-52 and tactical air strikes, little resistance came on the ground. For two days the two battalions prowled the deserted Tchepone region, including the shambles of the town itself, finding little but bodies of enemy soldiers killed in air strikes. The NVA response to the assault on Tchepone was to increase fire against RVNAF firebases, notably Lolo and A Luoi. On March 9

the battalions and the 2d Regiment command post set out on foot to climb the ridge to Firebase Sophia. Cautious about ambushes, the troops maintained radio silence so as not to disclose their location and moved their positions every two hours during the night. They arrived safely at the firebase the following day, and the RVNAF "occupation" of Tchepone, a principal terrain objective of Operation Lam Son 719, was complete.[69]

ARVN general Hinh summarized best: "By this time, Tchepone was a worthless objective. It was a ruined town and [NVA] caches were stored[70] in the forests and mountain tops." On 9 March, Thieu ordered the RVNAF out of Laos. Incredibly, with all of his intelligence assists, General Abrams urged that Thieu reinforce the RVNAF in Laos with one division.[71] This is difficult to understand. By this time, the RVNAF were outnumbered by perhaps as much as ten to one and Giap was pouring in more troops to annihilate the RVNAF in Laos. Thieu had halted the RVNAF advance and Giap had a great deal of time to reinforce. Why would Abrams want to send more troops into this meat grinder? Thieu of course refused to send more people into Laos. Nixon was not impressed and wanted to fire Abrams because of his incompetence. Nixon later reversed course based upon objections by Laid and others. Whatever one thinks of Nixon, he was a pragmatist. Abrams died before he could publish memoirs. Had he done so, it is unlikely that he would have revealed anything beyond what historians have already written. Abrams took his secrets to the grave. He was the only U.S. Army chief of staff to die in office.

On 9 March 1971, the RVNAF withdrawal from Laos started while the NVA intensified their buildup. The NVA ability to reinforce their use of tanks and anti-air to destroy RVNAF troops and support led to a rout. The NVA had every advantage: leadership, troop morale, firepower, terrain, weather and numbers. It was a slaughter of the RVNAF, which would be seen again in the fall of Vietnam in 1975. Some RVNAF units were simply surrounded and annihilated, like Custer at his last stand. While U.S. helicopters tried to evacuate the RVNAF from Laos, there were not enough due to many helicopter losses earlier in the campaign. As the NVA overran RVNAF bases in Laos, there were many accounts of RVNAF valor. One RVNAF survivor recalled what happened as ammunition ran out:

> Ammunition began to run out, however, and the next day the NVA overran the base. They launched the assault from positions inside the marine perimeter, supported by ten flame throwing tanks. NVA infantrymen rushed over the bodies of their slain comrades to charge into the base. The marines knocked out four tanks, then fell back. Trying to break out, the three battalions ran into NVA ambushes. The troops scattered. One survivor recounted: The last attack came at about 8:00 p.m. They shelled us first and then came the tanks moving up into

our positions. The whole brigade ran down the hill like ants. We jumped on each other to get out of that place. No man had time to look for his commanding officer. It was quick, quick, quick or we would die.... When I was far from the hill, with about 20 other marines, there was a first lieutenant with us. We moved like ghosts, terrified of being ambushed by the North Vietnamese. We stopped moving many times when there was firing—not daring to breathe.... Our group bumped into a North Vietnamese unit, and we ran again. like ants. And the lieutenant, he whispered to us, "Disperse, disperse, don't stick together or we will all be killed." After each firing, there were fewer and fewer of us. A marine who escaped Delta described the agony of the Vietnamese leaving their wounded comrades. They lay there crying, knowing the B-52 bombs would fall on them. They asked buddies to shoot them, but none of us could bring himself to do that. So the wounded cried out for grenades, first one man, then another, then more. I could not bear it. We ran out at 8:00 p.m. and about midnight we heard the bombs explode behind us. No more bodies! They all became dust.[72]

U.S. helicopters suffered heavy losses getting the RVNAF in, and after the failure of the RVNAF more helicopters were lost removing the South Vietnamese from Laos. In a pattern seen before and after, the RVNAF panicked during the withdrawal. One pilot reported that it was so bad that the U.S. crews had to grease the skids of the helicopters to prevent RVNAF soldiers from hanging on to the skids during takeoff and thus overloading the aircraft. South Vietnam announced 7,683 RVNAF casualties (slightly less than half of their force engaged). U.S. losses were 215 killed and 1,187 wounded.

It was very similar to the Ap Bac battle eight years earlier: The RVNAF were slow, ran in panic when under fire and left their wounded behind. Lam Son 719 demonstrated that the Saigon regime had learned nothing in the eight years after Ap Bac.

Tom Marshall, who was a helicopter pilot in 1971 moving RVNAF out of Laos during Lam Son 719, summarized:

Yesterday on Firebase 31, we hauled off enough damn dead people. They had 'em lined up out there like at a zoo. I've never seen anything like it. The RVNAFs don't even know what they're doing. You CA [Combat Assault] 'em out into an area, and they're so damn scared, they won't even move. That's the reason they're all getting killed. They won't even move. And when we come to pick up, they hang on the damn skids to try to get out of there. They're like a human wave attack on your damn helicopter. You've got to kick 'em in the mouth, kick 'em in the head, kick 'em everywhere, to keep 'em off. A Huey slick won't carry but about nine RVNAFs, and, hell, we have carried as many as twenty out, hanging on the slicks, grabbing, 'em by the head and pulling them in to try to keep 'em from getting killed. But I still can't help but feel sorry for those people 'cause they really didn't want this thing to happen. Just minding their own business. In fact, the people we CAd in Laos didn't even know they were going there until we put 'em down on the damn ground. That's pretty bad in my book. If you go into Laos, you have to do more than they're doing. I'm not saying it's the RVNAFs' fault as much as it is the command's [MACV's] fault. The command doesn't even know what the hell it's doing. I mean, it throws them out there on the damn mountaintop and expects them to do damn wonders. It's just like throwing a bunch of dinks—eight hundred dinks—can you imagine, eight hundred RVNAFs being attacked by six thousand NVA. I mean, you can see why they're getting their asses kicked. It's just that plain and simple. It's the United States' advisers and the Vietnamese higher-ups who don't know what in the hell they're doing. They're just dicking around with people's lives.[73]

At the conclusion of Lam Son 719, Highway 9 inside Laos had been turned into a junkyard of damaged or abandoned RVNAF vehicles and not a few corpses.[74] Many RVNAF dead and wounded were abandoned in Laos and the bodies of some U.S. flight crews were never recovered. The fate of Khe Sanh was now in question. It came under heavy fire and there were concerns that the NVA would follow the RVNAF out of Laos and attack Khe Sanh, but there was no attack. Hanoi was delighted with the results of the operation, and an attack on Khe Sanh was not necessary and dangerous given the threat of U.S. air superiority.

The blame game had started in a major way. Many were critical of RVNAF Lieutenant General Lam, who commanded the operation. JCS chairman Moorer made the following note for his diary after the operation:

After talking with Lieutenant General Davison [IIFFV commander] and recollecting my meeting with Davison, Abrams, Bunker [ambassador] and Sutherland in anticipation of LAM SON 719, I am appalled that: they did not take into consideration at that time General Lam's competence. As a matter of fact, none of my Army advisers (which included two full generals and four Lieutenant Generals) gave me any reason to believe that Lam could not hack it…. They failed to appreciate that the President had so much riding on this golden and last opportunity to punish the enemy. Davison criticized General Khang for going to Saigon frequently during the course of LAM SON 719, yet General Weyand took 10 days leave at Pearl Harbor and General Abrams simultaneously spent the weekend in Bangkok during the height of the action…. If the Army advisers knew so much about Lam's competence and the limited competence of the RVNAF in Military Region I to conduct this operation, they should never have let this operation be approved, or they should have moved a leader like General Tri with military experience in multi-division cross-border operations up to Military Region 1 to conduct it [it is surprising that the Chairman of the JCS did not know that Tri was dead].[75]

I call this the "Tennis Court Mentality" of the 1950s that was transferred to the war in Vietnam and was mimicked by the RVNAF. This meant that career officers could put away their sharpened pencils early each day so that they could go to play tennis or work out in the gym. Physical fitness in the army has always been a priority, as has been taking advantage of benefits like leave and other things. Most of us in the field stayed fit by humping heavy packs in the jungle. The point is that when you are at war some things need to be set aside, like a ten-day leave in Hawaii by Fred Weyand, Abram's deputy during Lam Son 719.

There is something terribly wrong here. I know that I never had leave during my first tour in Vietnam, nor did my fellow advisors. Too many things were going on. During my second tour, I planned a three day R & R to Bangkok, but many things were going bad and I kept delaying my R & R because of ongoing operations. I did get to Bangkok and got my three-day R & R and fretted about what was going on back at Pleiku while Weyand and Abrams were enjoying their vacations during Lam Son 719. My conclusion would be that ethics among the elite career officers in the U.S. Army were pathetic. The war was lost due to lack of leadership by both the U.S. and RVNAF officers. While U.S. Army generals were enjoying their "percs" good men were dying. Perhaps the Tennis Court Mentality shared by the United States and RVNAF is another reason why the war in Vietnam was lost.

Results

In many respects Lam Son 719 was a rerun of the Ap Bac disaster eight years earlier and demonstrated that the RVNAF and MACV had learned very little. The MACV disaster would not be repeated. Nixon decided that Lam Son 719 would be the last operation planned by the United States.[76]

In South Vietnam, the citizens wanted to know the truth. Thousands of RVNAF soldiers had been killed. On 1 April 1971 Thieu announced in his press conference that Lam Son 719 was still under way. This was a monumental lie matched by Nixon, who said that Lam Son 719 proved that Vietnamization was a success.

Kissinger was inclined to be lenient with the South Vietnamese for this failed operation. He blamed the lack of South Vietnamese planning and using only two divisions when four were needed: "On the whole, the South Vietnamese extracted themselves in tolerable fashion, except for unedifying and untypical television pictures of a few panicky soldiers clinging to the skids of helicopters." Nixon sent Alexander Haig on a fact-finding mission. Haig's account of Nixon's reaction to the disaster and his report are of interest.[77]

The President was in a cold rage. Without preamble he told me that he was relieving General Abrams of command in Vietnam immediately. "Go home and pack your bag," he said. "Then get on the first available plane and fly to Saigon. You are taking command."[78]

When Nixon called Laird and informed him of this, the unflappable Laid simply said, "Mr. President, that's all right, but I want you to know I'll be walking out of the front door of the Pentagon tomorrow [for the last time]."[79] Logic finally settled into the Oval Office: A brigadier general does not replace a four-star general, at least not instantly. Nixon relented. After Haig's return from Saigon he provided his conclusions to Nixon as to the causes of the disaster:

> The South Vietnamese troops, though in some cases poorly led by their higher-ranking officers, had fought bravely and performed well.... U.S. fire support and close air support had been inadequate.... This would never have been allowed to happen if American soldiers had been doing the fighting.[80]

Correspondents had a different conclusion:

> According to *Life* magazine "the NVA drove the invading forces out of Laos with their tails between their legs." *New York Times* reporter Gloria Emerson interviewed RVNAF survivors at Khe Sanh and concluded that their morale was "shattered": Through an interpreter they spoke of how the North Vietnamese outnumbered them and advanced in wave after wave, running over the bodies of comrades and never stopping.... It was a test, and now most South Vietnamese forces admit frankly that their forces failed.... What has dramatically demoralized many of the South Vietnamese troops is the large number of their own wounded who were left behind, begging for their friends to shoot them or to leave hand grenades so they could commit suicide before the North Vietnamese or the B-52s killed them.... Some soldiers who had been in the drive into Cambodia said they had never dreamed that the Laos operation would not be as simple. Since there was no significant fighting in Cambodia, these South Vietnamese felt that the enemy was no longer a threat. They learned differently in Laos and they will not soon forget it. In American helicopters they came out of Laos this week without their combat packs, their rations or their steel helmets—and sometimes without their weapons. Nothing mattered, they said, except getting out.[81]

It is not clear who Haig talked to during his trip to South Vietnam, but his conclusions are at odds with the facts. The RVNAF fled Laos in panic, leaving their dead and wounded behind as well as an enormous amount of equipment, including dozens of tanks and all of their engineering equipment. The NVA would use some of this equipment a year later during their invasion of South Vietnam. The air support during Lam Son 719 had a devastating effect on the NVA, who sustained as many as

20,000 casualties, mostly from B-52 bombing.[82] Their equipment losses were greater than the RVNAF's as a result of U.S. air support. Haig would later claim that "Lam Son destroyed the cream of the South Vietnam army and was far more serious and detrimental than was believed at the time. Our handling of that was very bad." He blamed "bureaucratic mischief in the Pentagon."[83]

As seen earlier, Lam Son 719 had the positive effect of causing the NVA to concentrate their forces, presenting lucrative targets for B-52 bombing raids. This leads to the question: Was this operation designed to do just that and everything else was secondary? If so, it was an unstated objective. The resulting NVA casualties, by some estimates as much as approximately half of the NVA force engaged, did nothing to delay Hanoi's planned 1972 NVA invasion of South Vietnam. Kissinger confirmed that the purpose of Lam Son was to delay the 1972 invasion of South Vietnam, but the invasion went forward as planned. In fact, Lam Son 719 strengthened the resolve of North Vietnam to invade the South when Giap observed the poor fighting ability of RVNAF and their vulnerability to tanks, anti-air, and heavy artillery. Kissinger would later blame Abrams for misleading him about the plan when Abrams obtained Kissinger's support. Abrams was dead by then and was not available to answer Kissinger's charge.[84] Historian Lewis Sorley, who transcribed tapes made by Abrams during this period, found that Abrams viewed the operation as a success: "I'm beginning to have a conviction about Lam Son 719 that it was really a death blow."[85] The question remains: Whose death blow? Military analyst General Phillip B. Davidson summarized:

> On 7 April, shortly after RVNAF's forced withdrawal from Laos, President Nixon, in a television broadcast to the nation, proclaimed, "Tonight I can report that Vietnamization has succeeded"—an Orwellian untruth of boggling proportions. Lam Son 719 had demonstrated exactly the opposite, that Vietnamization had not succeeded.[86]

Author Jeffrey Kimball wrote:

> Military analysts such as General Phillip Davidson, in his post war history of the war, not only agreed there were deficiencies but also viewed them as incurable. RVNAF military leadership was politicized; Thieu was wanting in judgment and nerve; several commanders were inept [such as Lam], many officers, without American advisory support, lacked the professional skills necessary to coordinate ground, tank, artillery, and air operations; RVNAF lacked offensive initiative and mobile fighting capability; and, like the Americans, the South Vietnamese relied too much on maneuver by helicopter when walking would have been swifter. American blunders—hasty planning, poor judgment,

inadequate coordination with the RVNAF, and inter-service rivalry—had compounded the RVNAF shortcomings.[87]

It was also evident that the performance of the United States from the White House down to and including MACV was abysmal. One of the goals of Lam Son 719 was to train and provide the South Vietnamese operational experience.[88] If Lam Son 719 was designed to train the RVNAF, it was training them what not to do.[89]

Press reporting of the disaster caused a national outrage:

In March 1971, a poll reported that public confidence in Nixon had dropped to 50 percent, the lowest rating since he had entered office. Support for his conduct of the war slid to 34 percent, another survey stated that 51 percent of Americans were persuaded that the conflict was "morally wrong."[90]

Street protests resumed, followed by a 200,000-strong march on Washington.[91] Laird agreed to deliver a speech at the University of Wisconsin, which was clearly one of the most unfriendly environments and a hotbed of student unrest. Laird canceled at the last minute and sent General "Chappie" James to give the address. James received a rather violent welcome, as would be expected at the University of Wisconsin during that period. Laird's biographer Dale Van Atta tells the story:

General "Chappie" James went in his [Laird's] place and received an antiwar reprimand from the chancellor and thirty-name petition protesting the war from the students serving the luncheon. Out in the cold were about two thousand antiwar protesters led by Rennie Davis, who had been convicted in the "Chicago Seven" trial of crossing state lines to incite a riot at the 1968 Democratic National Convention. He shouted to the demonstrators in Wisconsin, "If the government doesn't stop the war, we are going to stop the government." And he chided Laird for not showing up: "Laird is not all fool. If he would have come here today, we would have really kicked some ass!" On February 10, several hundred students at the University of Illinois in Champaign burned Laird in effigy.[92]

Bui Diem, South Vietnam's ambassador in Washington at this time, reported to Thieu:

The view is of thousands of students carrying the VC flag in the streets of Washington, and of ten thousand troops. All these images coalesce on the TV screen every night. These things undoubtedly provoke reflections from the American people who ask the question, more than ever—when will the war end? These reflections will perhaps push the ordinary man into a situation where he thinks it is better to give up than continue. And this situation is like a mirror staring back at Richard Nixon when he looks at the future of the war.... In the meantime, the antiwar elements have tried their best to put forward the idea that it is past time to think about such things as a schedule for withdrawing troops. Now it is simply—when will this war be ended? That is to say, the attitude is—we don't care about the consequences.[93]

While some suggested that the violent anti-war reaction to Lam Son 719 was less than the Cambodian incursion the year before,[94] both were disasters. The result of Lam Son 719 was further reduction in public support for the war.

From the standpoint of the RVNAF, any improvement in morale and fighting spirit over the past year was destroyed by Lam Son 719 when the public and all of the troops heard the result of the operation and the RVNAF rout and saw photos of panicked RVNAF soldiers hanging from helicopter skids. Combat losses to the allies were significant and difficult to replace given the drawdown schedule that had been established and would not be changed. Much was made by the U.S. government about losses to the NVA and disruption of the Ho Chi Minh Trail. Damage to the Ho Chi Minh Trail was quickly repaired. Human losses were never a concern for Hanoi. More troops would be immediately trained and sent south. The U.S. government stressed that Vietnamization was working, but it was not. The greatest argument used to prove the success of Lam Son 719 was that it had delayed the NVA invasion of South. Did it? There are two monsoons in Vietnam, and the one of concern in the North goes from in this case May (after Lam Son 719) through September 1971, with heavy rainfall into January 1972. Hanoi would not want to invade during the monsoon or bad weather since tanks and many other vehicles would bog down in bad weather, but as always, the infantry marches on. It is not clear that the results of Lam Son 719 had any effect. The politbureau in Hanoi debated the scale and timing of the invasion of South Vietnam. Hanoi did not expect to overrun South Vietnam but wanted to damage it so that later invasions (1975) after the United States left could destroy the South Vietnam regime. Finally, Hanoi decided to invade South Vietnam and the so-called Easter offensive was launched on 30 March 1972 in good weather. The invasion failed due to U.S. air support and U.S. weapons (for example, the anti-tank TOW).

There were some extravagant claims made about the adverse impact of Lam Son 719 on the NVA. These were made by French sources that most consider unreliable and subsequent events, such as the Easter Invasion less than a year later, would prove wrong:

> Subsequently a surprising source, the French military mission in Hanoi, concluded that "Lam Son 719 had a devastating effect upon the morale of the NVA and of the civilian population of North Vietnam." According to the French

analysis, said MACV J-2, "the destruction of nearly two North Vietnamese divisions, and increased defections during the same period, caused the morale of all but the NVA officer corps to disintegrate."[95]

Deputy Commander General Fred Weyand added to Lam Son 719 by saying, "I don't see how we can say anything other than that that operation was worth it. I think it's going to prove that it was terribly decisive."[96] The question was decisive for who? Subsequent events would show that it was a decisive victory for the NVA.

Lam Son 719 had the positive effect of causing the NVA to concentrate their forces and present lucrative targets for B-52 bombing raids. The NVA invasion in 1972 went forward as planned, since disruption on the Ho Chi Minh Trail was easily repaired within a week after the departure of the RVNAF. Another theory for the Laos incursion was that the MACV was using this operation as a training vehicle for the RVNAF general staff at a cost of thousands of RVNAF lives. It appears that all of those involved from the White House to MACV ducked responsibility for inventing the Laos invasion except Abrams. He died three years after departing South Vietnam, before he had a chance to write his memoirs that would no doubt have included the usual denials used when a bad plan goes predictably wrong. There is also significant evidence that Abrams invented the concept. At a meeting with Haig in 1970, Abrams suggested an invasion of Laos to cut the Ho Chi Minh Trail and thus delay the NVA invasion of South Vietnam.

When dealing with Lam Son 19, author A. J. Langguth points out that this was an incredible defeat of biblical proportions for the South Vietnamese, yet the deceit by the U.S. government and the South Vietnamese persisted. In Washington, Lam Son 719 was the sort of an orphaned defeat Jack Kennedy once described. U.S. ambassador to South Vietnam Bunker blamed the press for not conveying the RVNAF's great military performance.[97] In fact, Lam Son 719 proved that Vietnamization was a failure (and a fig leaf designed to justify our withdrawal from Vietnam) and the South Vietnamese and United States had learned nothing since Ap Bac.

The results of Lam Son 719 were mixed. For Hanoi it reaffirmed the opinion (perhaps shared by the world) that the South Vietnam bureaucracy was not capable of fighting a war without massive U.S. support. The RVNAF soldiers were brave and fighting well, but their leadership was pathetic and in many cases politicians in uniform answering to Saigon without regard to their troops. The NVA needed to restock after their massive losses during Lam Song 719 due to air strikes, but this would not take long.

For the RVNAF, any confidence in their fighting ability that had been built up over the past year was destroyed by Lam Son 719. While small units fought bravely against overwhelming odds, the senior RVNAF leadership continued to be viewed as incompetent and corrupt.

The question will always remain: How much of Lam Son 719 was Abrams's invention and how much was inflicted on him by CINCPAC and the JCS?[98] Secretary of Defense Laird said that after he received an unsatisfactory plan from the JCS he tasked Abrams to come up with a plan. If Lam Son 719 was inflicted on him the fact remains that he poorly planned and executed it.

It is evident that there was a total disconnect between Abrams and what Thieu ordered to be done. The most important of these was that Thieu directed that when the RVNAF reached Tchepone, they should withdraw as soon as possible without destroying any NVA supplies or doing anything to sever the Ho Chi Minh Trail. Abrams knew this but did nothing except push Thieu to reinforce when it was obvious to everyone that the battle was already lost. Of course Thieu refused and suggested that Abrams reinforce with U.S. troops, which everyone knew was prohibited by the Cooper-Church Amendment.[99] Nothing that Abrams did during this time period makes any sense, and at critical points during the operation both Abrams and his deputy General Weyand had left Vietnam and were on vacation.

For the United States, it became the blame game. Internally, everyone seemed to blame Abrams, as well they should, but from Nixon on down, everyone had approved the Abrams plan, which was detached from reality. There were too many correspondents in Vietnam reporting what had happened to allow Nixon, Kissinger, Haig and Abrams to cover up the truth, although they made a great effort to do that. For the U.S. government Lam Son 719 was a great victory, but the troops and the public did not care as long as we got out of Vietnam quickly.

The conclusion is that Lam Son 719 disrupted NVA operations in early 1971, but the NVA planned to invade South Vietnam in 1972, not 1971. The 1972 invasion went ahead as planned during the dry season in early 1972. Furthermore, it was a conventional attack across the DMZ and supplies followed the NVA advance as would be expected. Stockpiled supplies from the Ho Chi Minh Trail were therefore less important, but the supply losses during Lam Son 719 may have affected the invasion. The worst impact was on the RVNAF, whose morale had been building since the Cambodian incursion the previous year. The NVA sustained devastating casualties, but these troops were quickly replaced, including those pulled in from Indochina allies such as Laos. The 1972 invasion was thwarted in part by U.S. airpower. U.S. airpower would not be available as the NVA entered Thieu's palace in 1975.

What is the bottom line about Lam Son 719? While most U.S. historians consider it a failed operation, if there had been no Lam Son 719 it is possible that the NVA may well have swept through South Vietnam in 1972 rather than 1975, although this was not Hanoi's objective in 1972. Had that occurred in 1972, we would find many U.S. support troops and advisors still stuck in Vietnam while RVNAF soldiers were throwing away their uniforms and fleeing in panic as they did in 1975 ... and 1962 ... and 1971. Throughout the war we see incredible acts of bravery by small RVNAF units, but these were not enough to overcome the corruption of the Saigon regime. For Nixon, he won a landslide victory in the election of 1972 but was brought down by the Watergate scandal and resigned.

Chuck Gross, a helicopter pilot who supported Lam Son 719, observed the following a few days before the end of the operation:

> A few days before the close of Lam Son 719, I had been out flying single ship along the Laos border when we looked down and saw the ground underneath us erupting and being blown to shreds. My first thought was that we had flown right through an arc light (a B-52 drop). As we looked closer, we realized this was not an arc light but instead was an intensive NVA mortar attack. I had never seen anything close to this magnitude of a mortar attack before in my tour. The ground was billowing dust and flames. As we watched this mortar attack, I realized, right then and there, that the NVA were going to win this war. I knew that the RVNAF did not stand a chance without the help of the United States.[100]

After Lam Son 719, Laird was unhappy with an ongoing secret war in Laos, which for some reason came out of the DoD budget. He sent General John Vessey[101] to Saigon in an attempt to exert some control over operations run by the CIA and State Department:

> Laird visited Thailand in person and told Vessey to pack his bags and go to Laos. Vessey presented himself at the U.S. Embassy in Vientiane to report to Ambassador Godley. Godley's assistant, Monte Sterns, waylaid him and said, "The ambassador is pretty busy today and won't be able to see you. Why don't you get a room and look around and make contact with the other agencies?" Vessey made the rounds of the CIA and the Agency for International Development, which had a role in the war and provided cover for the CIA. In two days Vessey was back at the embassy. Sterns again came to the waiting room. "Well, the ambassador's still not ready," he said. But Vessey wasn't leaving. "I've been ordered to report to the ambassador. It seems to me I ought to see him." At that point, having overheard the conversation, Godley stormed out of his office and confronted Vessey. "I didn't ask for you and I don't want you here!" he bellowed. "Well, Mr. Ambassador, I didn't ask to come here, and I really don't

want to be here." Vessey retorted, "But I've been ordered to be here and it seems to me we ought to figure out how to make this work." Godley calmed down, but he set one ground rule: "The first thing I want to tell you is you can't send any back-channels to your military superiors!" Vessey fell back on good military order and said he couldn't cut off any means of communicating with his superiors, but he promised he would never send anything to Washington without showing it to Godley. Then he added, "Maybe we can work out the same arrangement." To his surprise, Godley agreed that the channel of communications would be open on both sides. While neither ever conceded that the other was the boss, Vessey was firmly in charge of the purse strings.[102]

Thieu managed to hold on to power until 1975, when the NVA tanks rolled into the imperial palace in Saigon. He vowed to fight to the end but ran to the airport with his gold to fly to Taiwan before the NVA overwhelmed Saigon.

In 1971 the 43rd Signal Battalion was in drawdown. We had few troops remaining in Vietnam. Since U.S. soldiers were prohibited from crossing into Laos, my battalion was in a support role and provided equipment to support the invasion. I lost two people killed in this action. At first we thought that they had been ambushed, but when we checked this out we found out that it was a traffic accident. They lost control of their vehicle. My driver and I identified the bodies of our soldiers. He looked at me and I at him and we said, "Yes, these are the soldiers identified by their dog tags." At that time and since then I thought that these good soldiers died in order to secure Nixon's reelection. Every few years I go to the Vietnam Memorial in Washington, D.C., and look up their names carved in stone. At first, our kids went with us and looked up at names of people they did not know. Now they go on their own, if they want. There was no point to Lam Son 719.

EIGHT

The Exit

Lam Son 719 was a disastrous defeat for the RVNAF and the United States. Both realized that South Vietnam was unlikely to survive long after the last U.S. combat troops were withdrawn. Many things were happening in 1972. The most significant event was the NVA invasion of South Vietnam that started in March 1972, described here. By this time the United States had withdrawn 400,000 troops and only 133,000 remained, and these would be withdrawn in six months.[1]

The Easter Invasion

Background

Nixon practiced the "Madman Theory" of foreign policy while in office. He explained it best during a discussion with his White House Chief of staff, H. R. Haldeman, quoted here:

> I call it the Madman Theory, Bob. I want the North Vietnamese to believe I've reached the point where I might do anything to stop the war. We'll just slip the word to them that "For God's sake, you know Nixon is obsessed about Communism. We can't restrain him when he's angry—and he has his hand on the nuclear button' and Ho Chi Minh himself will be in Paris in two days begging for peace."[2]

There are problems with using the madman approach to foreign policy. If you use it on a nuclear power such as the Soviet Union, they may launch a preemptive nuclear strike. During the Easter Invasion, Nixon proved that he was capable of anything. He threatened to mine Haiphong Harbor. This was risky business, since if a Soviet supply ship delivering

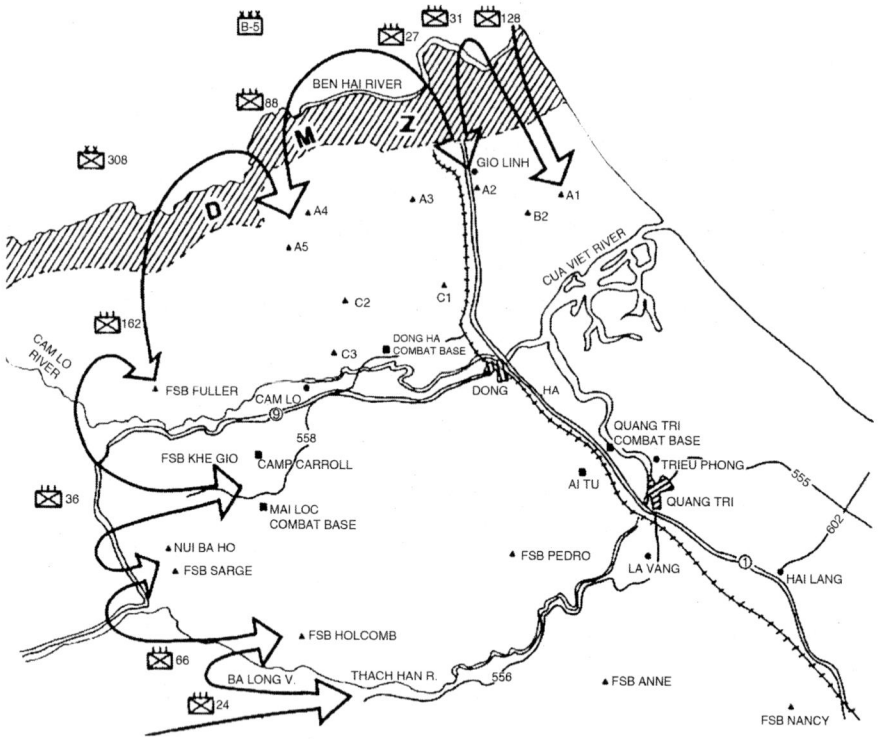

NVA Easter Invasion (courtesy of Ngo Quang Truong).

supplies to North Vietnam hit a mine and Soviet citizens were killed there could be major consequences and possibly confrontation between the United States and the Soviet Union. Nixon actually did order the mining in May 1972, but no Soviet citizens were injured. There is very little evidence that Nixon's madman approach achieved any positive result.

While Nixon was playing the madman in the Oval Office, Kissinger was negotiating with the Soviets over the Strategic Arms Limitation Treaty and also with China. Vietnam was in the background, but Kissinger tried to connect treaties with Soviet support for a Vietnam peace treaty. The problem was that the Soviets had less leverage on the North Vietnamese than the United States did on South Vietnam.[3]

At the same time, the United States was trying to negotiate a peace settlement with Hanoi with South Vietnam as a reluctant participant. These secret peace talks were going on in Paris and Kissinger, Nixon's National Security Advisor, represented the United States. At the same time, Nixon was under fire from Congress and the American people over the Vietnam War.

Since Lam Son 719 failed to delay the Hanoi invasion of South Vietnam, the NVA went forward as planned in March 1972. This invasion was called the Easter Invasion. By this time, many U.S. combat troops had been withdrawn from Vietnam and the NVA invasion would be countered by RVNAF units and U.S. air support.

The NVA had a good plan. They would strike across the DMZ in the north while other columns would attack east through the Central Highlands to the coast. In the south the attack was launched above Saigon. Giap committed 120,000 NVA troops plus thousands of VC. This was not an attempt to conquer South Vietnam but was intended to demonstrate to the United States that the RVNAF would always lose. In this way Hanoi hoped to influence the peace talks going on at that time. The attacks were launched on 30 March 1972.

The RVNAF numbers were impressive. South Vietnam had over 1 million men under arms and outnumbered the NVA by ten to one, but the RVNAF was a "straw dog." Nearly half of the force were local units tied to the ground. Thieu's maneuver battalions were spread across South Vietnam and had to counter three separate well-planned thrusts. Author Stanley Karnow summarized the situation:

> By now, only six thousand of the seventy thousand Americans remaining in Vietnam were combat troops, and their activities were restricted [stand-down]. The Saigon regime had more than a million men under arms, about half of them regulars and the rest in various local units—a force superior in firepower that outnumbered the enemy by a ratio of about five to one. Even so, Thieu's army was stretched thin, which gave the Communists the edge they hoped to exploit in the Mekong delta. For as Thieu rushed his big battalions away from the area to check the North Vietnamese offensive in other parts of the country, Vietcong guerrillas rapidly filled the vacuum left by their redeployment. Within two months, guerrillas overran or occupied more than a hundred abandoned government posts in the region, and pacification programs crumbled in several key provinces, such as Chuong Thien and Dinh Tuong. If a truce was to freeze the two sides in place pending a final political settlement, the Communists wanted to control as much of the rich and populous Mekong delta as possible. Figuring that domestic American pressures would prevent Nixon from reintroducing American forces in Vietnam, they were also out to cripple the Vietnamization effort. Pham Van Dong [Hanoi] publicly stated that it was necessary to prove the failure of Vietnamization to prove to Nixon that "he has everything to lose except the honorable exit we are determined to enable him to make." Melvin Laird, who had a vested interest in seeing Vietnamization work, acclaimed the South Vietnamese military performance as "astonishingly successful."

Nixon expressed the same optimism in public, but he was privately glum.

With the U.S. forces virtually out of action in Vietnam, America's position and prestige hinged on the Saigon regime—"the weak link in our whole chain," as he noted in his diary. "The real problem," he wrote, "is that the enemy is willing to sacrifice in order to win, while the South Vietnamese simply aren't willing to pay that much of a price in order to avoid losing."[4]

Karnow's numbers of U.S. troops remaining are a bit off (Langguth indicates 140,000 in January 1972),[5] but that is not the point. If the U.S. combat troops would not fight in this major NVA invasion, why were they not sent home in 1971? Author A. J. Langgruth provides the answer:

> As the New Year approached, Nixon considered making 1971 the last year of America's involvement in Vietnam. Just before Christmas, he had shared his thinking with Kissinger and Haldeman. In April 1971, Nixon said, he could go to South Vietnam, tour the country and reassure Thieu about the consequences of the impending final withdrawal. Then he would come home and announce that America's role in Vietnam was over. Kissinger strenuously protested Nixon's timetable. If U.S. combat troops came out by the end of 1971, he argued, the Communists could start trouble the following year. That meant the Nixon administration would pay the political price in the 1972 presidential election. Nixon should promise instead only that he would get American troops out by the end of 1972. That schedule would get him safely past his reelection. Nixon saw the wisdom in Kissinger's argument that guaranteeing his second term would require American soldiers to go on dying.
>
> All the same, Nixon wanted to make a major move in 1971, and he announced that draftees would no longer be sent to Vietnam. He also began talking about an attack into Laos. It would be like the invasion of Cambodia but done secretly this time and conducted by only RVNAF troops. As the plan developed, its code name became Lam Son 719, in honor of the village birthplace of Le Loi, a Vietnamese nationalist who had repelled Chinese invaders in 1428. Americans and RVNAF had already adopted the name once before for successful assaults on Communist bases in the A Shau Valley.[6]

The Invasion

The NVA made good progress. In the II Corps, one ARVN division fled in panic as the NVA approached Kontum, a province capital. The Montagnards who watched them flee called them "the rabbit soldiers."[7] General Nguyen Van Toan was a crony of Thieu. For years he had reaped profits from the cinnamon trade but was not an effective province commander. Thieu fired him during the Easter Invasion.[8] To the north in I Corps, Thieu replaced the incompetent Lam, who had failed during Lam Son 719, with General Ngo Quang Truong. One of two of Troung's divisions was made up of recruits and this division fled in panic at the time the NVA approached.[9] The division that fled was the 3rd ARVN Division, two regiments of which were made up of convicts, deserters and inept officers.[10]

This was déjà vu. In Ap Bac in 1962 and Tet in 1968, the world had watched the bravery of some RVNAF and the cowardice of others. It depended upon leadership. The same occurred during Lam Son 719 in 1971. The United States was not in South Vietnam to see the same performance in 1975. General Abrams was well aware of the RVNAF leadership problem and issued the following order: "Effective immediately, no Vietnamese commander will be air lifted out of a unit defensive position by U.S. fixed wing aircraft or helicopter unless such evacuation is directed personally by the RVNAF corps commander. Inform your counterpart."[11] Some examples of what occurred in the Easter Offensive of 1972 are provided here.

Cowardice and Deceit

As with most other RVNAF battles, the NVA invasion of South Vietnam in 1972 was met with bravery and competence by RVNAF soldiers and small-unit leaders, but the campaign was nearly lost by the corruption and cowardice of the RVNAF leadership. Author David Fulghum provides an example when he tells the story of Camp Carroll, an RVNAF position in I Corps that was under NVA attack:

> The sprawling firebase had endured three days of shelling, but as Easter Sunday dawned Camp Carroll, in Camper's [the U.S. senior advisor's] opinion, remained strong enough to survive at least another week. Unknown to Camper, however, Dinh, Phong, and other members of the 56th Regiment's staff had been talking to the NVA by radio, a common practice throughout the war. RVNAF troops seldom used codes or secure lines, and the NVA employed captured radios to monitor South Vietnamese conversations. Thus able to communicate, men of the two sides would frequently exchange polemics or taunting remarks. But this time, according to Col. Camper, the conversations between the 56th's staff and the NVA were anything but banter. At 2:30 p.m. on Easter Sunday, April 2, the RVNAF officers held a meeting closed to the Americans, Shortly after Dinh came to Camper at his bunker and told him that a cabal of disaffected RVNAF officers had forced him to negotiate a surrender of the camp complete with its artillery, ammunition, and American advisers. After being told by 3d Division headquarters that no reserves could be spared for Camp Carroll, Dinh said, in an interview aired on Communist radio after the fight, he believed "we would die if we remained in the base and we would also die in large numbers" if they tried to retreat. As a result, "The commanders of the various units reported to me that most of the soldiers did not want to resist the liberation forces anymore." The white flag was to go up in an hour. Col. Dinh offered to join Camper in a

suicide pact to preserve their "honor." When the American declined, Dinh suggested that they mix in with the surrendering soldiers and escape into the high grass. Camper turned down that offer too.[12]

Camper organized a U.S. airlift out. There were a few RVNAF soldiers who would refuse to surrender, and with his advisors Camper got out while the rest surrendered.

Also in I Corps, the NVA captured the province capital of Quan Tri on 1 May 1972. ARVN sergeant Nguyen Tho Hang provided his account of his effort to escape Quan Tri:

> First, we had trouble getting out of town because the streets were blocked by rubble from destroyed buildings. Then the road was crowded with so many people, civilians and soldiers, that we could only crawl along. It was like everybody in the area was on that road, and Communist shells were exploding everywhere. A shell fell about five yards in front of our jeep, damaging a tire and wounding a comrade in the leg. We abandoned the jeep and ran. The comrade couldn't run. We left him behind, and he was later killed. Soon we saw Communist tanks. I ran toward the sea, then doubled back, and finally got to a safe place. I had run all day, without stopping, and my feet were covered with blisters.[13]

Sergeant Hang's account tells us more about the RVNAF than many other accounts. First, he tells us that he ran instead of fighting. Second, he tells us that he was more concerned about his blisters than taking care of his comrade he left behind to be killed. The best that I can say is that when someone gets hit you scoop him up and get him back to your lines. There was no concept of "no one left behind" in the RVNAF.

At this point, Nixon stepped up the war and ordered bombing of targets in North Vietnam. He increased B-52 bombing of the invading NVA forces. He threatened that he would mine the North Vietnamese port Haiphong Harbor to stop the flow of supplies to Hanoi. On 8 May 1972, Nixon addressed the nation:

> After describing the North Vietnamese invasion, I outlined our three options: an immediate withdrawal, a negotiated peace, or a decisive military action to end the war. I said that I had rejected the first option because it would be immoral to abandon our South Vietnamese allies to Communist tyranny and because it would encourage aggression throughout the world. I explained that while I preferred the second option, "it takes two to negotiate" and the North Vietnamese had proven to be unwilling partners. Therefore, I said, the United States really had no choice at all: "There is only one way to stop the killing. That is to keep the weapons of war out of the hands of the international outlaws of North Vietnam." In order to leave the door open for later negotiations, I concluded with a reiteration of our basic terms for a fair peace settlement.

Antiwar critics and the news media competed with each other in denouncing our action. One senator remarked that the decision was "reckless and wrong." Another said that "the President must not have a free hand in Indochina any longer." One newspaper called the decision a "desperate gamble" and urged that Congress should cut off funds for the war to "save the President from himself and the nation from disaster." Another claimed that the President "has lost touch with the real world." One legislator topped them all when he breathlessly intoned that the President "has thrown down the gauntlet of nuclear war to a billion people in the Soviet Union and China…. Armageddon may be only hours away." There was nearly unanimous agreement that, as one network reporter put it, our action "practically kills prospects of a summit" with the Soviet leadership. Most *of* the members of Congress, my cabinet, and my staff shared the view that the summit would probably be off.[14]

The Invisible Army

While the RVNAF were fighting for their lives to survive the NVA Easter Invasion, the remaining U.S. forces numbered over 133,000. The question was what were the troops doing beyond writing letters and waiting to go home? The answer was that they were in stand-down mode, doing nothing, except for the advisors. U.S. Army forces would not be committed to counter the NVA invasion. Historian Lewis Sorley explained General Abrams's dilemma:

> Abrams noted the contribution of American support, and that it was only a contribution: "This invasion could not have been held at this point without U.S. air support; however, ten times the air power could not have done the job if the armed forces of South Vietnam had not stood and fought."
>
> And he concluded: "The South Vietnamese government, its armed forces and its people are holding together in this crisis. We can anticipate more heavy fighting and additional hardships for the people of South Vietnam in the coming weeks. The leaders of Hanoi are staking everything on military victory. The fabric of what the South Vietnamese have built here with our assistance has survived its severest test. The qualities demonstrated by the South Vietnamese people, in my judgment, assure that they will continue to hold."
>
> Because the drawdown had essentially stripped him of ground combat units, Abrams was, observed a contemporary account, "in a position almost unique in military history. Though a soldier all his life, General Abrams now finds himself fighting a war using massive American air and naval forces rather than ground-combat units."[15]

The Last Days of John Paul Vann

At the time of the Easter Invasion, John Paul Vann was the senior advisor to the RVNAF general commanding II CTZ. He had the equivalent

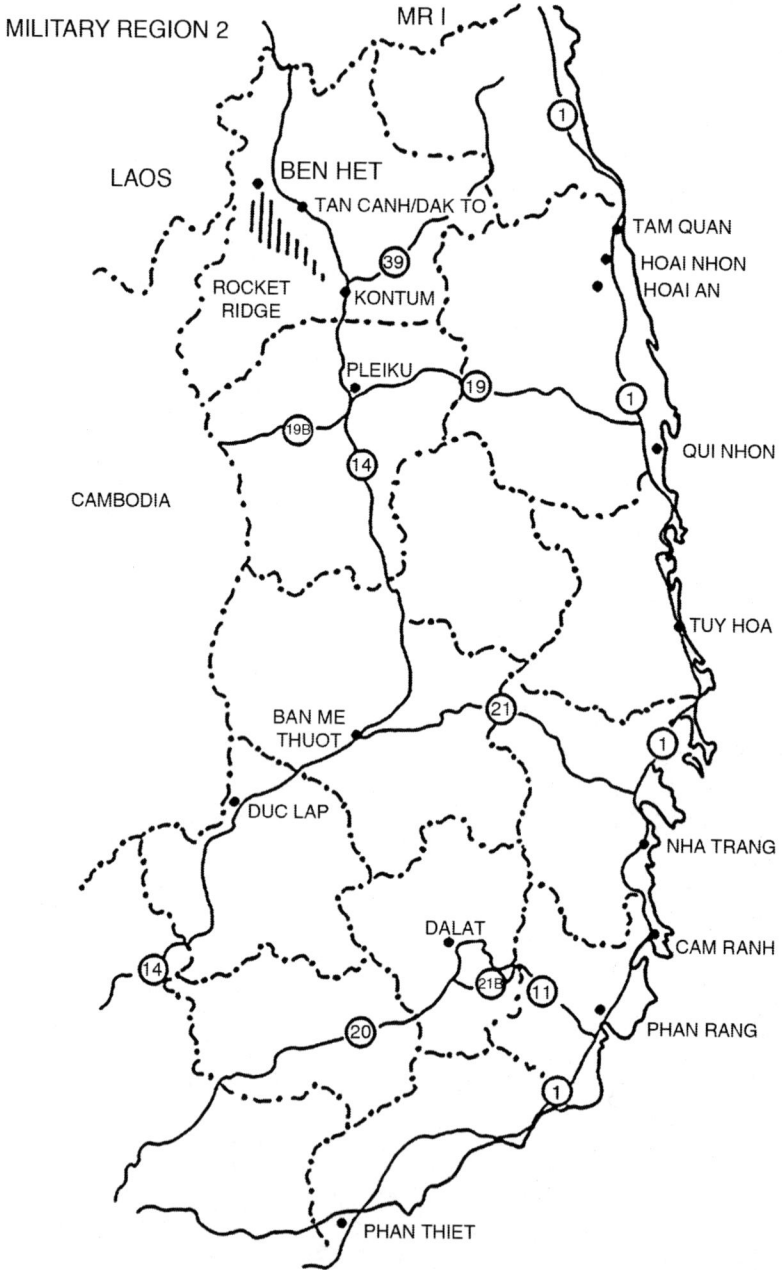

MILITARY REGION 2

MR I

LAOS

BEN HET

TAN CANH/DAK TO

ROCKET RIDGE

KONTUM

39

TAM QUAN

HOAI NHON
HOAI AN

1

PLEIKU

19

1

19B

14

QUI NHON

CAMBODIA

TUY HOA

BAN ME THUOT

21

1

DUC LAP

NHA TRANG

DALAT

CAM RANH

14

21B

11

20

PHAN RANG

1

PHAN THIET

Attack on Kontum (courtesy of Ngo Quang Truong).

rank of a U.S. major general. A year earlier when I spoke with Vann, U.S. troops were rapidly withdrawing. By the Easter Offensive, nearly all U.S. troops were out of II Corps. He commanded no U.S. combat troops, but as senior advisor he controlled U.S. advisors who remained in II Corps. Vann had a good ability to cajole and intimidate the RVNAF generals, motivating them to fight, a gift badly needed. One of the NVA strikes into South Vietnam had as its objective the small provincial capital Kontum, some miles north of Pleiku, the headquarters of II Corps. Kontum was the objective of one of the three strikes that the NVA made into South Vietnam. If the NVA took Kontum, they could proceed south and seize Pleiku and then east to the sea, cutting South Vietnam in half. Vann was in a key position. He commanded no troops, but he could control air assets.

This was mountainous terrain near the tri-border area. In order to seize Kontum, the initial objective of the NVA was Tan Canh. If the NVA could seize Tan Canh or the nearby firebase along Rocket Ridge, they could overrun Kontum. When I visited Tan Canh in 1970, we had a communications site there and the troops had dug in a splendid defensive position. As we talked and had a drink, I heard a faint "pop" and I asked what that was. The site NCOIC just said that it was another VC mortar round that had hit the top of the bunker. They were dug in so deep with several layers of protection that one could hardly hear the annoying VC rounds, yet the U.S. troops could go upstairs manning the bunkers and had fields of fire in all directions. As with all other things, we handed this over to the RVNAF. During the NVA Easter Invasion Tan Canh was overrun.

The NVA assembled 35,000 troops to attack Kontum under one its best generals, Hoang Minh Thao, one of General Giap's favorite commanders.[16] The NVA force was methodical in their advance. First came the engineers with earth-moving equipment to build roads at night. Sound carries great distances in the mountains and the defenders could hear the sounds of construction. Next came the NVA tanks, and the defenders could see the headlamps of the tanks from a very far distance as they moved toward them. This was a conventional war not seen before in South Vietnam. It was terrifying for the RVNAF.

There were limited effective RVNAF units in II Corps available to repel the NVA attack, but reinforcements were sent in. Vann coordinated air support and helped with resupply. He would fly through heavy fire to pinpoint targets, report results, adjust fire, and land in order to encourage RVNAF commanders and provide supplies. His efforts were instrumental in stopping the NVA attack in western II Corps.

After taking Tan Canh, the NVA stopped to resupply and reinforce before attacking Kontum City. This was a three-week delay, because the

NVA was focused on the other two fronts in I Corps and III Corps, which failed. While the NVA delayed the attack on Kontum City, U.S. B-52s destroyed NVA troops with concentrated bombings and the U.S. rushed anti-tank missiles to defeat the NVA tanks.[17] Vann coordinated most of this battle. The NVA retreated.

In eastern II Corps, Vann was faced with a different problem. In Binh Dinh Province on the coast, he was faced with RVNAF leadership cowardice on an unimaginable scale and Regional Forces/Popular Forces (RF/PF) troops were deserting by the thousands. The RVNAF commander of the 40th Regiment, Colonel Tran Heiu Duc, refused to fight and did not fire a round. As the NVA approached, he would withdraw his troops and fall back to higher ground and keep falling back until he ran out of higher ground. Vann tried to intervene. On 19 April 1972, he arranged air support and a convoy of M113s to allow Duc to withdraw in an orderly manner. At that point Duc fled in panic, leaving all of his remaining troops with the wounded behind. The Binh Dinh districts of Bong Son and Tam Quam easily fell before the NVA advance.

I recall in 1966 during Operation Masher that Bong Son was in VC country. The VC were entrenched and nothing had changed since then. In 1966, as we approached the airfield at Bong Son, the VC laid down a curtain of fire at the end of the runway while we were on final approach. The aircraft received many hits as it flew through the curtain of fire. At that point, we always sat on our flak jackets for obvious reasons. The inside of the cabin exploded with bullets, dust and debris. Thanks to the flak jackets, none of us was wounded. The pilot looked back at us. He was white faced; he looked terrified and was not the reassuring image of a commercial pilot today. He simply said, "Get ready; we are going down," and we did. Thanks to his skill, we successfully crash-landed and everyone survived the crash, and we limped out of the jungle to the assembly area. I was amazed. There were VC monuments to their dead in Bong Son. This was clearly a VC stronghold. Obviously, the RVNAF never ventured into this area. It would be dangerous to do so. Masher was a failure. It was designed to have the U.S. Marines in the north move south while Vietnamese units moved north to trap the VC. It was a bad idea because of all of the coordination required to trap the VC, who easily disappeared, with few casualties. By 1972 nothing had changed. RVNAF defense of Bong Son and Tam Quam districts collapsed and the NVA moved in. Two hundred thousand people in Binh Dinh Province were now under NVA control.[18]

There were worse examples of cowardice. RVNAF medical helicopters landed to pick up the wounded. While the wounded lay ready for pickup, the RVNAF Military Police (MPs) had concocted a scheme to extort money from the able-bodied RVNAF troops for a place on the medevac helicopters. Half of the loot went to the helicopter crews. As the wounded were left dying at the medevac site, the RVNAF MPs and helicopter crews counted their money.[19] The RVNAF had learned lessons from Lam Son 719: Allow the escape of able-bodied soldiers scrambling over the wounded, but also make a profit from it.

The distance between Pleiku, the RVNAF II Corps headquarters and the province headquarters at Kontum was 42 kilometers. In 1970 the 43rd Signal Battalion headquarters was located at Pleiku and we had a detachment at Kontum providing support. When I could get a chopper I loaded up with mail, beer and other nice things to drop off with our troops and then I could chat with them. The chopper would lift off, go high to avoid ground fire and then settle at the pad in Kontum. The terrain was mountainous with forests, as is most of the Central Highlands. If I could not get a chopper or it was bad weather, I drove, but choppers saved a lot of time.

On 9 June 1972, John Paul Vann loaded into his chopper at Pleiku. He needed to go to Kontum and it was night. By this time he was the senior U.S. person in II Corps and had a very busy schedule. He had always been a risk taker and would rather take a helicopter and save time than go by road or air the next day. By his actions he had secured a victory for the RVNAF in II Corps. After a celebration at Pleiku, he lifted off at 9:00 p.m. He said at the time, "I've been in Kontum every day since this thing got started."[20] En route Vann's helicopter crashed before it reached Kontum. It was dark and they went into the trees. There is no evidence to suggest that the crash was the result of enemy action. All aboard were killed. Vann's helicopter was flying low. The Montagnards cut trees and burn foliage to plant their crops. Vann did not know or had forgotten that there was a spot between Pleiku and Kontum where the Montagnards preserved a small grove of trees to bury their ancestors. All other terrain was devoid of any trees on this route. I remember this spot because I traveled the road between Pleiku and Kontum frequently. On that night, the pilot went in at maximum speed to the grove of trees and his helicopter exploded. ARVN rangers saw the crash and wanted payment for finding John Paul Vann's body, which was untouched by the crash because he was thrown free of the aircraft, but he was killed instantly. The Rangers robbed Vann's body of his wristwatch, wallet and Rutgers ring before returning Vann's body.[21] This might be one of the best summaries of why the South Vietnamese lost the war. There was no RVNAF leadership, no one in charge; every man for himself. The Easter Invasion proved that some units fought bravely, but many others fled in panic and most were only concerned about piling up money because they knew that the war was lost and they needed money to escape Vietnam and find a new life. The leadership of the corrupt Saigon regime was doing the same thing. It all came down to a lack of RVNAF professional leadership.

Neil Sheehan, Vann's biographer, was able to find the crash site several months after the crash. It was only 550 yards from the route that I had frequently used. Sheehan found that there were few helicopter parts that could be identified except for a twisted tail boom. He provided this summary at the end of his book:

> The wreckage was scattered around the grove for fifty to sixty yards. The speed at which the machine had hit the trees and the explosion of the fuel cells had shattered the little helicopter. The sole recognizable fragment was the twisted tail boom. The grove was beautiful. The trees were majestic in their natural state. The canopy of their branches gave deep shade. The sun came down in rays of gentle light. I wondered why the tribal people had left this grove of trees untouched. I saw a small, low square of hewn logs planted upright in the ground nearby and asked the Montagnard lieutenant what it was. "Dead men here," he said. "Dead men here," he repeated, sweeping his hand about. Then I saw the figures placed around another, larger square of hewn logs farther into the trees. I had not noticed them before, because I had been concentrating on the wreckage. They were carved of wood in the primitive fashion of the Montagnards, an ancient people who migrated into Indochina earlier than the Vietnamese. The figures were squatting, resting their chins on their hands and staring into space. I had seen figures like them at another tribal hamlet not far from this one nearly ten years before, and I knew now why the trees had not been touched. The grove was the hamlet graveyard. The tribal people had left the trees in their natural state to guard the graves and to provide shade for their burial rites. Now I also knew what had happened on that night. John Vann had come skylarking up the road, mocking death again, unaware that these figures of death were waiting for him in this grove.[22]

By mid–September 1972, the NVA Easter Invasion had petered out, thanks to massive U.S. air support and determined RVNAF resistance. The NVA had sustained as many as 100,000 casualties in this campaign.[23] In that year, 39,000 Saigon soldiers died.[24]

Nixon took advantage of this victory to push for a peace treaty. Kissinger negotiated a settlement with Hanoi, the VC, and Thieu as a reluctant participant (he refused to recognize the VC as a legitimate government). On 27 January 1973, the Paris Peace Accords were signed. The agreement stipulated that all U.S. advisors and other troops (about 23,700 people) would withdraw within 60 days and our remaining bases would be dismantled. All U.S. prisoners of war would be released.

One of the last to leave was Paul Michael Bryant, Sr.:

After wrecking the XO's jeep in January of 73, and after being in a coma for 70 some hours and a couple of weeks in the hospital, I was sent back to the 57th, and the XO was none too pleased that he no longer had a jeep for what everyone knew was the last months of the 57th time in Nam. I also wasn't recommended for flight school, which was one of the reason I went down out of my way on a non-authorized trip to see my friends down past the motor pool that were billeted next to the motor pits. Had I not went down there to take him his DEROS orders and to be honest *brag* that I was going to be a wobbly 01 warrant officer and

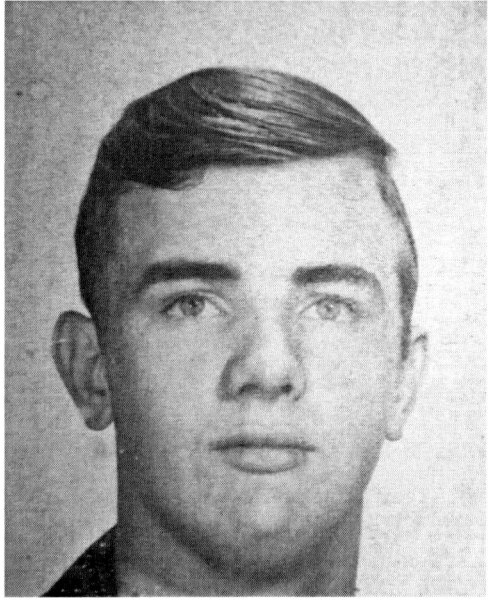

Paul Michael Bryant, Sr. (courtesy of Paul Michael Bryant, Sr.).

that they would have to salute me should we meet up back in the world. But in my defense, I had just turned 19 in country less than 6 months earlier, and was still quite immature and wet behind the ears. After wrecking the XO's jeep, I was assigned to the SSB green eyed monster or land line operating the telephones. It was the crank phones and when a call came in the little light on that line would flip over to green, then you had to answer and then plug in what looked like a electric guitar jack from there to where they wanted to talk to. It was a very uncomfortable job. It was upstairs over in the repair hangar for the birds. 4 hours on and 4 hours off for the rest of the time I was in country, well except for any time the XO could find a shit detail for me to do during my 4 hours off. At night it got so cold that I would take my poncho and crawl inside it with a Coleman lantern light down at my feet to try and get warm. Those that weren't upcountry didn't know how cold it could get up there at night. Working over in the hangar did have one advantage in that one of the mechanics made me a tail rotor chain watch band, he said something about it being made out of titanium and that it cost the government something like either 13 or 23 dollars a link and each link had 5 or more pieces every other one pointed in the opposite direction sort of like a bicycle chain but instead of only 2 long pieces in each link there were 13 or 23. I don't remember or it could have been as little as 5 or 6, I don't have it, because I pawned it outside of Ft. Knox after coming back to the world [*Paul Michael Bryant, Sr., 1973*[25]].

Paul G. Dailey's memoir can best be called "in retrospect":

You are not and will never be alone in your feeling of guilt for what we may have or may not have done during our Service in Vietnam.... We each hold a dark experience that we fight through regardless of our position in duty stations, we were all treated like crap for our service because of what a few did that society could not handle or understand. I have also opened up here and as Doug informed me at the time it's called "survivors guilt." We cannot change what has happened but we can look at the merits of derogatory remarks made by those who may have a bigger problem in excepting their own shortcomings. I will tell you right now that I will never deny any Vietnam Vet the opportunity to have my back, any man that stood and took the oath to protect the Constitution and the United States of America is not a coward. I don't care where a person was stationed in Nam, the same danger addressed all of us in one form or another. The military does not operate only on foot soldiers, somebody has to make sure he is fed, paid, clothed, housed and get medical treatment plus drive or fly his ass around and then you got all those who make sure that all that equipment keeps working so he is not walking everywhere. We that served and did not run from America but embraced her need: never have to feel guilty for we Served our Country in whatever capacity she asked of us. I challenge any servicemen to deny that at some point in their enlistment a clerk did not go above and beyond their pay grade to get them extra time off or fix the paperwork to extend leave or just plan cover someone's butt. The officers may have had the rank but the enlisted men had the power, especially those that controlled the flow of paperwork, I didn't intend to write a book, I apologize.... We can only assure you that you have nothing to feel guilty about, only pride for being willing to put your life in danger if asked to; you did by the action of going to Vietnam and not running to Canada. We cannot control what comes out of someone's mouth but question if that is in fact the location of the sound. Ultimately only you can come to terms with this problem but you're not alone and if you want to jump in that fox hole then trust us now! because we have your back. We experienced and we lived, there is a reason for that in itself. I was nearly killed my first days at the 604th when we were hit during the day by rocket fire and then again later during a night attack by mortars that landed only feet from me. I am here to tell you it wasn't any different than live fire at basic except you knew that they weren't controlled explosions. We all were 11 Bravo and then we had a job. We will never find peace in an apology, only in forgiveness. The lesson I had to learn [*Paul G. Dailey, 68/69*[26]].

The U.S. embassy staff remained until the final defeat of the South Vietnam regime in 1975. There were many other U.S. people such as aid workers, inspectors and staff who were to coordinate the U.S. withdrawal.

The first POWs were repatriated in February 1973. North Vietnam pledged that it would not try to reunify the country by force. An international control commission was set up to supervise the agreement. A sticking point throughout the negotiations was the status of remaining NVA troops in South Vietnam. Hanoi refused to withdraw these troops. In the end, Kissinger acquiesced and the United States signed with no guarantee that the NVA troops would be withdrawn. There was a vague reference to Hanoi not resupplying them. Kissinger said, "[A North Vietnam withdrawal] had been unobtainable for ten years.... We could not make it a condition for a final settlement. We had long passed the threshold." In response to criticism he said, "You don't understand. I want to meet their terms. I want to end this war before the election. What do you want us to do? Stay there forever?"[27] This left the South Vietnamese in a precarious position. With no U.S. forces to support them and a very dedicated force of NVA and VC within their border, it was only a matter of time before Hanoi would attack again. This set the stage for the last chapter in Vietnam.

The Final Chapter

While Nixon was enjoying the start of his second term as president, the new congress was busy at work to reduce his authority in Indochina by stopping all funding to that region. Congress was eventually successful. Meanwhile, Nixon became involved with the Watergate scandal and he ultimately resigned on 9 August 1974. Previously, Nixon's vice president, Spiro Agnew, had been convicted of crimes and stepped down. Jerry Ford had been appointed vice president and succeeded Nixon. If Thieu thought that he could count on Nixon's help in his coming conflict, that possibility was now gone.

Thieu's regime was in fairly good shape at the time of the Paris Peace Accords. The United States had been pouring in an enormous amount of equipment during Vietnamization and beyond until the treaty was signed. Still, there had not been time to adequately train the RVNAF to operate and maintain much of the equipment. Thieu controlled about 75 to 85 percent of his population.[28] It appeared that he had sufficient troops to defend South Vietnam, but numbers were always a mystery, because Hanoi had been secretly infiltrating troops into South Vietnam and exact numbers of these were not known. Most important, the RVNAF lacked the will to fight. Hanoi ordered its troops to attack only when they had clear superiority over the RVNAF and an enormous resupply campaign was initiated.

Hanoi's target was Saigon. If they could seize Saigon, it would end the war. They knew that Thieu would ultimately try to concentrate his forces to defend the Capital Military Region. The initial NVA attack was against Pruco Long Province in the southeast. It was a key junction on Route 14. The troops at the province capital of Pruco Binh were no match for the NVA and surrendered on 6 January 1975. There was no reaction from the United States. The Saigon regime was stunned. The U.S. Congress had done a good job of limiting the power of the president to reenter the war. The possibility of the United States reentering the war was not a concern for Hanoi. In the words of the Hanoi diplomat Pham Van Dong, "They won't come back even if we offered them candy."[29] The initial success of the NVA at Pruco Binh encouraged Hanoi to mount a full-scale invasion of South Vietnam. This was years ahead of their plan to destroy the South Vietnam regime and reunite their country.

Kissinger tried to use diplomacy to prevent an NVA invasion. He met with the Soviet Union and the Chinese to obtain their intervention and offered better relations with the United States as an incentive, but he was not successful.[30]

Hanoi chose Ban Me Thuot in the Central Highlands of South Vietnam as the target. Ban Me Thuot was a small village originally the hunting lodge of Emperor Bao Dai. It is high in the mountains, with a cool climate. I found it to be a very pleasant interlude from the sweat of the jungle when I visited it in 1966. This was also the location where the first U.S. advisors were killed during the Eisenhower administration. General Vien Tien Dung would command the invasion of South Vietnam. He would later succeed Giap as Hanoi's minister of defense. Ban Me Thuot was a very strange target for the invasion. It was many miles within South Vietnam's border, a long way to go. The NVA could have chosen a closer target, like Pleiku, which was a province capital where the II Corps headquarters was located. Dung was faced with an incompetent RVNAF regional commander, Phan Van Phu, who could assemble forces equal to those of Dung. Dung feinted an attack at Pleiku but concentrated his divisions far to the southeast.

It was a brilliant strategy and it worked because it was unexpected. The NVA concentrated three divisions at Ban Me Thuot on 10 March 1975 and the South Vietnamese defenders fled in panic. Thieu ordered Phu to retake Ban Me Thuot, but Phu had already abandoned his post in favor of safer places with his family.[31]

Corruption was not confined to the Saigon regime:

> Despite the alarm among many Americans, Thieu was getting no useful intelligence about the highlands from the CIA. Eighteen months earlier, its agent in Nha Trang had pocketed money earmarked for setting up a network of informants. Auditors discovered the embezzlement, and the man was sent home to Langley and early retirement. To avoid embarrassing the agency, he left with full pension and benefits. The incident helped to explain why Bill Colby had assured the White House earlier in the year that the CIA's latest National Intelligence Estimate foresaw no general offensive in 1975.[32]

At this point, Thieu lost his nerve and lost the war. He ordered the withdrawal of troops in II Corps south to retake Ban Me Thuot. When that failed, it became a headlong flight to Saigon. It was a horror story. All of the 8–5 RVNAF officers and soldiers who had roots down in II Corps now had to pack quickly, load their families and gold loot[33] acquired over perhaps as long as thirty years and get on the road east or south to escape (Highway 19 and others). The rich RVNAF officers such as Phan Van Phu abandoned their troops and ordered or bribed helicopter pilots to fly themselves, their families and gold to Saigon or Nha Trang.[34] That left behind about 200,000 soldiers and their families in II Corps who had been abandoned by their leadership.[35] For the rest it was a slaughter. As the RVNAF officers and soldiers with their families fled east and south in panic, throwing away their uniforms and weapons, the NVA waited along Highway 19 and other roads east and south. The most difficult path ran through Cheo Reo. Here, the NVA trapped the ARVN as they fled Pleiku. ARVN discipline collapsed and they went on a rampage, killing civilians and burning homes, searching for food or vehicles that would allow them to escape the NVA.[36] NVA estimates indicate 13,570 ARVN casualties. For the ARVN, it was the worst defeat of the war.[37] The NVA and VC ambushed and slaughtered thousands of the South Vietnamese, perhaps tens of thousands, as they fled in panic. There is no accurate count of the Vietnamese who were killed in II Corps due to Thieu's panic. Meanwhile Thieu sat in his palace in Saigon waiting for word about his army in II Corps and when it would arrive to help defend his Saigon regime. There was no longer an RVNAF II Corps army. The army in II Corps was now NVA.

By late March 1975, Da Nang, South Vietnam's second-largest city, on the northern coast in I Corps was a South Vietnamese stronghold and nearly a million refugees were streaming into Da Nang for safety. It did not work. On 29 March 1975, the NVA entered the city as the RVNAF threw away their uniforms and weapons and fled in panic. There are some remarkable videos taken at that time. While thousands of women and children waited to be airlifted out of Da Nang or by boat to safety, a U.S. commercial jet went to Da Nang to evacuate people. RVNAF soldiers pushed aside women and children and rushed the aircraft and quickly overloaded it. As the aircraft took off, many RVNAF soldiers were outside of the aircraft hanging on to the cargo hatch and other parts of the aircraft. As the aircraft gained altitude, they fell to their deaths. There are videos showing these ARVN soldiers as they tried to get on board the aircraft ... lack of discipline and lack of leadership.

At the port of Da Nang, things were much worse. Thousands of women and children crowded the docks to escape on fishing boats or other craft. RVNAF soldiers shot women and children in order to make room for themselves.[38]

In South Vietnam the economy was collapsing due to inflation, bribery, and corruption: "Quartermaster units often insisted on bribes in exchange for delivering rice and other supplies to the troops and even demanded cash to furnish fighting men with ammunition, gasoline and spare parts."[39]

General Cao Van Vien, the chairman of the South Vietnamese Joint General Staff, summarized. While complaining for the most part that the loss of South Vietnam was the fault of the United States (a common South Vietnamese theme), he finally got down to the facts:

> Finally, after many years of continuous war, South Vietnam was approaching political and economic bankruptcy. National unity no longer existed; no one was able to rally the people behind the national cause. Riddled by corruption and sometimes ineptitude and dereliction, the government hardly responded to the needs of a public which had gradually lost confidence in it. Despite rosy plans and projects, the national economy continued its course downward and appeared doomed short of a miracle. Under these conditions, the South Vietnamese social fabric gradually disintegrated, influenced in part by mistrust, divisiveness, uncertainty, and defeatism until the whole nation appeared to some to resemble a rotten fruit ready to fall at the first passing breeze.[40]

By this time the Hanoi strategy shifted. Based upon the collapse of the RVNAF seen so far, Hanoi decided to accelerate and destroy the Saigon regime, now rather than later. Dung received orders to liberate the South quickly, before the rains started in May. On 7 April 1975 Dung had planning under way. The offensive against Saigon would be launched no later than the last week in April.[41] At that time, there were six thousand Americans remaining in South Vietnam. The U.S. ambassador, Graham Martin, delayed evacuation because he believed that Saigon could be held. It was a fatal error for many South Vietnamese who should have been evacuated but were not because time ran out. Many of these South Vietnamese worked for the United States in sensitive positions such as intelligence support and would be targeted by the NVA for interrogation or even execution.

After a desperate fight at Xuan Loc thirty-five miles northeast of Saigon, the NVA broke through. This was the only battle where RVNAF soldiers put up a good fight. Thieu deserted his country on 25 April and flew to Taiwan with his gold. He was eventually replaced by General "Big" Minh, the man who had replaced Diem twelve years earlier.

At this time, General Nguyen Coa Ky flew over the battlefield and concluded that the NVA would win. He then flew his helicopter to land on a U.S. carrier.[42] Ky abandoned his nation and he died in the United States on 23 July 2011.[43]

As the NVA approached Saigon, the evacuation of U.S. citizens and some South Vietnamese was in full swing. It was a tight schedule to get people out to carriers and other ships standing by.

Many strange things happened as the South Vietnamese regime collapsed. South Vietnamese IBM employees were told to stay at their jobs because they were needed to process payrolls for the RVNAF. This was déjà vu. In the last days of Hitler in April 1945 as he prepared to commit suicide and the Soviet army was overwhelming Berlin, German army clerks were writing out requisitions for paper clips and other admin supplies that would be needed in 1946.

On 30 April 1975, NVA tanks rumbled through the gates of the South Vietnamese palace in Saigon. General Minh, the last Saigon regime head of state, prepared to meet the NVA representatives:

> Colonel Bui Tin, deputy editor of *Quan Doi Nhan Dan,* the North Vietnamese army newspaper, was covering the campaign as a correspondent. Having reported the capture of Ban Me Thuot, Da Nang, and Xuan Loc, he was eager to witness the "liberation" of Saigon, and had joined the armored spearhead at Bien Hoa. Now, riding a tank into the palace grounds, he prepared to play a dual role. As a journalist, he wanted to record the capitulation. But as the ranking officer with the unit, his first duty was to take the surrender.
>
> "I have been waiting since early this morning to transfer power to you," announced General Minh as Bui Tin entered the room.
>
> "There is no question of your transferring power," replied Bui Tin. "Your power has crumbled. You cannot give up what you do not have." A burst of gunfire erupted outside, and several of Minh's ministers ducked. Their nervousness provided Bui Tin with the pretext to deliver a short speech: "Our men are merely celebrating. You have nothing to fear. Between Vietnamese, there are no victors and no vanquished. Only the Americans have been beaten. If you are patriots, consider this a moment of joy. The war for our country is over."[44]

It was evident that the NVA did not want to interfere with the U.S. departure from Vietnam. A greater concern was renegade South Vietnam soldiers who would turn their guns on Americans trying to depart, but this did not occur. The final chapter captured by many cameras was U.S. helicopters landing and shuttling people out to the fleet. As far as is known, all U.S. personnel were evacuated, but many South Vietnamese key officials and intelligence people were left behind. By delaying the evacuation, Ambassador Martin caused the deaths of many South Vietnamese who were later executed by the NVA, but the total will never be known. Ambassador Martin was among the last to be taken out, clutching the U.S. flag with his wife. Their son was killed in Vietnam. The ambassador looked like a corpse. This was a very sad ending to a tragic war.

Summary

Throughout this conflict, public opinion and policy shifted a great deal from the early days in the Eisenhower administration, when they were preventing dominoes from falling, to the Kennedy years, when the press and the public realized that this was a bad war, to the LBJ years, when there were massive demonstrations against the war. By the time of Nixon's administration, the view was to get out at all costs. Since then there have been a spate of histories describing how we betrayed South Vietnam. These seem to forget that we lost over 58,000 of our people and a large part of our national treasure because of a corrupt Saigon regime. I would let the reader decide who betrayed whom. South Vietnam lost the war and there was nothing that we could do to prevent it.

My conclusion from the war in Vietnam after I spent a few years there is that as soldiers we did our best. The problem was that of leadership. The South Vietnamese had no adequate leadership. It was corrupt from the top down. From the South Vietnamese battalion commander I advised in 1965 to Thieu abandoning his country rushing to his plane to take him to Taiwan with all of his gold in 1975. The U.S. leadership was no better.

Author A. J. Langguth summarized: "South Vietnam's leaders deserved to lose. The American leaders for thirty years failed the people of the North, the people of the South and the people of the United States."[45]

Perhaps the most important part of this book is the oral histories of the U.S. enlisted soldiers and junior officers who fought there. Many contributed to this book, and their oral histories and mine are included. One thing that we learned is that you cannot dwell on this or any part of it. Move on, but do not forget. When I circulated the draft manuscript to veterans and posted it on my Web site, I got a surprisingly large response from many U.S. enlisted soldiers and junior officers who served in Vietnam. They said that at last there was someone who would tell their story and put it together in a book that also included the official history. This helped them understand better why they served in Vietnam. I did my best.

Like the Vietnamese, the only things that mattered to us were our family, our country and our dog if we were fortunate to have one. As others have said, "I want to be as good a man as my dog thinks I am." I am not sure that I measured up to his expectations, but I tried.

Biographical Dictionary

This section provides the history of the lives of the key participants mentioned in this book.

Creighton Williams Abrams, Jr., was born in Springfield, Massachusetts, on September 15, 1914. Abrams graduated from the U.S. Military Academy with the class of 1936. He was commissioned in the armor branch and served during World War II. He was an aggressive and successful armored commander, receiving two Distinguished Service Crosses for bravery. He served in the Korean War and was promoted to general in 1964. He was assigned as General Westmoreland's deputy in Vietnam and succeeded him on June 10, 1968. Abrams stressed pacification rather than Westmoreland's policy of search and destroy. Abrams returned to the United States and was appointed as U.S. Army Chief of Staff in June 1972. He died from cancer in September 1974. He was the only Chief of Staff to die in office.

Dean Gooderham Acheson was born on April 11, 1893, in Middletown, Connecticut. He attended Yale and served in the National Guard during World War I. He served in the State Department during World War II. He was appointed Secretary of State on January 21, 1949. He served four years in this position. He was accused of responsibility for the loss of China after Mao defeated the nationalists in 1949. Acheson returned to private life in 1953 and died of a stroke in Sandy Spring, Maryland, on October 12, 1971.

Bao Dai was the last emperor of Vietnam. He was born in Hue, Indochina, on October 22, 1913. His reign as emperor was from January

8, 1926, to August 25, 1945. He collaborated with the Japanese during World War II. From June 13, 1949, to August 25, 1955, he was chief of state of South Vietnam. He was accused of being too closely associated with France and was ousted by Ngo Diem. Bao Dai moved to France, where he died in Paris on July 30, 1997.

William Laws Calley is the U.S. Army officer convicted as a war criminal for the murders that he committed at My Lai, South Vietnam. Calley was born in Miami, Florida, on June 8, 1943. He dropped out of college due to failing grades and then held jobs such as bellhop and dishwasher before entering the army, where he graduated from OCS and was commissioned as second lieutenant in the infantry in 1967. He was deployed to South Vietnam as a platoon leader. He was not well liked by his troops, who described him as lacking in common sense. At My Lai he murdered unarmed civilians and was convicted of the murders and sentenced to life in prison. President Nixon later issued Calley a conditional pardon reducing the sentence to time served but upholding Calley's dishonorable discharge. After his release he resided in Atlanta, Georgia.

Christian de Castries was the French commander at the Battle of Dien Bien Phu in 1954. De Castries was born in Paris on August 11, 1902. He served in World War II and was assigned as the French commander at Dien Bien Phu in December 1953. After the defeat of the French, he was repatriated and retired from the French army in 1959. De Castries died in Paris on July 29, 1991.

Ngo Dinh Diem was born on January 3, 1901, in Quang Binh, French Indochina. Following the 1954 Geneva Accords and the departure of the French from Indochina, Diem became president of the Republic of Vietnam (South Vietnam). Diem was a Catholic and adopted oppressive polices toward the Montagnard natives and the Buddhist majority. His lack of popular support and his losing policies toward the war led the United States to support a coup to replace Diem. Diem was assassinated along with his brother Ngo Dinh Nhu on November 2, 1963, in Saigon.

Bernard B. Fall was the war correspondent and historian who covered the Vietnam War from its earliest days. Fall was born in Austria on November 19, 1926. He moved to France and after the fall of France during World War II fought with the Resistance against the Nazis. After the war, he moved to the United States and studied at Syracuse and Johns Hopkins University. Fall visited Vietnam several times, writing several books, including *The Street Without Joy*, which may have been his best. He predicted the defeat of the French and the United States because of their failure to understand the Vietnamese society and adopt tactics such as pacification. On February 21, 1967, while accompanying a U.S. unit in Vietnam, Fall stepped on a land mine and was killed.

Vo Nguyen Giap was born in Quang Binh Province, French Indochina, on August 25, 1911. He commanded NVA forces during the French war and the Vietnam War, which ended in 1975. Giap graduated from the University of Hanoi with a bachelor's degree in politics, economics and law. He fought with the resistance against the Japanese during World War II. During the French war, he defeated the French in the Battle of Dien Bien Phu in 1954. He continued in command of NVA forces in the war against the United States that ended with the surrender of the Saigon regime in 1975. Since his retirement after the war, he has written books and is active in political affairs in Vietnam.

Alexander Meigs Haig, Jr., was born in Philadelphia, Pennsylvania, on December 2, 1924. He studied for two years at the University of Notre Dame before entering the U.S. Military Academy, where he graduated in 1947. He served in the Korean War and commanded a battalion in Vietnam before returning to the United States, where he was assigned to the U.S. Military Academy in 1967. In 1969 he was appointed as an assistant to the National Security Advisor, Henry Kissinger. In that position, Haig helped negotiate the Vietnam cease-fire talks in 1972. When H. R. Haldeman resigned as Nixon's Chief of Staff due to the Watergate scandal, Haig was assigned to that position, where he served until 1974, when he became NATO Supreme Commander, and he retired from the army in 1979. After retirement he held various civilian positions in industry. When Ronald Reagan was elected president, he appointed Haig as Secretary of State. When Reagan was wounded in an assassination attempt on March 30, 1981, Haig committed what could be considered the most publicized gaff in U.S. history. Haig implied that he was in charge of the government until the vice president arrived in Washington from a trip. To the press Haig said, "Constitutionally, gentlemen, you have the president, the vice president, and the Secretary of State in that order.... I am in control here, in the White House, pending the return of the Vice President." Apparently, Haig had forgotten about the 25th Amendment to the Constitution, which places two people between the Secretary of State and the vice president. The media had a field day. After that, Haig continued as Secretary of State, resigning on July 5, 1982. He died on February 20, 2010. He is respectfully remembered by all who served with him, including Henry Kissinger, who gave Haig's eulogy at the Basilica of the National Shrine of the Immaculate Conception on March 2, 2010.

Paul D. Harkins was born in Boston, Massachusetts on May 15, 1904. He graduated from the U.S. Military Academy with the class of 1929. He advanced in rank to command U.S. forces in Vietnam (1962–1964). He was known by his staff as "General Blimp" because he inflated the success of the RVNAF. He was removed from command in Vietnam and retired in 1964. Harkins died in Dallas, Texas, on August 21, 1984.

Colonel Oran Henderson was court-martialed for his effort to cover up the My Lai massacre. Henderson was born in Indianapolis, Indiana, on August 25, 1920. At the time of the massacre, Henderson had twenty-five years of service in World War II and the Korean War and commanded a brigade in the American Division that was responsible for the My Lai massacre. Henderson was found not guilty. He died of pancreatic cancer in 1998.

Harold K. Johnson was born in Bowesmont, North Dakota, on February 22, 1912. He attended the U.S. Military Academy, graduating with the class of 1933. He was commissioned in the infantry and his assignments included the 57th Infantry (Philippine Scouts). With the fall of Bataan, Johnson became a prisoner of war of the Japanese. After World War II, he served in the Korean War and in Vietnam. He was appointed the U.S. Army Chief of Staff in 1964. Johnson retired from the army in 1967 and died of cancer in Washington, D.C., on September 24, 1983.

Henry Alfred Kissinger was born in Furth, Germany, on May 27, 1923. He and his family fled Germany in 1938 to escape persecution by the Nazis. They settled in New York City, where Kissinger attended high school and started community college. He was drafted into the army in 1943 and served in the 84th Division in Europe. Following the war, he earned his bachelor's degree, followed by his master's and Ph.D., at Harvard in 1954. He advanced in the academic community and was the director of the Harvard Defense Studies Program between 1958 and 1971. Nixon chose Kissinger to be his National Security Advisor in 1968 and Kissinger later served as Secretary of State under Nixon and Gerald Ford. Kissinger helped achieve a settlement to the war in Vietnam and also worked to achieve détente with the Soviet Union and the opening of China. Since retiring, he has authored several books and resides today in Kent, Connecticut, and New York City.

Samuel W. Koster was the commander of the U.S. Army Americal Division who tried to cover up the My Lai massacre that occurred in 1968. Koster was born in West Liberty, Iowa, on December 29, 1919, and graduated from the U.S. Military Academy with the class of 1942. Koster was investigated for his efforts to cover up the massacre, but charges were dropped due to lack of evidence. Subsequent investigations led to his demotion and he retired in disgrace after he was stripped of his Distinguished Service Medal in 1973. Koster died in Annapolis, Maryland, on January 23, 1986.

Nguyen Cao Ky was born in Hanoi, French Indochina, on September 8, 1930. Ky started as an infantry officer but was sent for pilot training by the French before Vietnam was partitioned. Ky moved to South Vietnam and joined the air force. He rose through the ranks and eventually became the commander of South Vietnam's air force. In November 1963, Ky participated in the coup that resulted in the assassination of Ngo Dinh Diem. In the succession of generals who followed Diem, Ky eventually sided with Nguyen Van Thieu, and the two ran for office in the 1967 with Thieu as president and Ky as his running mate. In the 1971 election, Ky was sidelined and Thieu won the presidency. When the NVA defeated the South in 1975, Ky fled to the United States and settled in Westminster, California, where he ran a liquor store. Ky died in Kuala Lumpur, Malaysia, on July 23, 2011.

Melvin R. Laird was born in Omaha, Nebraska, on September 1, 1922. Laird graduated from Carleton College in Minnesota and served in the navy during World War II. After the war, he succeeded his deceased father in the Wisconsin State Senate and in 1969 became Secretary of Defense under Richard Nixon. Laird became the architect of Vietnamization, the policy that allowed the United States to exit the war in Vietnam. He left office in 1973 and has written many articles since then.

Curtis Lemay was born in Columbus, Ohio, on November 15, 1906. Lemay worked his way through college, graduating from Ohio State University with a bachelor's degree in civil engineering. He received a reserve commission in the U.S. Air Force in 1929 and a regular commission in 1930. He served in World War II and directed a campaign of massive bombing of Japan that caused hundreds of thousands of Japanese casualties. He was appointed Chief of Staff of the U.S. Air Force in 1961. During the war in Vietnam he continued to urge the use of massive airpower to defeat Hanoi, and this may have caused Hanoi to return to the conference table in 1972. He retired in 1965 and died at March Air Force Base, California, on March 1, 1990.

Robert S. McNamara was selected by President John F. Kennedy to be his Secretary of Defense shortly after JFK took office. McNamara was born on June 9, 1916, and died on July 6, 2009. McNamara remained in office, serving Lyndon B. Johnson, after Kennedy was killed. McNamara was the longest-serving Secretary of Defense, 1961–1968. He resigned to head the World Bank and departed his position as Secretary of Defense during the Tet Offensive of 1968.

Doung Van Minh (*"Big Minh"*) was born in My Tho Province on February 16, 1916. Minh joined the French army at the start of World War II. He became a South Vietnamese general and politician who helped Ngo Dinh Diem consolidate power after Vietnam was partitioned in 1955. Later Minh led the coup that resulted in the death of Diem, for which he was blamed. He lasted only three months as president after Diem's death. Minh was replaced by General Khanh in a bloodless coup that occurred in January 1964. Khanh allowed Minh to remain in South Vietnam, but Minh was ultimately exiled. In 1975, as South Vietnam collapsed during the North Vietnamese invasion, Minh took over as president and surrendered to the NVA on April 30, 1975. Minh was allowed to leave the country and he died in Pasadena, California, on August 6, 2001.

Ho Chi Minh was born Nguyen Sinh Cung in Nghe An Province, French Indochina, on May 19, 1890. He used a number of aliases throughout his life in order to avoid arrest but is known today as Ho Chi Minh. Ho Chi Minh was educated in Hue and traveled extensively, visiting France, the United States, Russia, China and the United Kingdom. In 1941 he returned to Vietnam to lead the Vietminh independence movement. He led the Vietminh against the French and the Japanese, receiving support from the United States. At the end of World War II, Ho declared the independence of Vietnam under the title of the Democratic Republic of Vietnam. A war with France ensued that ended with the 1954 Geneva Accords that divided the country with Ho as leader in the North. The war with the South and the United States that followed ended in 1975. Ho Chi Minh died of a heart attack at his home in Hanoi on September 2, 1969.

Thomas Hinman Moorer was born in Mount Willing, Alabama, on February 9, 1912. He graduated from the U.S. Naval Academy with the class of 1933 and served as a pilot during World War II. Moorer served as

Chief of Naval Operations between 1967 and 1970. He became Chairman of the Joint Chiefs in 1970, retiring in 1974. Moorer died in the U.S. Naval Hospital in Bethesda, Maryland, on February 5, 2004.

Madame Nhu was born of a wealthy family in Hanoi, Indochina, on August 22, 1924. She married Ngo Dinh Nhu in 1943. He was the brother of Ngo Dinh Diem, who would become the president of South Vietnam. At the time of her marriage, she converted from Buddhism to her husband's religion, Catholicism. Since Diem was a lifelong bachelor, Madame Nhu became the First Lady of South Vietnam. She was considered by many to be a schemer like her husband and was prone to making candid public statements, sometimes critical of the United States. When Diem and Ngo Dinh Nhu were assassinated in a coup d'état on November 2, 1963, Madame Nhu was traveling in the United States. She moved to Rome in exile and later moved to France. Her property in Vietnam was confiscated by the new government. In her last years she returned to Rome, where she died on April 24, 2011.

Ngo Dinh Nhu was born in Phu Cam, French Indochina, on October 7, 1910. He was the younger brother of the first president of South Vietnam, Ngo Dinh Diem. Nhu received his bachelor's degree in literature in Paris. He pursued academic interests until the end of World War II, when he became politically active and helped in mobilizing support for his brother Diem. In 1963 the Buddhist majority rose up against the pro–Catholic regime of Diem. Both Nhu and his brother were assassinated on November 2, 1963.

Marshal Lon Nol was born in Prey Veng, Cambodia, on November 13, 1913. He served as prime minister and defense minister of Cambodia. In 1970 he mounted a successful coup against Prince Norodom Sihanouk, the Cambodian head of state. Lon Nol proclaimed himself to be the president of the Khmer Republic. He then gave Hanoi and the VC twenty-four hours to leave Cambodia and he closed the port Sihanoukville, a source of supply for them. Lon Nol suffered a stroke in 1971 and his effectiveness started to decline. He had relied on U.S. aid, but by 1975 he was only able to hold the capital, Phnom Penh, against the Khmer Rouge. On April 1, 1975, he resigned and fled the country to Indonesia and then to the United States while the Khmer Rouge took over. Lon Nol died in Fullerton, California, on November 17, 1985.

Bruce Palmer, Jr., was born in Austin, Texas, on April 13, 1913. He graduated from the U.S. Military Academy with the class of 1936. He served in World War II and commanded the XVII Airborne Corps, 1965–1967. In Vietnam he commanded II Field Force and became Acting Chief of Staff of the U.S. Army in 1972. Palmer retired from the army in 1974 and died on October 10, 2000.

William R. Peers was born in Stuart, Iowa, on June 14, 1914. He graduated from the University of California with a degree in education in 1937 and served during World War II, the Korean War and Vietnam. In Vietnam he commanded the IFFV and the 4th Infantry Division before being assigned to investigate the My Lai massacre in 1969. His report assigned blame and led to court-martials. General Peers died in San Francisco, California, on April 6, 1984.

Pol Pot was born in Kampong Thom Province, French Indochina, on May 19, 1925. He joined a Communist cell in 1951. He gained control of the Khmer Rouge movement in Cambodia and took Phnom Penh on April 17, 1975. With the Khmer Rouge in control of the country, a bloodbath started that caused the deaths of over a million people due to executions and starvation. In 1979 Vietnam took control of Cambodia and ended most of the deaths. Pol Pot died on April 16, 1998.

Prince Norodom Sihanouk was born in Phnom Penh, Cambodia, on October 31, 1922. He attended cavalry school in France and was selected as king of Cambodia in 1941. During World War II the Japanese took control of Cambodia. At the end the war, Sihanouk proclaimed Cambodia's independence and held a series of appointments as prime minister until 1960, when he was elected as head of state. Sihanouk worked to maintain Cambodia's neutrality during the Vietnam War but allowed North Vietnam and China to maintain bases in eastern Cambodia. He was deposed by Lon Nol in 1970 and fled to Beijing, China. Lon Nol was deposed by the Khmer Rouge in April 1975 and Vietnam invaded Cambodia and ousted the Khmer Rouge in 1979. Sihanouk returned to Cambodia and in 1993 became the king of Cambodia. He departed on a self-imposed exile in January 2004, first to North Korea and then to China, where he died on October 15, 2012.

Nguyen Van Thieu was born in Phan Rang, French Indochina, on April 5, 1923. Initially Thieu joined the Vietminh Communists, but he quit after a year and joined the South Vietnamese army, rising in rank to command a division by 1960. Thieu participated in the coup against Diem in November 1963 and became a member of the military junta after Diem's death. Thieu became head of state in 1965 and then president until the fall of Saigon in 1975. His regime was noted for corruption and the appointment of commanders based upon their politics and loyalty to him rather than their competence. He fled the country shortly before the Communists overran South Vietnam in 1975. Thieu died in Boston, Massachusetts, on September 29, 2001.

John Paul Vann was born in Norfolk, Virginia, on July 2, 1924. Vann enlisted during World War II and remained in the service after the war. He also served in the Korean War and Vietnam. He was an outspoken critic of the RVNAF at the Battle of Ap Bac and retired from the army in 1963. Vann returned to Vietnam as a U.S. civilian employee in 1965 and became senior advisor in the II Corps Tactical Zone. His greatest contribution may have been during the NVA Easter Invasion of South Vietnam, when he coordinated air support and was instrumental in the defeat of the NVA. Vann was killed in a helicopter crash near Kontum on June 9, 1972. He was posthumously awarded the Presidential Medal of Freedom and the Distinguished Service Cross for his actions from April 23 to 24, 1972.

William Childs Westmoreland was born in Saxon, South Carolina, on March 26, 1914. He attended the U.S. Military Academy, graduating with the class of 1936. He served in World War II and the Korean War and commanded U.S. forces in Vietnam. He has been criticized for his focus on search-and-destroy operations when most agree that pacification should have been our primary policy. The NVA Tet Offensive of 1968 was a military victory for the United States and its allies but was a political disaster in the United States and caused an increasing percentage of the population to turn against the war. Westmoreland was replaced by General Creighton Abrams in 1968 and then became U.S. Army Chief of Staff. Westmoreland retired from the army in 1972 and spent a good deal of the rest his life defending his reputation. Mike Wallace interviewed Westmoreland for a CBS special. Wallace implied that Westmoreland had lied about enemy strength prior to Tet '68 for political reasons. Westmoreland sued and a lengthy trial ensued. Westmoreland settled for an apology from CBS. Westmoreland died in Charleston, South Carolina, on July 18, 2005.

Names, Abbreviations and Terms

advisors—term applied to U.S. service personnel who provided advice and assistance to ARVNAF units.

APC—armored personnel carrier.

ARVN—Army of the Republic of Vietnam.

baby boomer—a person born in the United States between the end of World War II and 1964.

back channel—informal flag officer correspondence.

base area—Communist base camp. Usually containing fortifications, supply depots, hospitals, and training facilities.

B-52s—U.S. heavy bombers that composed the U.S. strategic response.

Black Panthers—a far left group founded in 1966 and active until 1982. Its doctrine called primarily for the protection of black neighborhoods from police brutality, but it also espoused Marxist-Leninist doctrine.

Cambodian Liberation Army—also called Khmer Liberation Army. Communist armed forces of National United Front of Kampuchea (FUNK).

Central Highlands—a highland area of the western part of all II Corps stretching roughly from Ban Me Thuot in Darlac Province north to Kontum Province and the southern border of I Corps.

Chinook—CH-47 cargo/troop-carrying helicopter.

CIA—Central Intelligence Agency.

CINCPAC—Commander-In-Chief, Pacific: commands all U.S. forces in the Pacific.

Cobra-Bell AH-IG Huey Cobra—fast attack helicopter armed with machine guns, grenade launchers, and rockets.

Cooper-Church Amendment—was enacted on 5 January 1971. It ended funding for U.S. ground troops and military advisors in Cambodia and Laos after 30 June 1970. It barred air operations in Cambodian airspace in direct support of Cambodian forces without congressional approval, and it ended American support for Republic of Vietnam forces outside territorial South Vietnam.

CORDS—the Civil Operations and Revolutionary Development Support was established under MACV in 1967. CORDS organized U.S. civilian agencies in Vietnam within the military chain of command.

corps—two or more divisions, responsible for the defense of a Military Region.

COSVN—Central Office for South Vietnam. Communist military and political headquarters for southern South Vietnam.

C rations/C rats—individual canned rations used in the field.

CTZ—Corps Tactical Zone. Identifies the four military regions that composed South Vietnam.

D day—a day set for launching a military operation.

DEROS—date eligible for return from overseas. The date a soldier's tour of duty was to end.

dog tags—metal tags soldiers carried or wore that identified their name and other information.

DMZ—demilitarized zone. Established by the 1954 Geneva Accords, provisionally dividing North Vietnam from South Vietnam along the seventeenth parallel.

domino theory—President Eisenhower articulated the domino theory, which expressed the belief that if a country fell to the Communists others would follow like dominoes.

drawdown—reduction in force.

FAC—Forward Air Controller. Pilot or observer who directs strike aircraft and artillery.

I Corps—RVNAF military command controlling forces in Military Region of South Vietnam's five northernmost provinces.

IFFV—I Field Force, Vietnam, located in Nha Trang, exercised control over U.S. forces located in II CTZ.

4ID—U.S. 4th Infantry Division.

fragging—killing or attempting to kill a fellow soldier or officer, usually with a fragmentation grenade.

Freedom Bird—term applied to all aircraft that carried U.S. service members back to the United States after serving in Vietnam.

friendly fire—fire directed on friendly troops by mistake.

FSB—Fire Support Base. Semifixed artillery base established to increase indirect fire coverage of an area and to provide security for the firing unit.

FULRO—the autonomous movement of Montagnards in Vietnam to separate themselves from the South Vietnamese regime.

Great Society—the LBJ program with a set of domestic programs that were aimed at the elimination of poverty and racial injustice. Antiwar Democrats complained that spending on the Vietnam War choked off the Great Society.

Hamlet Program—the rural peasants would be provided security, being physically isolated from Communist insurgents and support services in defended hamlets, thereby strengthening ties with the central South Vietnamese government. It was hoped this would lead to increased loyalty by the peasantry toward the government. In the end, the program led to a decrease in support for Diem's regime and an increase in sympathy for Communist efforts.

hooch—a small living quarter or hut.

Huey—helicopter that was used to move troops and provide fire support and medevac.

indirect fire—bombardment by mortars or artillery in which shells travel on a trajectory to an unseen target.

Indochina—a French term used to describe their colony in Southeast Asia that included Cambodia, Laos, and Vietnam.

JCS—Joint Chiefs of Staff. Consisting of chairman, U.S. Army Chief of Staff, U.S. Navy Chief of Naval Operations, U.S. Air Force Chief of Staff, and the U.S. Marine Corps Commandant. Advises the president, the National Security Council, and the Secretary of Defense.

JGS—Joint General Staff, the South Vietnamese military organization that directed the activities of the ARVNAF.

KIA—Killed In Action.

klicks—distance measurement in kilometers.

LAW—M72 light anti-tank weapon. A shoulder-fired rocket with a onetime, disposable launcher.

LRRP—Long-Range Reconnaissance Patrol.

MACV—Military Assistance Command, Vietnam. U.S. command for all U.S. military activities in Vietnam.

mad minute—concentrated fire by all weapons at maximum rate. Usually used to demonstrate firepower.

MARS—Military Auxiliary Radio System. Sponsored by the Department of Defense, this system manned by volunteers allowed service members to contact their family in the United States via radio from Vietnam.

medevac—medical evacuation by helicopter.

Me Generation—also called America's "worst generation," stemming from the fact that they were totally self-focused and did not wish to provide any service to their country: see also "baby boomers." The point is that many of these citizens served their country very well in Vietnam, the Peace Corps and other programs.

minigun—a weapons system composed of a series of Gatling-style rotating barrels that rotate and fire at a high rate powered by an electric motor.

M113—armored personnel carrier used by both ARVN and U.S. forces.

monsoon—a seasonal reversing wind accompanied by corresponding changes in precipitation: heavy rain for weeks that blocks roads.

Montagnard/Yards—minority mountain people who live in simple societies in the Central Highlands.

MPC—Military Payment Certificate. A form of currency used to pay U.S. military personnel in Vietnam and other overseas countries. This prevented the circulation of U.S. greenbacks that could be used for illegal purposes.

MR—Military Region. Term that replaced "Corps Tactical Zone." One of four geographic zones into which South Vietnam was divided for purposes of military and civil administration.

NCO—noncommissioned officer (noncom). Enlisted ranks including corporal and sergeant up to command sergeant major.

NLF—National Liberation Front, officially the National Front for the Liberation of the South. Formed on December 20, 1960, it aimed to overthrow South Vietnam's government and reunite the North and the South. NLF included Communists and non–Communists.

NVA—North Vietnamese Army.

OCS—Officer Candidate School provided a way for enlisted soldiers to obtain commissions after they entered active duty.

OER—Officer Efficiency Report, a primary tool for officer evaluations and promotions.

pacification—a process of countering a counterinsurgency by controlling the terrain to provide security for the population.

palace guard—in Vietnam these were units that could be called in to protect the South Vietnamese president against coup attempts.

pearls—During the French war in Indochina, captured French soldiers were held for ransom by the Vietminh until cash was paid for their release. For this reason, they were called pearls.

percs—benefits available to service members.

PF—Popular Forces. South Vietnamese village defense units.

Phoenix program (Phung Hoang)—an intelligence-gathering program designed to neutralize the Vietcong infrastructure through identification and arrest of key party cadres.

politburo—policymaking and executive committee of the Communist Party.

REMF—Rear Echelon Mother F——r. An expression to describe a soldier in rear areas who performed administrative duties and was not assigned to a combat unit.

RF—Regional Forces. South Vietnamese provincial defense units.

ROTC—Reserve Officer Training Corps: a college-based program for training commissioned officers of the U.S. Armed Forces.

RVNAF—Republic of Vietnam Armed Forces, including ARVN, PF, RF, VNAF, VNMC, and VNN.

SAM—surface-to-air missile.

sapper—NVA/VC sappers were commando raiders adept at penetrating allied defenses.

satchel charges—explosive packs small enough to be easily carried and placed on targets.

II Corps—RVNAF military command controlling forces in Military Region 2, the Central Highlands, and adjoining coastal lowlands.

IIFFV—II Field Force, Vietnam, located in Bien Hoa Province, exercised control over U.S. forces located in III and IV CTZ.

starlight scope—an optical instrument that allows images to be produced in levels of light approaching total darkness.

Strela—a series of Russian-manufactured anti-aircraft missiles.

Tet—Vietnamese lunar New Year holiday period.

III Corps—RVNAF military command controlling forces in Military Region 3, the area from northern Mekong Delta to the southern highlands.

TOW—Tube-launched, Optically tracked, Wire-guided anti-tank missile.

tracer—ammunition that has a small pyrotechnic charge in its base that allows the firer to track the flight of the bullet and adjust his fire.

tropospheric scatter/tropo—a method of transmitting and receiving microwave communications signals over long distances.

USMA—United States Military Academy located at West Point, New York.

Vietcong—a contraction of Vietnamese Communist.

Vietminh—term used in the French war to describe the Communist army under Ho Chi Minh.

ville—a small village.

VNAF—South Vietnamese Air Force.

VNMC—South Vietnamese Marine Corps.

VNN—South Vietnamese Navy.

The Presidents and U.S. Casualties

Dwight D. Eisenhower

With Eisenhower's Total Retaliation doctrine that promoted the nuclear war option, many had the opinion that conventional war was a thing of the past. The total number of our people killed in South Vietnam during the Eisenhower years was nine, including non-hostile deaths. Southeast Asia was not a major topic of interest for the American public at that time.

John F. Kennedy

The U.S. involvement under Kennedy expanded and its relationship to the Cold War was restated:

The chief purpose of the United States in Vietnam was to demonstrate American credibility as a military power and a reliable ally to its enemies and its allies around the world. The danger was that if the United States were perceived to be lacking in military capability, political resolve, or both, the Soviet Union and/or China and their proxies would act more aggressively, while U.S. allies, including important industrial democracies such as West Germany and Japan, would be inclined to appease the communist great powers.[1]

After the Bay of Pigs disaster Kennedy worried:

If he [Khrushchev] thinks that I'm inexperienced or have no guts, we won't get anywhere with him. So we have to act and Vietnam looks like the place.[2]

At that time, there were 11,326 U.S. servicepeople in South Vietnam. Three thousand were advisors and the rest were support people. The United States had twelve flag officers, a third more than the total generals in the RVNAF. None of the U.S. flag officers had counterinsurgency training.

At the time of John F. Kennedy's death, there were twenty-three thousand U.S. advisors in Vietnam and U.S. deaths totaled 170.[3]

Lyndon B. Johnson

President Johnson shared the same view of Vietnam and the Cold War as Eisenhower. The domino theory was back in the White House. The National Security Action Memorandum (NSAM) 288 approved by Johnson in March 1964 enlarged the objectives of the United States: "We seek an independent non–Communist South Vietnam.... Unless we can achieve this objective in South Vietnam almost all of Southeast Asia will probably fall under Communist dominance."[4] Earlier, we had as our objective to help the South Vietnamese win their contest against the Communist conspiracy. Johnson rejected the section of NSAM 288 that called for the assumption by U.S. officers of the overall command of the entire war in Vietnam. The rationale for the rejection was negative impact on the South Vietnamese. It may also have occurred to President Johnson (and not the Pentagon) that it is easier to get out if you are merely advising than if you have told the world that you have taken over the war. Like a vampire, this rejected section of the NSAM would be resurrected annually by the Pentagon, and rejected each time it was raised. The war would remain an advisors' war with the South Vietnamese in command of their own units.

During 1964 the Vietcong targeted U.S. advisors in a series of attacks across the country. In August 1964 the Gulf of Tonkin incident occurred and as a result Johnson had new war powers from Congress. In December 1964, the Politburo in North Vietnam introduced a major change to the war. The war would now be fought as an invasion of South Vietnam by the NVA. General Westmoreland, the new commander of MACV who had replaced Harkins, saw the sudden change in terms of NVA regiments arriving in South Vietnam. In early 1965 NVA attacks included the Central Highlands (II Corps Tactical Zone) at Qui Nhon and Pleiku, where an attack on the air bases (Chu Hon and Camp Holloway) occurred. The Advisory Team 21 compound at Pleiku was a relic of the French war, and on 7 February 1965 the NVA attacked. Specialist 5 Jesse Pyle was on duty and detected the NVA advance. He opened fire, alerting the advisory team. In the ensuing battle Pyle was killed, and he was later awarded the Silver

Star for his valor. President Johnson retaliated with air strikes on North Vietnam.

The war was changing rapidly. Battalion advisors became more liaison officers than advisors because U.S. troop units were pouring in. Liaison between the U.S. and RVNAF forces was badly needed.

By the time LBJ left the presidency, our forces in Vietnam had peaked at 543,000. A total of 30,000 Americans had been killed.[5]

Richard M. Nixon

Richard M. Nixon was elected president in 1968, in part because he said he had a plan to end the war in Vietnam. His election was a close victory with a margin of less than 1 percent in the popular vote over Hubert Humphrey. On Nixon's inauguration day in 1969, he received a message from the Soviets. The Soviet Union wanted to pursue arms reduction, and this started the period in U.S. foreign relations known as détente.[6]

> Nevertheless, after hearing Laird's cheery report on the prospects of transforming RVNAF and its sister services into a force capable of holding off the North, Nixon adopted Vietnamization as a national policy. Détente with Moscow would make it work, or so Nixon and Kissinger believed, by trading treaties and agreements with the Soviets in return for a radical reduction in Soviet arms and supplies that made Hanoi's military activity possible.[7]

Nixon did not view Communism as a single monolith entity but rather as superpowers that could be dealt with separately. In this way, he pursued arms reduction with the Soviets while seeking to improve relations and trade with China. In the coming years he would play off one superpower against the other to support U.S. national interests. Vietnam became a pawn that Nixon used in his dealings with the other superpowers. Specifically, he would ask the Soviets and China to assist the United States in obtaining a peaceful exit from Vietnam. Nixon would threaten to discontinue arms reduction negotiations if the Soviets did not intercede with their ally North Vietnam. Unfortunately, Nixon would learn that the Soviets had less leverage over its ally North Vietnam than the United States had over the South Vietnamese president, Nguyen Van Thieu.[8]

By the time that Saigon fell to the NVA in 1975, the U.S. death toll was 58,159. Dead and wounded among the North and South Vietnamese ran into millions.

APPENDIX C

Lam Son 719 Result

Damage assessment during this campaign was difficult since the NVA held the ground before, during and after the fight. People sent in to assess damage were faced with the problems that they could come under fire at any time and that much of the area around Tchepone was shredded. It was difficult to

ALLIED LOSSES			ENEMY LOSSES
UNITED STATES			**TROOPS**
Dead: 102			Dead: About 13,000
Wounded: 215			(Saigon government figure)
Missing: 53			Captured: About 50
			(Saigon government figure)
SOUTH VIETNAM	Official figure	Unofficial report	**WEAPONS**
			Captured or Destroyed:
Dead:	1,146	3,800	1,968 crew-served
Wounded:	4,236	5,200	4,545 individual
Missing:	246	775	
			VEHICLES
HELICOPTERS			Captured or Destroyed:
Destroyed: 92			100 tanks 291 trucks
Cost about $30 million			
Damages to others about			**SUPPLIES**
$10 million			Captured or Destroyed:
			128,000 tons of ammunition
PLANES			1.3 million drums of gasoline
Destroyed: 5			7,600 yards of pipeline
Cost about $8 million			Food, medicine and clothing

Lam Son 719 Result (courtesy of Nguyen Duy Hinh).

determine how much damage had been inflicted on the NVA. Aerial reconnaissance was hampered by the mountainous terrain, anti-aircraft fire and heavy foliage. RVNAF general Nguyen Duy Hinh produced the table seen here, which is a best-educated guess about the damage done to the NVA. B-52s and close air support were the cause of nearly all of the destruction to the NVA. On the friendly side, one can see how the Saigon regime downplayed the RVNAF losses.[1]

Chapter Notes

Preface

1. Michael A. Eggleston, *Letters and Papers, 1954–2008*, draft manuscript.
2. Philip Caputo, *A Rumor of War* (New York: Henry Holt, 1977), 193–194.
3. See the Peers Commission report quoted within.
4. Paul G. Dailey, unpublished memoir.

Introduction

1. Nguyen Duy Hinh, *Lam Song 719*, Indochina Monographs (Fort McNair, Washington, DC: U.S. Army Center of Military History, 1979).
2. Stanley Karnow, *Vietnam: A History* (New York: Viking Press, 1983).
3. Michael A. Eggleston. *Letters and Papers, 1954–2008*, draft manuscript.
4. Tom Marshall, *The Price of Exit* (New York: Ballantine Books, 1998), 180.

Chapter One

1. Karnow, 135.
2. Karnow, 85.
3. Ho was known by several names over the years, but in this history I refer to him by the last name that he used.
4. Karnow, 121.

5. Karnow, 140.
6. Karnow, 144.
7. Karnow, 145.
8. Not really; the Japanese were allowed to retain their emperor, Hirohito, who was not tried as a war criminal as some say he should have been.
9. Karnow, 147.
10. Karnow, 147.
11. Karnow, 135.
12. Karnow, 150.
13. I recall traveling the route that Dr. Fall described as the "Street without Joy" Route 1 in 1966. As we would say, this was "Indian Country." You could be attacked at any time and nothing had changed since the events that Dr. Fall described during the French war. I was ready to fight and I looked back at the seat behind me and there was a Vietnamese guard with his .45-caliber pistol out and ready. He swayed back and forth and did not look friendly. The muzzle of his .45 was aimed at the back of my head. I thought that if we got fired on he would blow my head off by accident or on purpose. We survived the trip without an ambush. To this day, I am not sure which side this guy was on.
14. Harold G. Moore and Joseph L. Galloway, *We Were Soldiers Once ... and Young: Ia Drang—the Battle That Changed the War in Vietnam* (New York: Harper-Collins, 1992).
15. Karnow, 169.
16. Karnow, 172–173.

17. Karnow, 178.
18. Karnow, 188.
19. Dean Acheson, *Present at the Creation: My Years in the State Department* (New York: W. W. Norton, 1969), 691.
20. Karnow, 188. In some ways this battle was similar to Lam Son 719, fought nearly twenty years later.
21. Karnow, 196.
22. Karnow, 191.
23. The United States had decided to shore up a weak, incompetent ally, France, by providing a small amount of air support, but it did not come close to what would be needed at Dien Bien Phu.
24. Karnow, 195.
25. Karnow, 196.
26. McGovern and Buford are not listed on the Vietnam Memorial wall, nor are several other people killed before the earliest casualties on the wall, which start with 1959. Conventions needed to be established when the people who conceived the wall got started, and for some reason best known to themselves Jan Scruggs, who founded the memorial, and others chose 1959 as the start of casualties on the wall. On the other end was the decision about whose names should be entered on the wall after the war. A good example is Lewis Burwell Puller, Jr. Puller was a marine like his father, "Chesty" Puller, and was badly wounded in Vietnam. Lewis survived but lost both legs and other body parts and was the subject of at least one book. He finally killed himself years later. It was decided that Puller's name should not be on the wall.
27. Karnow, 204.
28. A. J. Langguth, *Our Vietnam: The War 1954–1975* (New York: Simon & Schuster, 2000), 91.
29. Henry Kissinger, *Ending the Vietnam War: A History of American's Involvement in and Extrication from the Vietnam War* (New York: Simon & Schuster, 2003), 25.
30. Karnow, 238.
31. Karnow, 214.

Chapter Two

1. See appendix B.
2. Maurice Isserman and Michael Kazan, *America Divided: The Civil War in the 1960s* (Oxford: Oxford University Press, 2008), 88.
3. Kevin Daugherty and Jason Stewart, *The Timeline of the Vietnam War* (San Diego, CA: Thunder Bay Press, 2008), 50. Faking operations meant that the RVNAF planned an operation, did nothing, and then reported a fraudulent victory to Saigon. It was safe for the RVNAF in the field to do this since no one in Saigon checked. In addition to the Halberstam article on Ap Bac, U.S. advisors and helicopter crew members observed the RVNAF performance and word went back to the Pentagon.
4. Langguth, 202. Ap Bac was considered to be the first major victory of the Vietcong since Dien Bien Phu.
5. Isserman and Kazan, 87.
6. Langguth, 204–205; Neil Sheehan, *A Bright Shining Lie: John Paul Vann and America in Vietnam* (New York: Random House, 1988), 263–265.
7. George C. Herring, *America's Longest War: The United States and Vietnam, 1950–1975* (Boston: McGraw-Hill, 2002), 113.
8. Langguth, 208; Arthur M. Schlesinger, Jr., *A Thousand Days: John F. Kennedy in the White House* (New York: Houghton Mifflin, 2002), 985.
9. Deborah Shapley, *Promise and Power: The Life and Times of Robert McNamara* (Boston: Little, Brown, 1993), 250. Diem would be killed later in 1963. The point is that Diem's views and actions in 1963 were precisely the same as the South Vietnamese president Thieu's in 1971 during and after Lam Son 719. It seems that the South Vietnamese would never change their way of doing business.
10. Karnow, x.
11. This conclusion by Karnow is hard to support. It would appear that most historians provide evidence to prove that Ho was a communist and not a nationalist, but it all depends upon the time frame. When as a young man he appeared in 1919 in Geneva, where World War I peace accords were being discussed, he was obviously a nationalist and asked for an interview with Woodrow Wilson to promote Vietnam independence. Unfortunately, Ho's request to see President Wilson was denied.
12. Karnow, 11.

13. Karnow, 262
14. Karnow 262.
15. Sheehan, 313.
16. Sheehan, 316. Vann shared the same dry sense of humor with Sheehan. It made life livable.
17. Sully would return after Diem's death. He was later killed when his aircraft crashed.
18. Sheehan, 283.
19. Lewis Sorley. *Honorable Warrior: General Harold K. Johnson and the Ethics of Command* (Lawrence: University Press of Kansas, 1998), 153.
20. Maxwell D. Taylor. *Swords and Plowshares, A Memoir* (New York: Da Capo Press, 1972), 291.
21. Sorley, *Honorable Warrior*, 153.
22. Mark Moyar, *Triumph Forsaken: The Vietnam War, 1954–1965* (Cambridge: Cambridge University Press, 2006), 179.
23. Moyar, 201.
24. Moyar, 201.
25. Sheehan, 270–272.
26. Langguth, 204.
27. Karnow, 265.
28. Langguth, 216.
29. Karnow, 277.
30. Karnow, 310–311.
31. The concept was that villagers forced to leave their village and concentrated in a fortified hamlet in theory would be defended and safer.
32. Karnow, 324.
33. Karnow, 325.
34. Karnow, 326.
35. A fellow advisor told me that he got trapped and was faced with a charging Vietcong fellow who did not mean him well. My friend emptied his M2 carbine in this guy's chest and he kept coming. Finally, my friend pulled his .45 pistol and shot the guy in his face, which blew his head off. That stopped the attack.
36. Michael A. Eggleston. *Letters and Papers, 1954–2008*, draft manuscript.
37. Listen to the Pete Seeger song "Where Have All the Flowers Gone?" performed by Joan Baez.

Chapter Three

1. Sorley, *Honorable Warrior*, 241.

2. James Allan Long, unpublished memoir.
3.. Michael Cason, unpublished memoir.
4. Sheehan, 379; H. R. McMasters, *Dereliction of Duty: Johnson, McNamara, the Joint Chiefs of Staff, and the Lies That Led to Vietnam* (New York: Harper Perennial, 1997), 130.
5. Shapley, 600–601.
6. Shapley, 589.
7. Greg Mitchell, "When an Artist, in Vietnam Era, Tried to Drown Robert McNamara—and Nearly Did It," *Huffington Post*, July 7, 2009.
8. Karnow, 436–437.
9. Ken Fugate, unpublished memoir.
10. Jim Van Alstin, unpublished memoir.
11. Loren J. Kindler, unpublished memoir.
12. Ronald S. Simpkins, unpublished memoir.
13. Charles F. Bernitt, unpublished memoir.
14.. Olen. C. Phipps, unpublished memoir.
15. Years later, after a Mike Wallace broadcast accused Westmoreland of suppressing the truth, Westmoreland sued. An out-of-court settlement was arranged.
16. Karnow, 534.
17. Phillip B. Davidson, *Vietnam at War: The History 1946–1975* (New York: Oxford University Press, 1988), 486.
18. Forrest "Sonny" C. Ashcraft, unpublished memoir.
19. Bill Garbett, unpublished memoir.
20. Bill Comrey, unpublished memoir.
21. Danté M. Puccetti, unpublished memoir.

Chapter Four

1. Jack Harrigan, unpublished memoir.
2. Isserman and Kazan, 67–68.
3. Isserman and Kazan, 78.
4. Karnow, 358.
5. James Allan Long, unpublished memoir.
6. Michael A. Eggleston, *Letters and Papers, 1954–2008*, draft manuscript.
7. Caputo, xv.

8. Michael A. Eggleston. *Letters and Papers, 1954–2008*, draft manuscript.

9. Philip Duncan Hoffman, *Humping Heavy: A Vietnam Memoir* (2011), 195.

10. I do not believe that the world will ever understand why draft evaders who had committed criminal acts received unconditional pardons from President Carter. Carter was not reelected to the presidency.

11. Michael A. Eggleston. *Letters and Papers, 1954–2008*, draft manuscript.

12. James M. McPherson. *The Negro's Civil War: How American Blacks Felt and Acted During the Civil War* (New York: Vintage Books, 1965), 163.

13. Some dispute the blank check theory, but if one reads the public law the notion of a blank check is inescapable.

14. David Reynolds, *One World Divisible: A Global History Since 1945* (New York: W. W. Norton, 2000), 283.

15. Jeremy Varon, *Bringing the War Home: The Weather Underground, the Red Army Faction, and Revolutionary Violence in the Sixties and Seventies* (Berkeley: University of California Press, 2004), 123.

16. Varon, 157.

17. Sheehan, 717.

18. Richard Nixon, *No More Vietnams* (New York: Arbor House, 1985), 126.

Chapter Five

1. Sheehan, 380.

2. Keith William Nolan, *Into Laos: The Story of Dewey Canyon II/Lam Son 719, 1971* (Novato, CA: Presidio Press, 1986), 20–21.

3. Nolan, 22.

4. Nolan, 25.

5. Isserman and Kazan, 67.

6. David Fulghum, Terrance Maitland, and the editors of Boston Publishing Company, *The Vietnam Experience: South Vietnam on Trial: The Test of Vietnamization, 1970–1972* (Boston: Boston Publishing, 1984), 26.

7. General Bruce Palmer, Jr., *The 25 Year War: America's Military Role In Vietnam* (Lexington: University Press of Kentucky, 1984), 155.

8. Nolan, 23.

9. Fulghum et al., *The Vietnam Experience*, 43.

10. Eric Blaine Riker-Coleman, *Reflection and Reform: Professionalism and Ethics in the U.S. Army Officer Corps, 1968–1975* (Chapel Hill: University of North Carolina Press, 1977), 28–29.

11. Usually at least a Bronze Star with "V" and other awards.

12. Fulghum et al., 47–49.

13. A demonstration of the pathetic culture of flag officers during and after the Vietnam War occurred when a chief of naval operations during the Clinton administration falsified his record to indicate that his awarding of the Bronze Star was for valor and not achievement. Unsurprisingly, when his crime was discovered and publicized, he committed suicide in his Pentagon office.

14. Fulghum et al., 47.

15. Nolan, 26–27.

16. Nolan, 27.

17. Raymond Z. Fraley, unpublished memoir.

18. Fulghum et al., 36.

19. Military Pay Certificates (MPCs) were not new in Vietnam. They had been used in earlier wars. It was an attempt to stop the black market and the enemy from using our U.S. greenbacks to buy weapons and other things used against us.

20. Michael A. Eggleston, unpublished memoir.

21. James Hilton, *Lost Horizon*.

22. Fulghum et al., 9.

23. Fulghum et al., 8.

24. Fulghum et al., 9.

25. Michael A. Eggleston, unpublished memoir.

26. Lewis Sorley, *Westmoreland: The General Who Lost Vietnam* (Boston: Houghton Mifflin Harcourt, 2011), 242.

27. "Mad minute" is a reference to a firing demonstration when at the end everyone fires all of their ammunition to impress the spectators.

28. Fulghum et al., 15.

29. Jeremy Kuzmarov, *The Myth of the Addicted Army: Vietnam and the Modern War on Drugs* (Boston: University of Massachusetts Press, 2009).

30. See Vice Chief of Staff General Bruce Palmer's history.

31. Fulghum et al., 16.

32. Fulghum et al., 20.
33. Fulghum et al., 22.
34. Michael A. Eggleston, unpublished memoir.
35. I told our priest that when I died I wanted the choir to sing Daniel Powter's song "Bad Day." The priest could hardly stop laughing but in the end agreed. Maybe other veterans would like the same. We all had a bad day at one time or another in combat.
36. http://www.war-veterans.org/Maggie.htm.
37. Jim Lovins. Unpublished memoir.
38. Michael A. Eggleston, unpublished memoir.
39. Michael A. Eggleston, unpublished memoir.
40. Jim Lovins, unpublished memoir.
41. Michael A. Eggleston, unpublished memoir.
42. Fulghum et al., 37.
43. Fulghum et al., 38.
44. William C. Westmoreland, *A Soldier Reports* (New York: Doubleday, 1976), 332.
45. Shapley, 431.
46. Riker-Coleman, 31.
47. Caputo, 126.

Chapter Six

1. Morley Safer, *Flashbacks: On Returning to Vietnam* (New York: Random House, 1990), 203.
2. Alexander M. Haig, Jr., *Inner Circles: How America Changed the World: A Memoir* (New York: Warner Books, 1992), 226.
3. Nguyen Duy Hinh, *Vietnamization and the Cease-Fire*, Indochina Monographs (Fort McNair, Washington, DC: U.S. Army Center of Military History, 1984), 27.
4. Hinh, *Vietnamization and the Cease-Fire*, 32.
5. Hinh, *Vietnamization and the Cease-Fire*, 96.
6. Hinh, *Vietnamization and the Cease-Fire*, 96.
7. Fulghum et al., 63–64.
8. Sheehan, 739.
9. General Thomas Matthew Rienzi.

Communications-Electronics, 1962–1970, Vietnam Studies (Washington, DC: U.S. Government Printing Office, 1972), 172.
10. Ken Fugate, unpublished memoir.
11. Sheehan, 572.
12. I could describe it, but I do not want to provide a blueprint for crazy people who want to kill other human beings.
13. See the song by the Animals with Eric Burdon from this period, which was very popular in Vietnam, "We Gotta Get Out of This Place."

Chapter Seven

1. Lewis Sorley, *Thunderbolt: General Creighton Abrams and the Army of His Times* (Bloomington: Indiana University Press, 2008), 305.
2. Fulghum et al., 64–65.
3. Hinh, *Lam Song 719*, 8.
4. Kissinger, *Ending*, 163–164.
5. Jeffrey Kimball, *Nixon's Vietnam War* (Lawrence: University Press of Kansas, 1998), 211.
6. Nixon, 120.
7. Kissinger, *Ending*, 169–170.
8. Kissinger, *Ending*, 169.
9. Kissinger, *Ending*, 172–173.
10. Kissinger, *Ending*, 172–173.
11. Palmer, 103–104.
12. Willard J. Webb and Walter S. Pool, *The Joint Chiefs of Staff and War in Vietnam, 1971–1973* (Washington, DC.: Office of Joint History, 2007), 7.
13. Sorley, *A Better War: The Unexamined Victories and Final Tragedy of America's Last Years in Vietnam* (New York: Harcourt, 1999), 255.
14. Sorley, *Thunderbolt*, 307.
15. Dale Van Atta and President Gerald R. Ford, *With Honor: Melvin Laird in War, Peace, and Politics* (Madison: University of Wisconsin Press, 2008), 345.
16. Van Atta and Ford, 345.
17. Westmoreland glossed over his role in the JCS plan. All that he said in his memoirs (474) was: "Because of the prohibition on funds for American ground troops operating outside South Vietnam imposed by the United States Senate in December 1970, American ground troops were unable to participate in the opera-

tion, but the American command furnished much of the logistical, air, and long range artillery support primarily from a reactivated combat base at Khe Sanh. Not even American advisors were permitted to accompany RVNAF units." In keeping with the "blame game" Westmoreland then went on with a long rant blaming the South Vietnamese, but it was not that simple.

18. Haig gives us his account of Lam Son 719 but not his role in the JCS plan, although his role in the White House is very self-focused and self-serving. Haig's account of Lam Son 719 (274–278) tells history nothing that is not already known. There are a few exceptions. The blame game continued. Haig blamed U.S. air support (274). He then quoted Kissinger as saying, "Well, Al, your military finally got what it wanted, and they've____ it up" (274). Haig's comments seemed to be unrelated to the reality of what had happened. For example, Haig complained that the U.S. artillery was too far away from the action to affect the outcome, and of course they were: they were in South Vietnam and could not provide artillery support to an action miles away without any on-site fire control and since U.S. helicopters were being shot down with disturbing frequency, there was no fire control available by air. Haig blamed Abrams (276) like most others. He should have blamed himself for the whole debacle. Haig got one thing right: "On April 7 [1971] American pilots reported that NVA truck traffic on the Ho Chi Minh Trail appeared to be back to normal" (278).

19. Van Atta and Ford, 346.

20. Sorley, *A Better War*, 270–271.

21. Kissinger, *Ending*, 190.

22. Kissinger, *Ending*, 193.

23. Kissinger, *Ending*, 194.

24. Kissinger, *Ending*, 195.

25. Hinh, *Lam Son 719*, 168.

26. I worked for Al Haig at West Point during the period 1967–1968 and have the greatest respect for his abilities. He combined the attributes of a good soldier and a master politician. Beyond that he was quite a likeable person. He could deal with privates to presidents with great ease as the world has seen and they would like and respect him for that. At times, he could let his elegant rhetoric become detached from the facts.

27. Hinh, *Lam Song 719*, 8.

28. Hinh, *Lam Song 719*, 36–39.

29. Hinh, *Lam Song 719*, 30.

30. Hinh, *Lam Song 719*, 156.

31. Nolan, 30.

32. Fulghum et al., 72.

33. Kissinger, *Ending*, 196; Langguth, 576. While the Cooper-Church Amendment prohibited U.S. forces from entering Laos (and other countries), the use of airpower in Laos was allowed. In all cases, the United States limited access to planning because of the worry that the NVA would get the information from the RVNAF, which was a valid cause for concern.

34. Webb and Pool, 7.

35. Langguth, 577. The estimate of the number of NVA on the ground varies widely according to which historian one reads and what phase of the battle one is referring to. Estimates on the number of NVA run from twenty-two to sixty thousand.

36. Langguth, 577.

37. Fulghum et al., 70.

38. Karnow, 629.

39. At this time, U.S. citizens were encouraged to write to soldiers to encourage them and see how they were doing. Through some magic, soldier addresses were made available and citizens, kids, adults, whatever, wrote to the troops. I kept all of the letters sent to me and they were really a morale booster for all of us.

40. Davidson, 646.

41. Hinh, *Lam Song 719*, 57; Davidson, 644. It was not only quantity but quality of NVA anti-air that was a concern. During Lam Son 719 some accounts indicate that the NVA had radar-controlled guns that increased their lethality. The results speak for themselves: During this operation 107 U.S. helicopters went down. The RVNAF had additional aircraft losses.

42. Karnow, 629–630. This is disputed by others who claim no such order was given, but the fact remains that Thieu stopped the attack for reasons not explained.

43. Kissinger, *Ending*, 198.

44. Kissinger, *Ending*, 198.

45. Kissinger, *Ending*, 198; Sorley, *A Better War*, 243–271.

46. This is similar to British prime minister Neville Chamberlain's speech on the eve of World War II "Peace in Our Time."

47. Karnow, 632.

48. Fulghum et al., 70; Sorley, *A Better War*, 246.

49. Fulghum et al., 72–73.

50. Fulghum et al., 88.

51. Fulghum et al., 70.

52. The ambush was at Mang Yang Pass near An Khe and is considered to be the last battle of the French war. See the account by Dr. Bernard Fall in his book *Street Without Joy: The French Debacle in Indo China* (Mechanicsburg, PA: Stackpole Books, 1994).

53. I recall being near a B-52 bombing raid, though still some distance away. There was no sound of aircraft, no sound of anything, until what I can only describe as a severe earthquake lifted me off of the ground and dropped me hard.

54. Webb and Pool, 7.

55. Fulghum et al., 75.

56. Fulghum et al., 82.

57. Fulghum et al., 83.

58. Hinh, *Lam Song 719*, 55.

59. Fulghum et al., 83.

60. Sorley, *Thunderbolt*, 308.

61. Karnow, 629–630.

62. Kissinger, *Ending*, 200.

63. Van Atta and Ford, 347.

64. Nixon, 137.

65. Kissinger, *Ending*, 200–201.

66. Van Atta, 348.

67. Sorley, *Thunderbolt*, 309.

68. Kissinger, *Ending*, 188.

69. Fulghum et al., 85–86.

70. Hinh, *Lam Song 719*, 90.

71. Fulghum et al., 86.

72. Fulghum et al., 87.

73. Marshall, 230–231.

74. Van Atta and Ford, 349–350.

75. Webb and Pool, 16–17.

76. Kimball, 246; Langguth, 579.

77. Karnow, 629; Kissinger, *Ending*, 193; Langguth, 579; Henry Kissinger, *White House Years* (Boston: Little, Brown, 1979), 1009.

78. Haig, 275.

79. Van Atta and Ford, 350.

80. Haig, 274.

81. Webb and Pool, 15.

82. Davidson, 650.

83. Davidson, 248.

84. Davidson, 674, 65, 653, 640–641.

85. Van Atta and Ford, 350.

86. Davidson, 660.

87. Kimball, 247.

88. Sorley, *Thunderbolt*, 306.

89. The success of Vietnamization was a myth of unimaginable proportions. In my discussions with John Paul Vann at that time, he was dismayed by the lack of South Vietnamese ability and will to fight. He wanted me to return my troops and replace the South Vietnamese at his location. It was too late. My troops were boarding airplanes to go home and I would soon follow.

90. Karnow, 632.

91. Karnow, 632.

92. Van Atta, 351.

93. Bui Diem, *In the Jaws of History* (Bloomington: Indiana University Press, 1999), 287.

94. Van Atta, 351.

95. Sorley, *A Better War*, 262.

96. Sorley, *A Better War*, 262.

97. Langguth, 579.

98. Sorley, *A Better War*, 231–235.

99. Davidson, 649.

100. Chuck Gross, *Rattler One-Seven: A Vietnam Helicopter Pilot's War Story* (Denton: University of North Texas Press, 2004), 180.

101. I worked for General Vessey when I was on the Army Staff and later when I was on the Joint Staff and he was chairman of the JCS. When I disagreed with him (as a junior officer can only respectfully do), he would just say, "Okay, good, let me think about what you and the others have said before I make my decision. I'll let you know." He always did. We were both Minnesotans. I was from Saint Paul and he was raised in Anoka, a small nearby town. I do not think that he knew that, but even if he did, it would not have affected the way that he treated me or anyone else as one of his subordinates.

102. Van Atta and Ford, 352.

Chapter Eight

1. Nixon, 141–142.

2. H. R. Haldeman, *The Ends of Power* (New York: Time Books, 1978), 122.

3. Karnow, 644.

4. Karnow, 642.

5. Langguth, 596.

6. Langguth, 576.

7. Sheehan, 775.
8. Karnow, 641.
9. Karnow, 639–641.
10. Langguth, 598.
11. Sorley, *Thunderbolt*, 322–323.
12. Fulghum et al., 140.
13. Karnow, 641.
14. Nixon, 146.
15. Sorley, *Thunderbolt*, 320.
16. Sheehan, 755.
17. Davidson, 709.
18. Sheehan, 760–763.
19. Sheehan, 763.
20. Sheehan, 785.
21. Sheehan, 786.
22. Sheehan, 789.
23. Sorley, *Thunderbolt*, 328.
24. Sheehan, 785.
25. Paul Michael Bryant, Sr., unpublished memoir.
26. Paul G. Dailey, unpublished memoir.
27. Karnow, 648.
28. Karnow, 657.
29. Karnow, 664.
30. Karnow, 664.
31. Langguth, 647; Karnow, 665.
32. Langguth, 647.
33. In Saigon one could visit what we would today call a "mall." There were many vendors selling gold in all forms at the prevailing rates. The convenient thing was that aside from gold bars (bulky and heavy) one could purchase gold leaf sheets. These were small and light, the sort of thing that you could split up among your family members if you were fleeing for your lives.
34. General Cao Van Vien, *The Final Collapse* (Honolulu: University Press of the Pacific, 2005), 119. The extent to which the RVNAF would go to mask cowardice and corruption within their ranks is amazing. Vien tells the reader that Phu was admitted to a hospital in Saigon because he was no longer mentally able to exercise command. General Davidson was more candid: "Phu and most of the other senior officers of II Corps abandoned the troops and flew to Nha Trang before the operation even started" (778). Phu killed himself as the NVA entered Saigon.
35. Karnow, 665.
36. George J. Veith. *Black April: The Fall of South Vietnam, 1973–75.* (New York: Encounter Books, 2012), 210.

37. Veith, 216.
38. Karnow, 666.
39. Karnow, 661.
40. Vien, 155.
41. Karnow, 666.
42. Langguth, 658.
43. In 1966, all advisors at Pleiku assembled at Pleiku Airbase to welcome General Nguyen Coa Ky on his visit to see the troops. It was a real treat. Out jumped Ky from his aircraft and his wife quickly followed. They were wearing his and hers matching flight suits. In Mandarin style, the RVNAF generals rushed forward to pay tribute to Ky. Bob Mulholland, a fellow advisor, was standing next to me and started to break up over the scene. I gave him a sharp elbow and said, "For God's sake don't laugh or we'll all get into trouble." We suppressed our laughter until Ky left. Our takeaway was that this whole war was a charade designed to make the RVNAF leadership look good while they shipped funds to their Swiss bank accounts. They were ridiculous clowns.
44. Karnow, 669.
45. Langguth, 668.

Appendix B

1. Michael Lind, *Vietnam, The Necessary War* (New York: Simon & Schuster, 1999), 34.
2. Mark C. Carnes and John A. Garraty, *American Destiny: Narrative of a Nation*, vol. 2, *Since 1865* (New York: Penguin Academics, 2006), 831.
3. Tamara Roleff, *The Vietnam War* (San Diego, CA: Greenhaven Press, 2002), 16.
4. Davidson, 314–315.
5. Karnow, 601.
6. Henry Kissinger, *White House Years*, 132.
7. Haig, 228–229.
8. Carnes and Garraty, 847.

Appendix C

1. Hinh, *Lam Song 719*, 128.

Bibliography

Primary Sources

BOOKS

Acheson, Dean. *Present at the Creation: My Years in the State Department.* New York: W. W. Norton, 1969.

Baker, Mark. *Nam.* New York: William Morrow, 1982.

Caputo, Philip. *A Rumor of War.* New York: Henry Holt, 1977.

Dockery, Martin J. *Lost in Translation: Vietnam: A Combat Advisor's Story.* New York: Ballantine Books, 2003.

Dooley, George E. *Battle for the Central Highlands: A Special Forces Story.* New York: Ballantine Books, 2003.

Ellsberg, Daniel. *Secrets: A Memoir of Vietnam and the Pentagon Papers.* New York: Penguin, 2002.

Frost, David. *Frost/Nixon: Behind the Scenes of the Nixon Interviews.* New York: Harper Perennial, 2007.

Giap, Vo Nguyen. *How We Won the War.* Philadelphia: Recon, 1976.

Haig, Alexander M., Jr. *Inner Circles: How America Changed the World: A Memoir.* New York: Warner Books, 1992.

Joyce, James. *Pucker Factor 10: Memoir of a U.S. Helicopter Pilot in Vietnam.* Jefferson, NC: McFarland, 2003.

Just, Ward, ed. *Reporting Vietnam: American Journalism 1959–1975.* New York: Literary Classics of the United States, 2000.

Kerry, Bob. *When I Was a Young Man: A Memoir.* New York: Harcourt, 2002.

Kissinger, Henry. *Ending the Vietnam War: A History of American's Involvement in and Extrication from the Vietnam War.* New York: Simon & Schuster, 2003.

_____. *White House Years.* Boston: Little, Brown, 1979.

Kitchin, Dennis. *War in Aquarius: Memoir of an American Infantryman in Action Along the Cambodian Border During the Vietnam War.* Jefferson, NC: McFarland, 1994.

Lanning, Michael Lee. *The Only War We Had: A Platoon Leader's Journal of Vietnam.* New York: Ballantine Books, 1987.

Lawrence, A. T. *Crucible Vietnam: Memoir of an Infantry Lieutenant.* Jefferson, NC: McFarland, 2009.

Loving, John C. *Combat Advisor: How America Won the War and Lost the Peace.* New York: iUniverse, 2006.

Luan, Nguyen Cong. *Nationalist in the Vietnam Wars: Memoirs of a Victim Turned Soldier.* Bloomington: Indiana University Press, 2012.

Manchester, William. *Remembering Kennedy: One Brief Shining Moment.* Boston: Little, Brown, 1983.

Marshall, Tom. *The Price of Exit.* New York: Ballantine Books, 1998.

Moore, Harold G., and Joseph L. Galloway. *We Are Soldiers Still: A Journey Back to the Battlefields of Vietnam.* New York: Harper Perennial, 2008.

_____. *We Were Soldiers Once … and Young: Ia Drang—the Battle That Changed the War in Vietnam.* New York: HarperCollins, 1992.

Moore, Robin. *The Green Berets.* New York: Crown, 1965.

Nesser, John A. *Ghosts of Thua Thien: An American Soldier's Memoir of Vietnam.* Jefferson, NC: McFarland, 2008.

North, Oliver L. *Under Fire: An American Story.* New York: HarperCollins, 1991.

Park, Stephen L. *Boots: An Unvarnished Memoir of Vietnam.* Boston: Writers Amuse Me Publishing, 2012.

Pezzoli, Ray, Jr. *A Year in Hell: Memoir of an American Foot Soldier Turned Reporter in Vietnam 1965–1966.* Jefferson, NC: McFarland, 2006.

Safer, Morley. *Flashbacks: On Returning to Vietnam.* New York: Random House, 1990.

Santoli, Al. *Everything We Had: An Oral History of the Vietnam War.* New York: Ballantine Books, 1981.

Schwarzkopf, General H. Norman. *The Autobiography: It Doesn't Take a Hero.* New York: Bantam Books, 1992.

Taylor, Maxwell D. *Swords and Plowshares: A Memoir.* New York: Da Capo Press, 1972.

Terry, Wallace. *Bloods: An Oral History of the Vietnam War.* New York: Ballantine Books, 1985.

Tram, Dang Thuy. *Last Night I Dreamed of Peace: The Diary of Dang Thuy Tram.* New York: Three Rivers Press, 2007.

Uhl, Michael. *Vietnam Awakening: My Journey from Combat to the Citizens' Commission of Inquiry on U.S. War Crimes.* Jefferson, NC: McFarland, 2007.

Veith, George J. *Black April: The Fall of South Vietnam, 1973–75.* New York: Encounter Books, 2012.

Vien, General Cao Van. *The Final Collapse.* Honolulu: University Press of the Pacific, 2005.

Westmoreland, William C. *A Soldier Reports.* New York: Doubleday, 1976.

WEB SITES

http://thewall-usa.com [last visited on 1 December 2012].

http://www.war-veterans.org/Maggie.htm [last visited on 15 June 2013].

UNPUBLISHED MATERIALS

Ashcraft, Forrest "Sonny." Unpublished memoir.

Bernitt, Charles F. Unpublished memoir.

Bryant, Paul Michael, Sr. Unpublished memoir.

Cason, Michael. Unpublished memoir.

Comrey, Bill. Unpublished memoir.

Dailey, Paul G. Unpublished memoir.

Eggleston, Michael A. *Letters and Papers, 1954–2008.* Draft manuscript.

_____. Unpublished memoir.

Fraley, Raymond Z. Unpublished memoir.

Fugate, Ken. Unpublished memoir.

Garbett, Bill. Unpublished memoir.

Harrigan. Jack. Unpublished memoir.

Kindler, Loren J. Unpublished memoir.

Long, James Allan. Unpublished memoir.

Lovins, Jim. Unpublished memoir.

Phipps, Olen C. Unpublished memoir.

Puccetti, Danté M. Unpublished memoir.

Simpkins, Ronald S., Sr. Unpublished memoir.

Van Alstin, Jim. Unpublished memoir.

Secondary Sources

BOOKS

Abu-Lughod, Janet L. *Race, Space, and Riots in Chicago, New York, and Los Angeles.* Oxford: Oxford University Press, 2007.

Allen, Michael J. *Until the Last Man Comes Home: POWs, MIAs and the Unending Vietnam War.* Chapel Hill: University of North Carolina Press, 2009.

Anderson, Louis E. *John F. Kennedy.* Stamford, CT: Brompton Books, 1992.

Andreas, Peter, and Kelly M. Greenhill. *Sex, Drugs and Body Counts: The Politics of Numbers in Global Crime and Conflict.* Ithaca, NY: Cornell University Press, 2010.

Apply, Christian G. *Working Class War: American Combat Soldiers in Vietnam.* Chapel Hill: University of North Carolina Press, 1993.

Arnett, Peter. *Live from the Battlefield.* New York: Simon & Schuster, 1994.

Association of Graduates, United States Military Academy. *The Register of Graduates and Former Cadets of the United States Military, 2010.* West Point, NY: Association of Graduates, 2010.

Atkinson, Rick. *The Long Gray Line: The American Journey of West Point's Class of 1966.* New York: Henry Holt, 1989.

Berman, Larry. *No Peace, No Honor: Nixon, Kissinger, and Betrayal in Vietnam.* New York: Free Press, 2001.

Berman, Paul. *A Tale of Two Utopias: The Political Journey of the Generation of 1986.* New York: W. W. Norton, 1996.

Bradley, Mark Phillip. *Imagining Vietnam and America: The Making of Postcolonial Vietnam, 1919–1950.* Chapel Hill: University of North Carolina Press, 2000.

Braestrup, Peter. *The Big Story.* Novato, CA: Presidio Press, 1994.

Carey, Elaine. *Plaza of Sacrifices: Gender, Power, and Terror in 1968 Mexico.* Albuquerque: University of New Mexico Press, 2005.

Carnes, Mark C., and John A. Garraty. *American Destiny: Narrative of a Nation. Vol. 2: Since 1865.* New York: Penguin Academics, 2006.

Carter, James M. *Inventing Vietnam: The United States and State Building 1954–1968.* New York: Cambridge University Press, 2008.

Central Intelligence Agency, Office of Current Intelligence. *Lam Son Summary.* 1973.

Chafe, William H. *Civilities and Civil Rights: Greensboro, North Carolina, and the Black Struggle for Freedom.* Oxford: Oxford University Press, 1980.

_____. *The Unfinished Journey: America Since World War II.* New York: Oxford University Press, 2007.

Clodfelter, Michael. *Mad Minutes and Vietnam Months: A Soldier's Memoir.* Jefferson, NC: McFarland, 1988.

Coleman, J. D. *Incursion.* New York: St. Martin's Paperbacks, 1991.

_____. *Pleiku: The Dawn of Helicopter Warfare in Vietnam.* New York: St. Martin's Press, 1988.

Colodny, Len. *Silent Coup.* New York: St. Martin's Press, 1991.

Daugherty, Kevin, and Jason Stewart. *The Timeline of the Vietnam War.* San Diego, CA: Thunder Bay Press, 2008.

Daugherty, Leo, and Gregory Louis Mattson. *Nam: A Photographic History.* Singapore: Michael Friedman Publishing, 2001.

Davidson, Phillip B. *Secrets of the Vietnam War.* Novato, CA: Presidio Press, 1990.

_____. *Vietnam at War: The History 1946–1975.* New York: Oxford University Press, 1988.

Diem, Bui. *In the Jaws of History.* Bloomington: Indiana University Press, 1999.

Dudziak, Mary L. *Cold War Civil Rights: Race and the Image of American*

Democracy. Princeton, NJ: Princeton University Press, 2000.

Duong, Van Nguyen. *Tragedy of the Vietnam War: A South Vietnamese Officer's Analysis.* Jefferson, NC: McFarland, 2008.

Fall, Bernard B. *Street Without Joy: The French Debacle in Indo China.* Mechanicsburg, PA: Stackpole Books, 1994.

Fitzgerald, Frances. *Fire in the Lake: The Vietnamese and the Americans in Vietnam.* New York: Back Bay Books, 1972.

Flamm, Michael W. *Law and Order: Street Crime, Civil Unrest, and the Crisis of Liberalism in the 1960s.* New York: Columbia University Press, 2005.

Foley, Michael S. *Confronting the War Machine: Draft Resistance During the Vietnam War.* Chapel Hill: University of North Carolina Press, 2003.

Fulghum, David, Terrance Mailtand, and the editors of Boston Publishing Company. *The Vietnam Experience: South Vietnam on Trial: The Test of Vietnamization, 1970–1972.* Boston: Boston Publishing, 1984.

Goldman, Peter, and Tony Fuller. *Charlie Company: What Vietnam Did to Us.* New York: William Morrow, 1983.

Goldstein, Joseph, Burke Marshall, and Jack Schwartz. *The My Lai Massacre and Its Cover-up: Beyond the Reach of the Law? The Peers Report with a Supplement and Introductory Essay on the Limits of Law.* New York: Free Press, 1976.

Green, Anna, and Kathleen Troup. *The House of History: A Critical Reader in Twentieth-Century History and Theory.* New York: New York University Press, 1999.

Gross, Chuck. *Rattler One-Seven: A Vietnam Helicopter Pilot's War Story.* Denton: University of North Texas Press, 2004.

Halberstam, David. *The Fifties.* New York: Random House, 1993.

_____. *The Making of a Quagmire.* New York: Ballantine Books, 1964.

Haldeman, H. R. *The End of Power.* New York: Time Books, 1978.

Herring, George C. *America's Longest War: The United States and Vietnam, 1950–1975.* Boston: McGraw-Hill, 2002.

_____. *LBJ and Vietnam. Administrative History of the Johnson Presidency.* Austin: University of Texas Press, 1994.

_____. *The Pentagon Papers.* New York: McGraw-Hill, 1993.

Hinh, Nguyen Duy. *Lam Song 719.* Indochina Monographs. Fort McNair, Washington, DC: U.S. Army Center of Military History, 1979.

_____. *Vietnamization and the Cease-Fire.* Indochina Monographs. Fort McNair, Washington, DC: U.S. Army Center of Military History, 1984.

Historical Division Joint Secretariat. *History of the Joint Chiefs of Staff and the War in Vietnam 1971–1973.* Washington, DC: Department of Defense, 1970.

Hoffmann, Philip Duncan. *Humping Heavy: A Vietnam Memoir.* Self-published, 2011.

Isserman, Maurice, and Michael Kazan. *American Divided: The Civil War in the 1960s.* Oxford: Oxford University Press, 2008.

Johnson, Haynes. *The Best of Times: The Boom and Bust Years of America Before and After Everything Changed.* New York: Harcourt, 2002.

Johnson, Lt. Col. Richard M. *Lam Son 719: Perils of Strategy.* Carlisle, PA: United States Army War College, 1996.

Karnow, Stanley. *Vietnam: A History.* New York: Viking Press, 1983.

Kimball, Jeffrey. *Nixon's Vietnam War.* Lawrence: University Press of Kansas, 1998.

Krepinevich, Andrew F., Jr. *The Army and Vietnam.* Baltimore, MD: Johns Hopkins University Press, 1986.

Kurlansky, Mark. *1968: The Year That*

Rocked the World. New York: Random House, 2005.

Kuzmarov, Jeremy. *The Myth of the Addicted Army: Vietnam and the Modern War on Drugs*. Boston: University of Massachusetts Press, 2009.

Langguth, A. J. *Our Vietnam: The War 1954–1975*. New York: Simon & Schuster, 2000.

Lawrence, John. *The Cat from Hue: A Vietnam War Story*. New York: Perseus Books, 2002.

Lee, J. Edward, and H. C. "Toby" Haynsworth. *Nixon, Ford and the Abandonment of South Vietnam*. Jefferson, NC: McFarland, 2002.

Lind, Michael. *Vietnam: The Necessary War*. New York: Simon & Schuster, 1999.

Loyte, Colonel J. F., Jr. *Project CHECO, Southeast Asia Report, Lam Son 719, 30 January–24 March 1971: The South Vietnamese Incursion into Laos*. 7th Air Force, HQ PACAF, 1971.

Lung, Hoang Ngoc. *The General Offensive of 1968–69*. Indochina Monographs. Fort McNair, Washington, DC: U.S. Army Center of Military History, 1978.

MacDonald, Peter. *The Victor in Vietnam: Giap*. New York: W. W. Norton, 1993.

Maraniss, David. *They Marched into Sunlight: War and Peace Vietnam and America, October 1967*. New York: Simon & Schuster Paperbacks, 2003.

McCullough, David. *Truman*. New York: Simon & Schuster, 1992.

McMasters, H. R. *Dereliction of Duty: Johnson, McNamara, the Joint Chiefs of Staff, and the Lies That Led to Vietnam*. New York: Harper Perennial, 1997.

McNamara, Robert S. *In Retrospect: The Tragedy and Lessons of Vietnam*. New York: Vintage Books, 1995.

McPherson, James M. *The Negro's Civil War: How American Blacks Felt and Acted During the Civil War*. New York: Vintage Books, 1965.

Moyar, Mark. *Triumph Forsaken: The Vietnam War, 1954–1965*. Cambridge: Cambridge University Press, 2006.

Murphy, Edward F. *Dak To: America's Sky Soldiers in South Vietnam's Central Highlands*. New York: Pocket Books, 1993. New York: Ballantine Books, 2007.

Nelson, Deborah. *The War Behind Me: Vietnam Veterans Confront the Truth About U.S. War Crimes*. New York: Basic Books, 2008.

Nixon, Richard. *No More Vietnams*. New York: Arbor House, 1985.

Nolan, Keith William. *Into Laos: The Story of Dewey Canyon II/Lam Son 719, 1971*. Novato, CA: Presidio Press, 1986.

Novick, Peter. *That Noble Dream: The "Objectivity Question" and the American Historical Profession*. Cambridge: Cambridge University Press, 1998.

Oates, Stephen B., and Charles J. Errico. *Portrait of America*. Vol. 2. Boston: Houghton Mifflin, 2007.

Olson, Rocky. *Sgt. Rock: Last Warrior Standing*. Roy, Utah: Zeroed-In Press, 2010.

Palmer, General Bruce, Jr. *The 25 Year War: America's Military Role in Vietnam*. Lexington: University Press of Kentucky, 1984.

Prochnau, William. *Once upon a Distant War: Young Correspondents and the Early Vietnam Battles*. New York: Random House, 1995.

Project CHECO Southeast Asia Report. *Lam Son 719: The South Vietnamese Incursion into Laos, 30 January–24 March 1971*. HQ PACAF, 1971.

Reynolds, David. *One World Divisible: A Global History Since 1945*. New York: W. W. Norton, 2000.

Ricks, Thomas E. *The Generals: American Military Command from World War II to Today*. New York: Penguin Press, 2012.

Rienzi, General Thomas Matthew. *Communications-Electronics, 1962–1970*. Vietnam Studies. Washington, DC: U.S. Government Printing Office, 1972.

Riker-Coleman, Eric Blaine. *Reflection and Reform: Professionalism and Ethics in the U.S. Army Officer Corps, 1968–1975*. Chapel Hill: University of North Carolina Press, 1977.

Roleff, Tamara. *The Vietnam War*. San Diego, CA: Greenhaven Press, 2002.

Schlesinger, Arthur M., Jr. *A Thousand Days: John F. Kennedy in the White House*. New York: Houghton Mifflin, 2002.

Schulman, Bruce J. *The Seventies*. New York: Da Capo Press, 2001.

Shapley, Deborah. *Promise and Power: The Life and Times of Robert McNamara*. Boston: Little, Brown, 1993.

Sheehan, Neil. *A Bright Shining Lie: John Paul Vann and America in Vietnam*. New York: Random House, 1988.

Simmons, David B. *Our Turn to Serve: An Army Veteran's Memoir of the Vietnam War*. Bloomington, IN: Xlibris, 2011.

Singer, Daniel. *Prelude to Revolution: France in May 1968*. New York: Hill and Wang, 1970.

Sorenson, Theodore C. *Kennedy*. New York: Harper & Row, 1988.

Sorley, Lewis. *A Better War: The Unexamined Victories and Final Tragedy of America's Last Years in Vietnam*. New York: Harcourt, 1999.

_____. *Honorable Warrior: General Harold K. Johnson and the Ethics of Command*. Lawrence: University Press of Kansas, 1998.

_____. *Thunderbolt: General Creighton Abrams and the Army of His Times*. Bloomington: Indiana University Press, 2008.

_____. *Westmoreland: The General Who Lost Vietnam*. Boston: Houghton Mifflin Harcourt, 2011.

Summers, Harry G. *On Strategy: A Critical Analysis of the Vietnam War*. New York: Random House, 1972.

Suri, Jermi. *Power and Protest: Global Revolution and the Rise of Detente*. Cambridge: Harvard University Press, 2003.

Tang, Truong Nhu. *A Viet Cong Memoir: An Inside Account of the Vietnam War and Its Aftermath*. New York: Vintage Books, 1986.

Tho, Brig. Gen. Tran Dinh. *The Cambodian Incursion*. Indochina Monographs. Fort McNair, Washington, DC: U.S. Army Center of Military History, 1979.

Thomas, Evan. *Robert Kennedy: His Life*. New York: Simon & Schuster, 2000.

Truong, Ngo Quang. *The Easter Offensive of 1972*. Indochina Monographs: Fort McNair, Washington, DC: U.S. Army Center of Military History, 1980.

Van Atta, Dale, and President Gerald R. Ford. *With Honor: Melvin Laird in War, Peace, and Politics*. Madison: University of Wisconsin Press, 2008.

Varon, Jeremy. *Bringing the War Home: The Weather Underground, the Red Army Faction, and Revolutionary Violence in the Sixties and Seventies*. Berkeley: University of California Press, 2004.

Vien, Cao Van. *The Final Collapse*. Indochina Monographs. Fort McNair, Washington, DC: U.S. Army Center of Military History, 1984.

Vuic, Kara Dixon. *Officer, Nurse, Woman: The Army Nurse Corps in the Vietnam War*. Baltimore, MD: Johns Hopkins University Press, 2010.

Webb, Willard J., and Walter S. Pool. *The Joint Chiefs of Staff and War in Vietnam, 1971–1973*. Washington, DC: Office of Joint History, 2007.

Whalon, Pete. *The Saigon Zoo, Vietnam's Other War: Sex, Drugs, Rock 'n' Roll*. Conshohocken, PA: Infinity Publishing, 2009.

Widmer, Ted. *Listening In: The Secret White House Recordings of John F. Kennedy*. New York: Hyperion, 2012.

Wilensky, Robert. *Military Medicine to Win Hearts and Minds: Aid to Civilians in the Vietnam War*. Lubbock: Texas Tech University Press, 2004.

Williams, Kieran. *The Prague Spring*

and Its Aftermath: Czechoslovak Politics, 1968–1970. Cambridge: Cambridge University Press, 1997.

ARTICLES

"The Invasion Ends." *Time,* 5 April 1971.

"Look down the Road." *Time,* 19 February 1965.

Mitchell, Greg. "When an Artist, in Vietnam Era, Tried to Drown Robert McNamara—and Nearly Did It." *Huffington Post,* July 7, 2009.

Index